Battlefields
of the
CIVIL WAR
A Guide for Travellers
Volume 2

Battlefields
of the
CIVIL WAR
A Guide for Travellers
Volume 2

Harper's Ferry, Fort Sumter, Richmond,
Cumberland Gap, Appomattox,
Andersonville, the Peninsula Campaign,
Sherman's March through Georgia,
the Shenandoah Valley

Blair Howard

HUNTER
PUBLISHING INC

Hunter Publishing, Inc.
300 Raritan Center Parkway
Edison NJ 08818
(908) 225 1900
Fax (908) 417 0482

ISBN 1-55650-685-6

Maps by Kim André

Cover photo: K.L. Giese/*Photo Network*

Acknowledgments

Writing the acknowledgments for a book is always a gratifying experience, but more than that it's a time to say thank you to the people who've not only made the book possible, but an enjoyable experience too. Firstly, I would like to thank my publisher and editor, Michael Hunter, for his confidence, both in me and in the project, for his enthusiasm for the Civil War, and for struggling through the hundreds of pages of text. Secondly, I would like to thank Kim André, map-maker extraordinaire, and professional in every sense of the word. Finally, I want to thank all those professionals and historians who were kind enough to help me with the details, but are far too numerous to list here. To you all, I extend my grateful appreciation and best wishes.

Contents

List of Maps

Introduction

From 1st Manassas on the Bull Run river to Appomattox Court House, from Shiloh to Chancellorsville, and from Gettysburg to Antietam, Chickamauga, Vicksburg, and Fredericksburg, the great battles of the Civil War have all become household names, names that stir the blood and conjure a thousand images of heroism and despair. But while almost every American is familiar with the most famous of our great fields of war, it should be remembered that the conflict was fought over many such battlefields, some only a shade less well known than their much-publicized counterparts, and many more now long forgotten but nonetheless important to the fate of the nation.

The American Civil War has, over a century and a half, taken on a new appeal. The stories of individual heroism, desperate battles, and great men have passed into legend. Today, all that remains to remind us of those dreadful days so long ago are a few acres carefully set aside and dedicated to the memory of those who died there – quiet places where one can be alone, close to the men whose names ring out as clearly today as they did in the throes of fearful conflict: Lee, Jackson, Sherman, Grant and a hundred more.

The battles that helped to shape the nation continue to hold our attention. Every year thousands of people flock to the one-time killing fields to watch as the generals and their armies meet again in realistic re-enactments of those terrible contests.

The Eastern United States, from Washington to Key West, from Savannah to Kansas City, contains a wealth of Civil War sites and military parks. They are all pleasant spots where one can go to spend an hour or two away from the hustle and bustle of city life or a quiet afternoon out with the kids. Unfortunately, very few of the people who do take the time to visit these magical places have any real idea of their significance and they know even less of the monumental events that took place there. It is hoped that this book will help to change all that.

Within these pages you will find the stories behind some 25 of our nation's battlefield parks and historic sites, many well known, others less familiar, and some that are well off the beaten path. By telling the story of the action as it took place, by bringing back to life many of the principle characters, and by the telling of the deeds they performed while under the greatest stress imaginable, we hope to make your visits to these special places much more enjoyable and rewarding. You will, we hope, leave them with the feeling that your afternoon in the sunshine was much more than a simple picnic and that you are a little richer for the experience.

The book is designed as a guide to your chosen "Field of Glory." Read it as you tour the battlefield. Ponder the great events that took place there – events that surely changed the face of our nation.

Chapter 1

The Road to War

From April, 1861 to April, 1865 there was a storm over the land. The nation became involved in a great civil war. In the early days it was a romantic war. Few thought it could last for more than a week or two. Men of both sides donned heroic uniforms, waved good-bye to their loved ones, and sallied forth laughing and boasting of the great deeds they would do. By April 1st, 1862, almost a year after the opening shots had been fired at Fort Sumter, the war had spread across almost the entire southern half of the divided nation. Major battles had been fought from Virginia to Florida, and as far west as Southern Missouri. And, although the battles of 1st Bull Run in Virginia, Wilson's Creek in Missouri, Gulf Islands in Florida, Forts Henry and Donelson in Tennessee, and Pea Ridge in Arkansas had been bloody enough, they had given little indication of the carnage that was to come. The concept of war on both sides was still a romantic one. Thoughts of great deeds and personal heroism were bolstered by the swashbuckling attitudes of the officers and by the stirring new tunes of glory. The Battle of Shiloh on April 6th and 7th, 1862 brought home to both nations all the horrors of war in an avalanche of death and destruction the like of which had never been seen before. Then came Stones River, Antietam, Fredericksburg, Chancellorsville, Gettysburg, Chickamauga, and some 5,000 lesser known altercations until, by the time the war ended, the nation had paid a price incomprehensible at its beginning. More than 620,000 young Americans had given their lives for one cause or the other. Scarcely a family on either side emerged from the conflict without having lost a relative or close friend. More Americans died fighting in the Civil War than in all the wars thereafter combined, including World War I, World War II, The Korean War, The Vietnam War, and The War in the Gulf. That's a staggering statistic.

In the beginning, ministers left the pulpit and became generals. Lawyers put away their books and took up the sword. Ordinary folk who once stood side by side in church on Sunday fought one against the other for causes they never quite understood – causes that could and would change the course of the nation forever. Pious, gentle men who once might have lived next door to one another engaged in such blood-letting as the world had never seen before

Before the outbreak of war in 1861, the North consisted of 23 states and seven territories with a combined population in excess of 20 million people. The economy was, for the most part, an industrial one. The North produced more food, and its manufacturing capacity was at least five times greater, than that of the South. Most of the nation's railroads were in the North, and most of the nation's money was on deposit in Northern banks. The North had some 4 million men eligible for military duty but it was not felt at the time that the South, should the situation deteriorate into war, would be a military threat. Unfortunately, almost no one bothered to take into account the South's vast superiority in military leadership.

The South numbered 11 states and a population of only 9 million, of whom more than 3 million were slaves. Theirs was an agrarian economy, but one with essentially only one crop – cotton.

When war broke out, the South had a little more than 1 million men eligible for military duty against the 4 million available in the North. The odds were almost evened, however, by the extraordinary number of Southern West Point graduates, almost all of whom defected to answer the Confederate call to arms. Many of the officers in the United States Navy did the same. They, too, returned to their homeland to form the nucleus of the Confederate Navy.

The events leading to the War Between the States are too many and too diverse to examine fully here, but a brief look at some of the major milestones will help to set the scene.

It has been said that slavery was the cause of the conflict between the states, and certainly it did play a very large part in the march toward the outbreak of war. After all, Thomas Jefferson's Declaration of Independence in 1776 declared a self-evident truth that all men are created equal. But slavery was only a part of the problem, and by 1850 the interpretation of Jefferson's Declaration depended largely upon where the interested parties might reside. In the north it was literally interpreted to mean that all human beings were created equal; in the South it was generally agreed that slaves were not human beings and that the Declaration was intended to protect individual state's rights as much as it was to protect the individual, and that the harsh, discriminatory Protected Tariff Laws inflicted by the Federal government upon the southern slave-holding states in 1824 and 1828, laws that favored the interests of the Northern States, were reason enough to declare the Union dissolved. These were laws that caused the president of South Carolina College in Columbia to ask, "Is it worthwhile to continue this Union of States, where the North demands to be our masters and we are required to be their tributaries?"

William Lloyd Garrison.

So, in November, 1832 South Carolina nullified the Tariff Acts of 1824 and 1828 and declared itself prepared to secede from the Union if the government decided to use force.

By 1856 events were rapidly approaching the boiling point. The new slave state of Texas had been admitted to the Union in 1845. William Lloyd Garrison had been publishing *The Liberator*, a newspaper dedicated to the abolition of slavery, for 25 years and the North, once largely indifferent to the fate of slaves, had been well and truly converted to the cause of abolition. But the differences between the North and South went much deeper. The slave-owning aristocracy in the South not only enjoyed an economic advantage, they also felt a "class-superiority" over the predominantly blue-collar society in the North.

So, while slavery was by now a driving issue, the quarrel was in fact a political and constitutional one. The northern states tenaciously held on to the Federalist conceptions of Alexander Hamilton, while the South was firmly dedicated to Jefferson's ideas that sovereign state rights were inalienable.

The spark that caused the explosion came on October 16th, 1859. John Brown, a fanatical abolitionist, together with four of his sons and a group of five blacks and a dozen whites, attacked the Federal arsenal at Harper's Ferry in Virginia. A force of United States Marines under the command of Colonel Robert E. Lee, a man who would soon become a legend in his own time, was sent to put down

John Brown.

the insurrection. After a short fight and some loss of life, Brown, severely wounded, was captured, put on trial along with six of his confederates, found guilty of treason and sentenced to death. He was hanged in Charlestown, in western Virginia, on December 20, 1859.

Then came the Presidential election of 1860. In February a southern senator by the name of Jefferson Davis demanded the repeal of the Personal Liberty Laws and that the North cease to interfere with the Fugitive Slave Law of 1850. He demanded the Federal government protect the rights of the slave states. In the meantime, Abraham Lincoln was eloquently espousing the anti-slavery cause in the North while his Democratic opponent, Stephen Douglas, was talking of compromise. This caused a split in the Democratic party that made Lincoln's election to the presidency inevitable. The eleven cotton states in the south put forth their own candidate, the incumbent Vice President of the United States, John Cabel Breckinridge of Kentucky. Breckinridge stood as a Southern Rights candidate. Then the scene became even further complicated when Senator John Bell, also of Kentucky, decided to run as a Constitutional Unionist; he was, in fact, nothing more than an old-fashioned Whig.

In that fateful campaign of 1860 secession was never an issue, but it was widely felt that the South would secede if Lincoln won. Contrary to popular opinion today, it seems that slavery did become the dominating and all-embracing topic of that turbulent campaign. Lincoln and his fellow Republicans wanted to prohibit slavery in

Abraham Lincoln, President-elect, 1860.

the emerging Territories and confine it within its existing limits. Stephen Douglas and most of the Democrats were for non-intervention in the Territories, Breckinridge and his supporters were demanding that slavery in the Territories should be protected by law, and John Bell buried his head in the sand hoping that by ignoring the issue it would soon be forgotten. On November 6th, 1860, Lincoln was elected president with only 40% of the popular vote. Douglas ran second while Breckinridge, who didn't gain a majority even in the South, ran third.

Finally, on December 20, 1860, the government of South Carolina passed an ordinance that proclaimed the dissolution of the Union between that state and other states united with her under the compact entitled "The Constitution of the United States of America." One month later, on January 21, 1861, the senior Senator from Mississippi, Jefferson Davis, announced the separation of the State of Mississippi from the United States. Florida, Alabama, Georgia, Louisiana, and Texas quickly followed South Carolina and Mississippi into secession. On February 20th, 1861, in Montgomery, Alabama, Jefferson Davis took the

Jefferson Davis.

oath as first President of the Confederate States of America. On April 13th, 1861, Confederate forces accepted the surrender of the Federal Garrison at Fort Sumter in South Carolina, and two days later President Lincoln issued a proclamation that called into service 75,000 militia for a period of three months, thus effectively declaring war upon the fledgling Confederacy. And so it began.

Virginia, although unwilling to take a stand on the issue of slavery, had stood firm on the perceived constitutional principle that every state in the Union enjoyed the same inalienable sovereign rights. It wasn't until Lincoln's call to arms that she made her fateful choice and joined her southern sister states in secession, and in so doing decided the future conduct of one of the noblest Americans who ever lived.

General Winfield Scott, USA, June 10, 1862.

Robert E. Lee was the son of "Light Horse" Harry Lee, colonel and hero of the American Revolution. His marriage to Mary Custis, a descendent of Mrs. George Washington, made him the master of Arlington, the great house, and now National Cemetery, that overlooks the national capital. He graduated from West Point in 1807, 2nd in his class of 46, and was General Winfield Scott's Chief of Engineers during the Mexican War. By the time Virginia decided to leave the Union, Lee already had served with distinction in the United States Army for more than 25 years. He was opposed to slavery and secession, but he had been taught from his earliest years that his first allegiance was to the state that was his home, Virginia.

Off to war. 1st Rhode Island Infantry at the rail depot in Providence, April, 1861.

In March 1861 Lee was summoned to Washington. On leaving for that fateful meeting he told a friend that, "If Virginia stands by the old Union, so will I. But if she secedes, then I will follow my native state with my sword, and if need be with my life." Lee spent more than three hours with General Winfield Scott, wrestling with his conscience and with the mighty problems now at hand. Then, on April 16th, he was, on Lincoln's authority, offered the post of Commander in Chief of the Union Armies. He declined the offer and a day later, on receiving the news that Virginia had seceded from the Union, he resigned his commission and, with great sadness, left his home at Arlington for good.

It should be said at this point that Lee, unlike his most favored lieutenant, Thomas "Stonewall" Jackson, never hated his Northern enemy. Indeed, he thought the decision to secede was a deplorable one, and many believe that even in the optimistic days of 1861 he foresaw its inevitable consequences.

Chapter 2

The Civil War Soldier
& His Equipment

An army of the Civil War was organized into a series of fighting units. The smallest of these was "the company," comprised of some 60 to 100 men and commanded by a captain and two lieutenants. Each company was divided into four squads, each commanded by a sergeant.

Next in size was "the regiment." The regiment was the unit for which the soldier of the Civil War lived and died. It was how he identified himself and was the source of great pride. A regiment was commanded by a full colonel assisted by a lieutenant colonel and a major and was, theoretically, made up of 10 companies, each with three officers. Artillery and cavalry regiments were larger, composed of 12 companies.

The basic infantry unit was "the brigade." Brigades usually numbered anywhere from 2,000 to 3,500 men and would be made up of four to eight regiments. But sometimes, as resources might dictate, a brigade might have as few as two regiments. A brigade, again theoretically, was commanded by a brigadier general. In fact, the smaller brigades were often commanded by the senior regimental colonel. A brigade was a large unit with a full compliment of staff officers: a quartermaster, ordinance and commissary officers, and several clerks, as well as the usual complement of line officers.

The next largest unit in the army of the Civil War was "the division." A division was made up of two or more brigades and, as circumstances allowed, would be commanded by a major general. In fact, many divisions were commanded by a brigadier general. With some 6,000 to 10,000 officers and men in the ranks, the division was a small army in itself.

Finally, there was the corps, the largest unit in the army, some 15,000 to 30,000 officers and men in two or more divisions, commanded by a major or lieutenant general.

The Federal armies were named for rivers: The Army of the Potomac, The Army of the Cumberland, The Army of the Tennessee. Confederate armies were named for states: The Army of Tennessee, The Army of Northern Virginia, and so on.

Federal units within the army were identified by number: XIV Corps, Second Division, 3rd Brigade, 38th Indiana, Army of the Cumberland. Confederate army units were identified by a mixture of names and numbers: Longstreet's Corps, Hood's Division, Anderson's Brigade, 7th Georgia, Army of Northern Virginia.

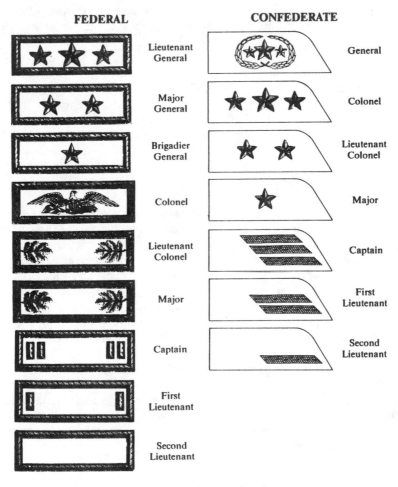

Civil War badges of rank.

On both sides the army was comprised of three branches: the infantry, the artillery, and the cavalry, all with the support of a medley of non-combatant ancillaries, such as catering, clerical, and medical. The latter was still in a very primitive stage of development.

The Generals

Federal general officers were identified on their shoulder straps as follows: a brigadier general wore one star, a major general two stars, a lieutenant general three stars, and full general four stars. Confederate generals were identified by a collar badge with three stars enclosed within a wreath of gold leaves and by the piping on the sleeve of their uniforms. They, too, rose in rank from brigadier general to full-general.

The general officer on both sides was, for the most part, a well-educated man, preferably a graduate of the Military Academy at West Point, and always ready to lay down his life at a moment's notice. He had to be, especially at the brigade level, because the Civil War general did not have the advantages of field communications and command that modern-day commanders enjoy; they commanded from the front, leading their troops into battle at the head of the brigade or division. Mortality among brigade commanders was very high. Second only to color bearers, they were the targets for every sharp-shooter in the opposing army.

The first general to die in the Civil War was Union Brigadier General Nathaniel Lyon at the Battle of Wilson's Creek on August 10th, 1861. Six generals were killed and 12 seriously wounded in a single day during the Battle of Antietam. At the Battle of Franklin on November 30th, 1864, five Confederate Generals, including Major General Patrick Cleburne, and one Union general were killed, five more were wounded, and Confederate Brigadier General George W. Gordon was captured. Robert E. Lee lost eight of his generals at the Battle of the Wilderness in 1864, and Major General George Pickett lost every one of his field commanders, either killed or seriously wounded, during his famous charge on the third day of the Battle of Gettysburg in July, 1863.

It's no wonder, then, that the life expectancy of a brigadier general during the Civil War was only a few months at best. Many did manage to survive the war, however, and most of those that did went on to achieve greatness in that other war-like arena, politics. The last Confederate general on official duty during the Civil War was Brigadier General Stand Watie, the Cherokee general, who surrendered his command of Creek, Seminole, Osage, and Cherokee Indians to Lieutenant Colonel Asa C. Matthews on June 23rd, 1865.

Brevet Ranks

The brevet rank was an honor awarded to officers by the President, usually for gallant actions or meritorious service in combat or, more commonly, to allow them to serve in a staff position. Many Union officers held brevet commissions higher than their actual rank. The Civil War caused an escalation of the practice of awarding brevet commissions, both to regular and volunteer army officers. Army regulations stipulated that an officer functioned at his brevet rank when on special assignment of the President in commands composed of different corps and when in detachments or on courts-martial composed of different corps. In these circumstances the officers received pay at their brevet rank.

Although there was a provision for brevet commissions in the Confederate Army regulations it is doubtful if any were ever awarded. Certainly there is no documented evidence of such an award.

The brevet commissions caused great confusion among the Federal officer class. By the end of the war as many as 1,700 officers held brevet ranks of brigadier or major general. This caused problems of title and recognition. For a long time after the war, the army had real problems deciding the official title of an officer and what rank he was entitled to show on his uniform. For instance, although George Armstrong Custer was only a lieutenant colonel when he died on the Little Big Horn, he held brevet major general commissions in both the regular and volunteer armies.

The practice of awarding brevet commissions had all but been abandoned by the turn of the century and the last brevet commission was awarded to Tasker H. Bliss in 1918.

Infantry

The majority of Civil War soldiers of both sides served in the infantry. These were the people who inflicted and suffered most of the casualties – the people who won or lost the battles.

The army of the Civil War was a great, unwieldy beast numbering anywhere from 30,000 men to 150,000 or more. The logistics of maneuvering such great numbers created problems of monumental proportions. Remember, battlefield telecommunication was still in its infancy, there were no trucks, and no air-transport, just a few sparse and primitive railway systems that often went where nobody wanted to go. The army of the Civil War moved primarily on foot, often covering great distances in a matter of only a few days. Stonewall Jackson was able to move his corps around the country so quickly it soon became known as "Stonewall's Foot Cavalry."

The Civil War soldier, although he became hardened and even used to the long marches, was never comfortable. In the summertime he endured long miles of choking dust. He ached with thirst, his throat was always sore, his nostrils became clogged and inflamed, his lips cracked and bled, and his mouth was always full of grit and dirt. The heavy woolen clothing he wore became wet with sweat and the dust worked its way inside so that it became an instrument of torture that turned his skin red and raw.

In the winter he trod the long miles of dirt road, often up to his ankles in thick mud or semi-frozen slush. Shoe leather turned into so much soggy paper and his uniform hung like a wet rag from his body. At night he was often forced to sleep in the rain or snow with only the dripping trees and a sodden blanket for cover.

On top of all this he had to carry his knapsack, a crude affair strapped to his back and around his chest, containing 20 or 30 pounds of equipment, including his rations for several day's march and all his worldly belongings. He also had to carry his rifle and up to 200 rounds of ammunition. It's no wonder, then, that the Civil War soldier would often arrive on the battlefield in a state of near exhaustion.

The private soldier, Federal and Confederate, was an uncomplicated individual, often illiterate, often confused as to what he was doing or why he was doing it, but almost always inordinately brave. The uniform he wore was often crude and inadequate, being made from a thick woolen cloth that was extremely uncomfortable to wear during the hot summer months, and stayed wet or damp all winter long. His training consisted largely of a few weeks marching back and forth in some quickly constructed boot camp; then he was thrown into battle at the first convenient opportunity. Many of those who went into battle for the first time didn't even know the complicated routine for loading their rifles. There are many documented cases of new recruits on the eve of battle desperately hunting for someone who could tell them which end of the bullet to put into the muzzle first, and there were thousands of weapons picked up on the battlefields found to contain as many as eight or nine charges rammed down the barrel, one on top of the other, without the weapon ever being fired. The majority of the Civil War infantrymen were poor marksmen. That being so, the infantrymen were almost always formed in line of battle in two ranks, one behind the other, to afford the maximum fire power. Such a formation could deliver a formidable volley of fire, a virtual wall of death, and thus eliminated the need for good marksmanship.

Away out in front of the line of battle would be the advance guard – the skirmish line – a widespread screen of soldiers deployed in loose formation who protected the main body of the army and gave warning of the advancing enemy. They would engage the enemy, draw his fire, and thus establish his position so that the army commander could develop his strategy. It was an effective, though somewhat primitive, way of doing business.

The basic weapon of the infantryman on both sides was the muzzle loading rifle musket. It was a little more than five feet long, weighed about nine pounds, and fired a large caliber bullet called a minie ball. The minie ball varied in caliber from .54 to .69. The rifle musket at a range of 300 yards was absolutely lethal, deadly accurate up to 500 yards and, in expert hands, could easily kill a man at 1,200 yards.

The most popular rifle musket of the Civil War was the 1861 model Springfield, .58-caliber rifle musket. It was a little over 58 inches long, weighed nine and one-quarter pounds, and fired a minie bullet propelled by 60 grains of black powder. The weapon was equipped with a ramrod and a 21-inch angular bayonet.

Also popular, especially among the Confederate troops, was the English-made, 1853 model Enfield rifle musket. The Enfield fired a .577-caliber minie bullet and it, too, was equipped with an angular bayonet, although a few were equipped with the not-so-popular sword bayonet introduced by the French during the 1840s. Sword bayonets were heavy and unwieldy, and by early 1864 had virtually been discontinued. The Enfield was a well-made rifle, dependable, and just as accurate as the American-made Springfield.

.58-caliber minie ball.

The name "minie ball," implies that it was both small and round; it was neither. It was named for one of its two French inventors: Claude-Etienne Minié (Henri-Gustave Delvigne was the other). Both were officers in the French army. The minie, a hollow-base, conical bullet, was developed to make better use of the new French rifles. Before the minie bullet, the rifle projectile had to be seated in such a way as to take to the grooves in the barrel. The only way to do that was to use a tight-fitting ball and wrap it a patch. The ball was then rammed down the barrel by brute force. It was a slow and far from satisfactory method, far less efficient than the relatively simple loading procedure of the smooth-bore musket with its loose-fitting ball. The new bullet, however, was made slightly undersized and its hollow base was designed to expand under the pressure of the gasses caused by the exploding black powder, thus forcing it into the grooves inside the barrel. Minié added an iron cup to the base of the bullet which was forced into its base by the explosion, thus adding to its efficiency.

The minie ball brought a new dimension to warfare in the 19th century. The accuracy of the new rifles combined with the deadly effect of the low-velocity, large caliber projectiles had a devastating effect upon all troops in all branches of the army. A wound inflicted by a low-velocity minie ball almost always had disastrous consequences. Bones were shattered beyond repair and the surgeon could do little more for the victim than remove the shattered limbs. Head and body wounds caused by the impact of a minie ball were of such a horrendous nature they were almost always fatal.

Artillery

Although artillery played an important part in the Civil War, and was in a constant state of development and improvement, it was still effective only when the cannoneer could see his target, and even though the cannon of the period could shoot much farther, its effective range was only about 1,500 yards. It was therefore limited in both its use and effect.

12-pounder Napolean gun.

12-pounder bronze field howitzer.

10-pounder Parrott rifle.

Three-inch ordnance rifle.

There were two basic types of Civil War cannon: the bronze smoothbore – namely the six and 12-pounder Napoleon and the 12-pounder mountain howitzer – and the iron rifled gun of which the three-inch ordnance rifle was the most popular, with the three-inch Parrott rifle a close second. There were, of course, many more, most of them imported from Europe and bearing the names of their makers – the Blakely, the Whitworth, the Armstrong and so on. The rifled gun had an increased range and greater accuracy than its bronze counterpart. Both types of cannon fired solid iron round-shot, two types of explosive shell, canister and, to lesser degree, grape-shot.

Artillery shells were of two types, both hollow iron containers. One was filled with black powder and equipped with a fuse lit by the explosive charge that propelled the shell. The fuse exploded it at a prescribed distance. Or an impact device was used to explode the shell on contact. Either way, this type of shell was designed to inflict maximum destruction at the extreme range of the gun used.

The other type of explosive shell was the shrapnel or case-shot, a thin, hollow iron sphere filled with explosives and a lethal payload of metal balls. The case-shot was equipped with a Bormann fuse – a crude but effective device calibrated in quarter seconds – timed to explode the shell some five seconds (about 1,200 yards) into its flight in front of the target. The case shot was designed as an extension of the canister. The explosive charge was sufficient only to rupture and strip away the iron case, leaving the load of metal balls to continue on their way without the spread of the canister at long ranges.

The devastating anti-personnel canister, too, could be fired by either type of gun. The canister, unlike the case-shot, was a soft metal can full of sawdust and large caliber lead or iron balls and was designed to burst open upon leaving the muzzle of the can-non, very much like a giant shot-gun shell. At close range the effect of canister was always deadly, especially when hard-pressed can-noneers would double and triple-load their pieces. Canister was effective only at a range of 300 to 600 yards. Beyond that the balls became so dispersed they were ineffective. The piece was con-structed with iron plates top and bottom, over which the ends of a sheet metal cylinder were bent. Iron balls, usually 48 in number, were tightly packed with sawdust inside the can in four tiers.

Grape shot was similar in principle to canister. It, too, consisted of an iron plate top and bottom. The load consisted of nine much larger metal balls than those of the canister arranged in three tiers. The whole thing was held together by several soft metal straps. Grape shot, like the canister, was designed to break apart on leaving the muzzle of the cannon, thus inflicting terrible damage at close range. Grape shot, however, was not popular with field artillery and, by 1864, had all but been discontinued.

Each type of projectile was fitted with a charge of gunpowder in the form of a powder bag. When double-loading canister, the cannoneer was supposed to knock the powder bag from the second load to ensure the barrel of the weapon wouldn't burst under the strain of a double load of explosive. Often, though, the gunners became carried away by the urgency of the moment and forgot, in which case the great weapons would bound high into the air under the recoil of an overloaded explosive charge.

Each gun was served by a crew of nine men: a sergeant (the chief of caisson), a corporal (the gunner whose job it was to aim the weapon), and seven cannoneers. A full and experienced crew could maintain a rate of fire anywhere from two to three rounds per minute.

Operating a Civil War cannon was something of a complicated affair. The Gunner would sight the weapon; the Number One man would stand to the right of the muzzle with rammer and sponge; Number Two stood to the left of the muzzle and inserted the ammunition; Number Three stood to the right of the breech and put his right thumb, in a leather stall, over the vent during sponging and loading (to prevent drafts igniting unburned powder left in the breech). Number Three also pricked the cartridge (the powder bag) through the vent, thus exposing the powder to the flash caused by the primer. Number Four stood to the left of the breech and inserted the friction primer into the vent (the primer, or striker, delivered a flash of fire down the vent to the powder bag causing it to explode), hooked his lanyard to it, and pulled on the command to fire; Number Five carried the ammunition five yards from the limber to the gun and handed it to Number Two. Number Six was stationed at the limber and cut fuses or handed ammunition to Number Seven, who the handed it on to Number Five. In theory, everything was supposed to go like clockwork, and usually it did. In the early days of the war, however, with the rush to get into battle, things did not go quite so smoothly and it wasn't unusual to find instructors on the field at the height of battle training rookie gun crews.

The light artillery cannon was an extremely mobile weapon. It could be quickly transported from one area of a battlefield to another by use of a two-wheeled limber that was pulled by a team of six horses and three drivers. The horses were harnessed in three pairs, one behind the other, with a driver mounted on each pair, usually on the left-hand side of the team. The limber also carried a single ammunition box with a variety of ammunition, fuses, and primers. Each cannon was supported by a caisson – a four-wheeled carriage that carried three more ammunition boxes. It, too, was pulled by a team of six horses and three drivers.

A typical Confederate artillery battery would be outfitted with four six-pounder guns and two 12-pounder field howitzers. The average Union battery consisted of four guns, all of the same caliber. A battery would be commanded by a captain of artillery and each section of the battery (two guns) would be in the charge of a lieutenant.

Cavalry

The romantic concept of the dashing cavalryman charging into battle, the reins between his teeth, a pistol in one hand and a sword in the other is largely a myth. The cavalry acted mostly as the intelligence – the eyes and ears – of the army. When it became necessary for them to fight, they would dismount and fight just like infantrymen. Every fourth man would stay back behind the firing line and hold the horses while his comrades engaged the enemy. The basic weapon of the cavalryman was officially the single-shot carbine and, during the later years of the war, the Spencer seven-shot repeating carbine. More often than not, however, the more popular weapon of the saddle was a sawed-off 12-gauge shotgun loaded with buckshot. The effect of such a weapon at close range was devastating. The cavalry of the Civil War on both sides produced some of the most romantic characters of the period. On the Confederate side, there was Nathan Bedford Forrest, Joseph Wheeler, and Jeb Stuart, and on the Union side George Armstrong Custer and Philip Sheridan, to name but a few.

For most of the enlisted men, and for the officers too, whether they were a part of the infantry, artillery, or cavalry, there was nothing romantic about the Civil War or what they did. They were, after all, expected to fight and die in the fields for cause and country, and more than 620,000 of them did just that.

The Ambulance Corps

At the beginning of the Civil War, most American doctors, Union and Confederate, had little idea of the numbers of casualties they would be called upon to deal with. After the debacle that was the Battle of First Manassas, or Bull Run, they soon realized that what was to come would require an effort without any precedent.

With few resources at the start, the Union Medical Department, assisted by the U.S. Sanitary Commission, was by the end of the war able to build and supply a remarkably efficient ambulance corps. The Confederacy, however, mainly because of the lack of resources, handled things more on a situation-by-situation basis. The fate of the wounded, then, depended very much upon which side held the field at the end of the battle.

The first real effort at creating an efficient field medical corps was made by Federal Surgeon General Charles S. Tripler, who commanded the Medical Department of the Army of the Potomac. Although he was, at that time, unable to transfer the ambulance

Union wounded.

corps from the Quartermaster's Department, he *was* able to regulate its use and configuration. He discarded the old, two-wheeled version in favor of a new four-wheel model. He established a fleet of 250 of the new ambulances and serviced them with crews of well-trained stretcher-men.

Unfortunately for Tripler, at the Battle of Second Manassas the new wagons were so fragile that they broke down and were abandoned on the field. Drivers panicked, broke open the supplies, and stole the whiskey. Tripler was replaced on July 4th, 1862, by Jonathan Letterman, who persuaded General George McClellan that the Army of the Potomac needed its own autonomous ambulance service.

Letterman organized the new service into corps and division units and began strenuous training of support staff under the direction of the Medical Department. Each infantry regiment had a complement of two surgeons, and each corps had a fleet of ambulances. From that point on the medical services for Federal armies improved steadily until the end of the war, by which time the situation in the Confederacy had deteriorated rather than improved.

There are thousands of stories of the horrors of the battlefield hospitals, most of them true. The advent of the new rifle muskets and the low-velocity minie ball brought devastating wounds to the

Camp of Chief Ambulance Officer in General Burnside's IX Corps at Petersburg.

operating tables. But these were not the only problems the doctors of the day were forced to deal with. More men died of disease than from battle wounds. Battlefield physicians were mostly country doctors, ill suited to coping with the devastating wounds, dysentery, measles, diphtheria, tuberculosis, and other diseases that often reached epidemic proportions.

The battlefield surgeon operated for days on end under terrible conditions, often without anesthetics. Time was always of the essence. Limbs often were removed simply because the surgeon had no recourse and even less time available to save them. It's no wonder, then, that "Sawbones" became the nickname for field surgeons.

After initial treatment in the field, the wounded might be evacuated to hospitals in the major cities. Those that were had a fair chance of survival. For those that ended up in the hastily constructed field hospitals, where the conditions were often dirty and poorly ventilated and the doctors ill equipped, the chances were somewhat more limited.

By the end of the war there were some 350 army hospitals in operation, most of them Federal. But the Confederacy, too, worked hard to develop its medical corps. The doctors and nurses were caring and conscientious and they received help from the aid societies that existed in many of the southern cities, but shortages of personnel and supplies made the Confederate hospital a less than desirable destination for the thousands upon thousands of wounded soldiers that arrived daily from the battlefields.

The ever-increasing number of casualties continued to tax both North and South until the end of the war.

Chapter 3

Fort Sumter

April 12-14, 1861

Major Robert Anderson, his hair already turning silver, was 56 when he became the first Union hero of the Civil War. He was a deeply religious man, cautious and reflective, but also very courageous, as his actions during the first few days of the war would demonstrate. Anderson, a southerner by birth and a graduate of West Point in 1825, 15th in his class, fought in the Black Hawk and Seminole Indian wars, served with General Winfield Scott in Mexico and, from November 1860, was the commander of the Federal garrison at Charleston Harbor. Even as he took up his command at Fort Moultrie, the political rift between North and South was rapidly approaching the point of no return, but he had little idea of the momentous events that were about to sweep him away on the winds of war.

The Story of the Battle

Less than a month after he took command on December 20th, 1860, South Carolina became the first state to secede from the Union. Anderson was, in effect, now in command of three military installations located in the heart of a hostile foreign country: Fort Moultrie on Sullivan's Island, Castle Pinckney at the mouth of the Cooper River, and Fort Sumter, still under construction on a man-made island some three miles from Charleston in the main ship channel. It's no wonder, then, that all eyes turned toward Charleston harbor and Anderson's tiny command. So, on December 26th, under cover of darkness, he moved his men out of Fort Moultrie and across the harbor to Fort Sumter. Within days, Confederate forces occupied Anderson's abandoned positions at Fort Moultrie and Castle Pinckney, as well as Fort Johnson on Cummings Point and a floating battery off Sullivan's Island; Fort Sumter was completely surrounded by Confederate batteries.

As the New Year began, President Buchanan sent some 200 reinforcements and supplies to Anderson in an unarmed merchant

Major Robert Anderson.

ship, the *Star of the West*. On January 9th, as the ship tried to pass around the point into Charleston harbor, the Confederate batteries on Morris Island opened fire and turned it back. Anderson, with only 85 men and dwindling supplies, would have to face the enemy, now more than 5,000 strong.

Tensions continued to mount as, during the following month, Mississippi, Florida, Alabama, Georgia, Louisiana, and Texas all seceded from the Union.

On February 28th, 1861, representatives of the seven seceding states met in convention in Montgomery, Alabama, organized a government, and elected Jefferson Davis as the Confederacy's first president. The situation for Federal forces deployed in the southern states now became exceedingly uncomfortable and so, with the exception of Fort Sumter in South Carolina and Fort Pickens at Pensacola, all Union garrisons surrendered their positions to the new authorities and returned home.

By the time Lincoln was inaugurated on March 4th, it had become evident that the North would use force to subdue the rebellion and maintain the Union and that Fort Sumter would be the focal point for both North and South.

In late March, Jefferson Davis ordered Brigadier General P.G.T. Beauregard to Charleston to take command of the Confederate forces there.

In the meantime, Anderson informed Washington that Confederate forces had heavily fortified Charleston and the harbor, and that he lacked sufficient manpower, food and ammunition to meet the threat. Lincoln, although he was very much aware of the delicate situation, informed the governor of South Carolina, Frances W. Pickens, that he intended to send a relief expedition to Fort Sumter to re-supply the garrison with food and provisions. Once again,

Lincoln, Anderson, and the world settled down to wait. They didn't have to wait long.

On April 1st General Beauregard telegraphed a message to President Davis that he was ready to address the situation at Fort Sumter. On April 10th Governor Pickens informed President Davis of Lincoln's intention to resupply the fort. Later that day the Confederate Secretary of War, Leroy P. Walker, ordered Beauregard to demand of Major Anderson the immediate evacuation of the fort. If the demand was not met, then Beauregard was to *"proceed in such a manner as you may determine, to reduce it."*

Pierre Gustave Toutant Beauregard, a vain and egotistical man, was considered a competent engineer and an able field commander; as a combat tactician, though, his abilities were somewhat limited.

Beauregard was born in St. Bernard Parish, Louisiana of wealthy Creole parents on May 28th, 1818. His upbringing was entirely French, he spoke the French language better than he spoke English, and he was educated at a French military academy in New York. From there he entered West Point where he instructed by... none other than Robert Anderson, now the defender of Fort Sumter.

Beauregard graduated from West   *General P.G.T. Beauregard.*
Point in 1838, 2nd in a class of 45.
He was commissioned a second lieutenant in the Corps of Engineers and sent to Newport, Rhode Island. During the Mexican War he served as an engineer under General Winfield Scott, was wounded twice, and received two brevets for bravery. In January he was appointed superintendent of West Point, a position he held only a matter of days before being removed for his outspoken Southern sympathies.

On February 20th, Beauregard resigned his commission in the Federal Army and on March 1st accepted a commission as briga-

Inside Fort Sumter.

dier general in the Confederate States Army. By the end of March he was in Charleston, South Carolina, at the end of a long journey that had once again brought him face-to-face with his one-time instructor, Major Robert Anderson.

On April 11th, 1861, a three-man delegation from General Beauregard arrived at the fort carrying an ultimatum. The message read as follows: *"I am ordered by the Government of the Confederate States to demand the evacuation of Fort Sumter. My aides, Colonel Chestnut and Captain Lee, are authorized to make such a demand of you. All proper facilities will be afforded for the removal of yourself and command, together with company arms and property, and all private property, to any post in the United States which you may select. The flag which you have upheld for so long and with so much fortitude may be saluted by you on taking it down."*

Anderson refused to surrender the fort, but stated that if he did not receive supplies he wouldn't be able to hold out for more than a few days. The Confederate delegation reported this to Beauregard, who immediately wired Secretary Walker for instructions. Walker gave Beauregard leave to hold his fire until he received a commitment from Anderson as to when he would leave the fort.

The delegation returned to Fort Sumter a little after midnight on the morning of April 12th and offered Major Anderson the following new conditions: *"In consequence of the verbal observation made by you to my aides, Messrs. Chestnut and Lee, in relation to the condition of your supplies and that you would in a few days be starved out if our guns did not batter you to pieces, or words to that effect, and desiring no useless effusion of blood, I communicated both the verbal and your written answer to my communications to my Government.*

"If you will state the time at which you will evacuate Fort Sumter, and agree that in the meantime you will not use your guns against us unless ours shall be employed against Fort Sumter, we will abstain from opening fire upon you. Colonel Chestnut and Captain Lee are authorized by me to enter into such an arrangement with you. You are, therefore, requested to communicate to them an open answer."

Anderson conferred with his officers and sent word to General Beauregard that, unless he was fired upon, received new supplies or orders from Washington, he would evacuate the fort on April 15th. The answer was deemed unacceptable and Colonel James Chestnut told Anderson that, *"Sir: By the authority of Brigadier General Beauregard, commanding the provisional forces of the Confederate States, we have the honor to notify you that he will open fire of his batteries on Fort Sumter in one hour from this time."* The American Civil War was about to begin.

True to his word, exactly one hour later at 4:30 a.m. on April 12th, 1861, Beauregard ordered his batteries to open fire. Lieutenant Henry S. Farley fired the first shell from Fort Johnson on James Island. For more than two hours the shelling continued without the Federal garrison returning fire. Then Captain Abner Doubleday, more famous for his invention of the game of baseball, fired a 32-pounder at the Confederate battery on Cummings Point. He had this to say of his action: *"In aiming the first gun at the Rebellion I had no feeling of self-reproach, for I fully believed that the contest had been inevitable. My first shot bounded off from the sloping roof of the battery opposite without producing any apparent effect. It seemed useless to attempt to silence the guns there, for our metal was not heavy enough to batter the work down.*

"...Our firing became regular, and was answered by fire from the Rebel guns which encircled us on four sides of the pentagon upon which the fort was built. The other side faced the open sea. Showers of balls and shells poured into the fort in one incessant stream. When the immense mortar shells, after sailing high in the air, came down in a vertical direction and buried themselves in the parade ground, their explosions shook the fort like an earthquake."

Interior of Fort Sumter, 1863.

At the time when Major Anderson moved his 85 men from Fort Moultrie, Fort Sumter, a pentagonal structure with walls 40 feet high and 12 feet thick, was still incomplete. Of the 140 seacoast cannon planned, only 40 had been installed, and only 21 of those were in a position where they could be used. That, compounded by a lack of powder and fuses for what few shells they did have, reduced the garrison to firing solid round-shot at the Confederate batteries.

All that night and the rest of the day the Confederate batteries pounded the tiny Federal garrison, with little in reply from the beleaguered fort. The following morning the bombardment resumed with increased vigor. Red-hot projectiles fell from the sky, setting the barracks and officers' quarters inside the fort ablaze, threatening the powder magazine, and choking the defenders with dense black smoke. All through the morning of the 13th Anderson's men huddled beneath the ramparts as shot and shell rained in upon them, firing a few hurried rounds at the enemy with each lull in the Confederate bombardment.

A Federal Assistant Surgeon, Dr. Crawford, having no sick to attend to, volunteered to take command of one of the fort's batteries and later had this to say of the action: *"All of the woodwork was in flames. The officers, seizing the axes that were available, exerted themselves in cutting away whatever woodwork was accessible. It soon became evident that the magazine with its 300 barrels of powder was in* danger from the flames, and every man that could be spared was placed upon the duty of removing the powder, toward which fire was gradually progressing, now separated from the magazine by only one set of quarters. Not a third of the barrels could be removed; so thick was the cloud of smoke and burning cinders, that penetrated everywhere, that a cause of serious danger arose from the exposed condition of the powder taken from the magazine, and Major Anderson ordered that all but five barrels be thrown into the sea."

Late in the morning the Federal supply ships appeared at the mouth of Charleston harbor but made no attempt to run the Confederate defenses. They stood off and watched as, slowly but surely, Fort Sumter was reduced to rubble

Surgeon Dr. Crawford.

around its defenders until, by early afternoon, with ammunition almost exhausted, Major Anderson decided to surrender the fort in order to spare his men from the relentless barrage.

On Sunday the 14th of April, 1861, with permission of General Beauregard, Major Anderson commenced a 100-gun salute to his flag before it was struck from above the fort. On the 50th firing, the great gun exploded, killing one man and wounding several more – the only casualties of the engagement. The formal transfer of troops began at 4 p.m. and the Confederate and South Carolina flags were hoisted side by side over the battered fort.

During the battle more than 3,400 rounds of cannon fire fell upon the fort, so damaging it that it was never rebuilt.

The battle of April 12th and 13th, 1861 was not the only action seen by Fort Sumter during the Civil War. On April 7th, 1863, Union Rear Admiral Samuel F. Du Pont with a flotilla of seven monitors – the most formidable warships afloat – along with the ironclads *Keokuk* and *New Ironsides*, launched an attack on Charleston. Each ship carried a formidable array of weaponry, including one 11-inch and one 15-inch cannon. The fleet opened fire at noon on April 7th and was answered by 77 huge seacoast guns of the Confederate batteries located at Fort Sumter and at strategic points around the harbor.

The barrage from the monitors' huge guns further reduced the wreckage of Fort Sumter, but they too suffered heavy damage. Nothing could withstand the mighty projectiles from the shore-based batteries. Confederate gunners found their marks some 400 times. Decks were holed, armor plating ripped away, smokestacks torn from their mountings, and guns put out of commission. The *Keokuk* was shattered with more than 90 hits and sank during the night after the attack had been abandoned; the *Nehant* was hit 51 times, the *Weehawken*, 53 times. All of the monitors suffered extensive damage and Admiral Du Pont lost his command as a result of this failure.

On the 14th of April, 1865, Robert Anderson, now a retired brigadier general, returned to Fort Sumter to raise again the flag he had hauled down four years to the day earlier.

The National Park Service took over the administration of the monument in 1948 and of Fort Moultrie 14 years later when work began on restoration. By 1961, half of Fort Sumter had been excavated and a museum installed. Fort Moultrie was ready for visitors in time for the American Bicentennial. Today, the damage Fort Sumter sustained during the Civil War is still very much in evidence. The battered walls, reduced from three stories to one, the embedded projectiles, and the great guns that once again stand silent guard over Charleston harbor, all remain a symbol of the destruction of those dark, far-off days.

Visitors can take a self-guided tour of both Fort Moultrie and Fort Sumter, taking advantage of interpretive services provided by the park rangers. There is a museum and a gift shop at Fort Sumter, and a Visitor Center with interpretive exhibits at Fort Moultrie.

Fort Sumter is located on a man-made island in Charleston harbor and can be accessed either by private boat or by the Fort Sumter Tour Boat. The Tour Boat leaves from the Municipal Yacht Basin at Lockwood Boulevard, just south of US 17 in Charleston, and from the Patriots Point Navel Museum at Mt. Pleasant in Charleston. To reach Patriots Point take US 17 north from Charleston and follow the signs. The boat tour lasts a little more than two hours and reservations are recommended.

Fort Moultrie is located on Sullivan's Island, and is reached via US 17 to SC 703; turn right and follow the signs.

The Fort Sumter National Monument (includes Fort Moultrie) is open daily from 9 a.m. until 6 p.m., June 15th through Labor Day. Opening hours vary during the rest of the year.

What to See, Where to Stay

Charleston

Visitor Information. The Charleston Visitor Reception Center offers an assortment of information on points of interest, tours, campsites, fishing trips, cultural events, maps, and a self-guided tour of the city. PO Box 975, Charleston, 29402. Telephone 803-853-8000.

Annual Events

Southeastern Wildlife Exposition. More than 500 exhibitors display wildlife arts, antique collections, and crafts for sale in 18 downtown historical locations in mid-February. Telephone 803-723-1748.

Festival of Houses and Gardens. Many of the city's finest homes and gardens are open to the public from mid-March through mid-April. Afternoon and candlelight tours are available and reservations are recommended. Telephone 803-722-3405.

Spoleto Festival, USA, and Piccolo Spoleto. An internationally acclaimed arts and music festival held in late May and early June. A counterpart to the arts festival in Spoleto, Italy, founded by Gian Carlo Menotti. Opera, ballet, dance, visual arts, theater, classical music, jazz, and choral performances. The Piccolo Spoleto is for children and is held next to the main festival. Telephone 803-722-2764.

Fall House & Garden Candlelight Tours. Evening tours of privately owned homes and gardens in the historic district of Charleston. Late September through October. Telephone 803-722-4630.

Resorts

Seabrook Island. 1002 Landfall Way, John's Island, SC 29455. Telephone 800-845-2475. 136 villas, 1-3 bedrooms. 7 pools, wading pool, lifeguard. Supervised children's activities. Golf, honeymoon, and family packages. Convention facilities. Tennis pro. Golf course, private beach, sailboat and windsurfer rentals, deep-sea fishing, bicycles, health club privileges, game room, entertainment. Sunset cruises available. Accepts credit cards.

Wild Dunes. 5757 Palm Blvd., Isle of Palms, SC 29451. Telephone 800-845-8880. 240 villas and 24 cottages. Pools, wading pool, whirlpool, pool-side service, lifeguard. Playground. Supervised children's activities. Convention facilities. Valet service. 36-hole golf course, swimming beach, boats and rentals, fishing guides, bicycle rentals, grills on the beach. Accepts credit cards.

Hotels

Marriott. 4770 Marriott Drive, Charleston, SC 29418. Telephone 803-747-1900. 295 rooms, Weekend rates. Indoor/outdoor pool. Meeting rooms, gift shop, entertainment, dancing, tennis & golf privileges, exercise equipment. Luxury concierge level with private lounge, honor bar, complimentary continental breakfast, and refreshments. Accepts credit cards.

Mills House. 115 Meeting Street, Charleston, SC 29401. Telephone 803-722-2400. 214 rooms. Elevated pool, restaurant, meeting rooms. Reproduction ante-bellum furnishings, antiques, carriage for sightseeing. Accepts credit cards.

Omni Hotel at Charleston Place. 130 Market Street, Charleston, SC 29401. Telephone 803-722-4900. 440 rooms. Indoor/outdoor pool, poolside service, restaurant, entertainment, convention facilities, golf & tennis privileges, exercise room, whirlpool, sauna, steam room. Luxury Club Level with private lounge, free continental breakfast, refreshments and newspaper. Accepts credit cards.

Inns

Anchorage. 26 Vendue Range in the Historic District (Charleston, SC 29401). Telephone 803-723-8300. A renovated ante-bellum warehouse adjacent to the harbor and Waterfront Park with 19 rooms and 2 suites. Children over 12 years old only. Garage parking. Free coffee in the lobby, breakfast, complimentary tea/sherry, antiques, library/sitting room. Accepts credit cards.

Barksdale House. 27 George Street, Charleston, SC 29401. Telephone 803-577-4800. A town house built in 1778 with 10 rooms, porches, and a courtyard. Children over 10 years old only. Free continental breakfast, complimentary tea and sherry. Accepts credit cards.

Church Street. 177 Church Street, Charleston, SC 29401. Telephone 803-722-3420. Located in the historic market area with 31 suites, some with balconies. Municipal garage parking. Free coffee. Free buffet breakfast. Valet service, antique reproductions, courtyard. Accepts credit cards.

Guilds. 101 Pitt Street, Mount Pleasant, NC 29464. Telephone 803-881-0510. Six rooms, free crib, continental breakfast. Tennis & golf privileges. A restored clapboard building (circa 1888) furnished with period reproductions. Close to the ocean, fishing three blocks, swimming beach three miles. Accepts credit cards.

Indigo. 1 Maiden Lane, Charleston, SC 29401. Telephone 803-577-5900. Children under 12 stay free, crib free, free coffee in rooms, free continental breakfast. Circa 1850, antique furnishings, courtyard. Accepts credit cards.

John Rutledge House. 116 Broad Street, Charleston, SC 29401. Telephone 803-720-2615. Children under 12 stay free, crib free, free continental breakfast, valet service, fireplaces. Historic home built 1763, antique furnishings, library. Accepts credit cards.

Kings Courtyard. 198 King Street, Charleston, SC 29401. Telephone 803-723-7000. Children under 12 stay free. Three-day package plans. Free continental breakfast, room service, dining room, bar, meeting rooms, whirlpool, fireplaces, two courtyards. Built in 1853. Accepts credit cards.

Lodge Alley. 195 E. Bay Street, Charleston, SC 29401. Telephone 803-722-1611. Children under 12 stay free, crib free, honeymoon plans, free morning coffee in sitting room, dining room, complimentary sherry, valet service, tennis & golf privileges, fireplaces, antiques, built in 1773. Accepts credit cards.

Maison Du Pre. 317 E. Bay Street, Charleston, SC 29401. Telephone 803-723-8691. Crib free, free continental breakfast, complimentary tea/wine. Three Charleston town houses and two carriage houses combined into one. Enclosed porches and three fountains. Built in 1804.

Meeting Street. 173 Meeting Street, Charleston, SC 29401. Telephone 803-723-1882. Honeymoon plans, free crib, free continental breakfast, bar, entertainment Friday & Saturday, whirlpool, courtyard, miniature formal garden, walking tours. Accepts credit cards.

Middleton. 61 Ashley River Road, SC 29414. Telephone 803-556-0500. Set on 7,000 acres overlooking the river. Children under 12 stay free, crib free, pool, free continental breakfast, complimentary wine and cheese, meeting rooms, valet service, tennis, fireplaces. Free admission to adjacent Middleton Place Gardens. Accepts credit cards.

Planters. 112 N. Market Street, Charleston, SC 29401. Telephone 803-845-7082. Located in the heart of the scenic, historic district. Family rates, crib free, cafe, free continental breakfast in rooms, meeting rooms, valet service, tennis and golf privileges, many antiques. Accepts credit cards.

Vendue. 19 Vendue Range, Charleston, SC 29401. Telephone 803-577-7970. A circa 1824 structure with rooftop terrace overlooking the harbor. Free continental breakfast (full breakfast in suites), afternoon refreshments, bar, cafe, valet service, some fireplaces. Accepts credit cards.

Victoria House. 208 King Street, Charleston, SC 29401. Telephone 803-720-2944. A Romanesque-style building circa 1889. Children under 12 stay free, crib free, free coffee in rooms, free continental breakfast, complimentary tea/sherry, cafe adjacent, room service (breakfast only), valet service, health club privileges. Accepts credit cards.

Motor Hotels

Best Western Northwoods Atrium Inn. 7401 Northwoods Blvd., North Charleston, SC 29418. Telephone 803-577-2644. Under 18 stay free, crib free, free continental breakfast, room service, bar, cafe, free airport, rail station & bus depot transportation, pools, pool service, exercise equipment, whirlpool, sauna, game room. Accepts credit cards.

Hawthorn Suites. 181 Church Street, Charleston, SC 29401. Telephone 803-577-2644. Under 18 stay free, crib free, free full breakfast, room service, valet service, bar, dancing, laundry, gift shop, exercise equipment. some wet bars. Accepts credit cards.

Holiday Inn-Riverview. 301 Savannah Highway, Charleston, SC 29407. Telephone 803-556-7100. Under 19 stay free, crib free, pool, cafe, room service, bar, dancing, laundry, valet service, free historic district transportation, balconies. Located on the river. Accepts credit cards.

Quality Suites. 5225 North Arco Lane, Charleston, SC 29418. Telephone 803-747-7300. Under 18 stay free, crib free, free full breakfast, room service, bar, cafe nearby, free airport transportation, pool, exercise equipment, bicycles, some bathroom telephones. Accepts credit cards.

Sheraton Airport Inn. 5991 River Avenue, Charleston, SC 29418. Telephone 803-744-2501. Under 17 stay free, crib free, free continental breakfast, room service, bar, free airport transportation, pool, exercise equipment, whirlpool, sauna, game room. Accepts credit cards.

Motels

Comfort Inn. 5055 North Arco Lane, Charleston, SC 29418. Telephone 803-554-6485. Under 18 stay free, crib free, free continental breakfast, free airport transportation, pool, whirlpool. Accepts credit cards.

Cricket Inn. 7415 Northside Drive, Charleston, SC 29420. Telephone 803-572-6677. Under 18 stay free, crib free, pool, free coffee in lobby, continental breakfast, cafe nearby, accepts credit cards.

Days Inn Airport. 2998 W. Montague Avenue, Charleston, SC 29418. Telephone 803-747-4101. Children under 12 stay free, crib free, pool, playground, free airport transportation. Accepts credit cards.

Hampton Inn Airport. 11 Ashley Pointe Drive, Charleston, SC 29418. Telephone 803-744-1621. Children under 18 stay free, crib free, valet service, meeting rooms, free coffee, free continental breakfast, tennis & golf privileges, pool, playground. Accepts credit cards.

Holiday Inn Airport. 6099 Fain Street, Charleston, SC 29418. Telephone 803-744-1621. Children under 18 stay free, crib free, room service, bar, laundry, entertainment, dancing Monday to Friday, meeting room, valet service, game room, tennis, pool, playground, free airport transportation. Accepts credit cards.

Knights Inn. 2355 Aviation Avenue, Charleston, SC 29418. Telephone 803-744-4900. Family rates, suites, crib free, two pools, free coffee in lobby, bar, laundry, free airport transportation. Accepts credit cards.

La Quinta. I-26 N at Ashley Phosphate Road, Charleston, SC 29218. Telephone 803-797-8181. Under 18 stay free, crib free, heated pool, free morning coffee, cafe adjacent, room service, meeting rooms, valet service, picnic tables, grill. Accepts credit cards.

Masters Inn. 300 Wingo Way, Mount Pleasant, SC 29464. Telephone 803-884-2814. Under 18 stay free, pool, free coffee, continental breakfast, cafe nearby, laundry, meeting room. Accepts credit cards.

Ramada Inn. West Montague Avenue, Charleston, SC 29418. Telephone 803-744-6230. Children under 18 stay free, room service, bar, entertainment, dancing, valet service, meeting rooms, free airport transportation. Accepts credit cards.

Red Roof Inn. 7480 Northwoods Blvd., Charleston, SC 29418. Telephone 803-572-9100. Children under 18 stay free, crib free, free coffee in the lobby. Accepts credit cards.

Town and Country Inn. 2008 Savannah Highway, Charleston, SC 29407. Telephone 803-571-1000. Children under 18 stay free, crib free, bar, laundry, entertainment, dancing Tuesday to Saturday, valet service, meeting rooms, golf privileges, pool. Accepts credit cards.

Restaurants

Barbados Room. At Mills House Hotel (listed). Telephone 803-577-2400. 6:30 am to 3 pm, 5:30 pm to 10:30 pm. Reservations accepted, continental menu, wine list, specializes in seafood. Own baking, piano in the evenings, valet parking. Accepts credit cards.

Carolina's. 10 Exchange Street. Telephone 803-724-3800. Reservations accepted, bar, à la carte entrées, specializes in grilled seafood, pasta, and regional cuisine. Accepts credit cards.

Colony House. 35 Prioleau Street in the historic district. Telephone 803-723-3424. Reservations accepted, bar, à la carte entrées, specializes in seafood, and Low Country cuisine. Parking. Renovated 1830 warehouse. Accepts credit cards.

82 Queen. 82 Queen Street. Telephone 803-723-7591. Reservations accepted, bar, à la carte entrées, specializes in seafood and Low Country cuisine. Outdoor dining. Accepts credit cards.

Ferrante's. 32 Market Street. Telephone 803-723-3624. Reservations accepted. Italian menu, bar, semi-à la carte. Specialties: scallops Ferranti, veal scaloppini. A restored seaman's church: stained glass windows, high-arched ceiling, brass chandeliers, mural of ancient Rome. Accepts credit cards.

Fish Market. 12 Cumberland Street. Telephone 803-723-1600. Reservations accepted, continental menu, bar, entertainment Wednesday through Sunday, wine cellar, à la carte entrées. Specializes in Maine lobster and fresh seafood. Valet parking. Accepts credit cards.

Garibaldi's. 49 S. Market Street. Telephone 803-723-7153. Italian menu. Specializes in fresh seafood, pasta, and veal. Own deserts. Outdoor dining, bistro atmosphere, located in the center of the historic district. Accepts credit cards.

Jilich's. 184 Bay Street. Telephone 803-577-4338. Reservations accepted, regional American menu, à la carte entrées, lunch and dinner. Accepts credit cards.

Le Midi. 337 King Street. Telephone 803-577-5571. French menu, wine list. Specializes in seafood, rabbit, and chicken. Own deserts. Accepts credit cards.

The Library at Vendue. (See Vendue Inn). Telephone 803-723-0485. Reservations accepted, continental menu, bar, wine cellar, semi-à la carte menu. Specializes in wild game, seafood, and veal. Own baking and soups. Intimate dining. Accepts credit cards.

Louis' Charleston Grill. (See Omni Hotel). Telephone 803-577-4522. Reservations accepted, à la carte entrees. Specializes in crabmeat & lobster cakes, beef, veal, and fresh local seafood. Own baking and soups. Accepts credit cards.

Magnolia. 185 E. Bay Street. Telephone 803-577-7771. Reservations accepted, bar, semi-à la carte, lunch and dinner. Specialties: salt & pepper fried shrimp and skillet grits cake. Accepts credit cards.

Marianne. 235 Meeting Street. Telephone 803-722-7196. Reservations accepted, French menu, bar, à la carte entrées. Specializes in beef, lamb, and seafood. French bistro decor. Tableside cooking. Accepts credit cards.

Mistral. 99 S. Market Street. Telephone 803-722-5708. French menu, bar, semi-à la carte. Specializes in fresh seafood, veal, and desserts. Accepts credit cards.

Papillon. 32 Market Street. Telephone 803-723-3614. Northern Italian menu, semi-à la carte. Specializes in grilled seafood, meat pie, and pastries. Accepts credit cards.

Pier 61 Ltd. 652 St. Andrews Blvd. Telephone 803-571-7533. A la carte entrées, wine, beer. Specializes in seafood and prime rib. Parking. Accepts credit cards.

Poogan's Porch. 72 Queen Street. Telephone 803-577-2337. Reservations accepted, regional Low Country cuisine, bar, à la carte entrées. Specialties: Cajun shrimp, bread pudding, and Creole jambalaya. Outdoor dining. Garden room, intimate dining. Accepts credit cards.

Chapter 4

Wilson's Creek

August 10th, 1861

Wilson's Creek National Battlefield is located 10 miles to the south of Springfield, Missouri, and three miles east of Republic. From Springfield take Interstate 44 west to exit 70. From there take Missouri Highway MM south to US 60, cross US 60 and go for about three-fourths of a mile to Missouri Highway ZZ. Take Missouri ZZ and go two miles to the park entrance. You may also take US Highway 60 from Springfield to Missouri ZZ, and from there turn south and go two miles to the park entrance.

The park is open daily from 8:00 a.m. until 7:00 p.m. in the spring, fall, and winter, and from 8:00 a.m. until 9:00 p.m. during the summer months. For more information, contact the Park Headquarters, Wilson's Creek National Battlefield, Route 2, Box 75, Republic, MO 65738. Telephone 417-732-2662.

The Story of the Battle

The Battle of Wilson's Creek was fought just 10 miles to the south of Springfield, Missouri, on August 10th, 1861. Although the numbers engaged were relatively small (a total of about 15,000 for both sides) compared with the more than 60,000 engaged at the Battle of First Manassas, the armies went at it like two packs of hungry dogs fighting over a fresh-killed carcass.

The political atmosphere in Missouri at the time was volatile. Although the general consensus among Missourians was that the state should remain neutral, a large portion of the population's sympathies, including those of the governor, Claiborne F. Jackson, lay with the fledgling Confederacy. Missouri was strategically important to both sides for several reasons. First, there were the two great waterways, the Missouri and the Mississippi Rivers. Secondly, she was blessed with an abundance of natural resources and manpower. Then there was the issue of slavery.

Gov. Claiborne Fox Jackson.

For many years the question of slavery had hung like a great dark cloud over Missouri. In 1854 the problem flared into bloodshed when Missourians tried to force slavery onto the free Kansas settlers. For three years the "Bloody Kansas Affair" continued, with raiding, looting, burning, and murder. Then, as the national political situation began to turn sour, the powers that were in Missouri turned their attentions to matters of greater importance.

By 1861 it had become obvious to all that Missouri would not be allowed to remain neutral. When, after the fall of Fort Sumter early in April, President Lincoln called for troops to put down the rebellion, Governor Jackson refused the request saying, *"Your request is illegal, unconstitutional, revolutionary, inhuman, diabolical, and cannot be complied with."* And, with that, he immediately ordered the state's military units to Camp Jackson near St. Louis to make preparations to seize the U.S. Arsenal there. But he underestimated the resourcefulness and fierce patriotism of the Arsenal's commander, Captain Nathaniel Lyon.

Lyon, upon learning of Jackson's intentions, moved quickly. First he moved most of the Arsenal's weapons, ammunition, and supplies to Illinois. Then, on May 10th, he marched upon Camp Jackson with a force of more than 7,000 men and forced its surrender. Governor Jackson, however, continued to enlarge and arm the Missouri State Guard with the express intention of using it to remove Missouri forcefully from the Union. But things were not progressing quite as Jackson intended. Strong opposition, led by Republican Congressman Frank Blair and the now Briga-

Brig. General Nathaniel Lyon.

Maj. General Sterling Price.

dier General Nathaniel Lyon, commander of all Federal forces in Missouri, forced Jackson into talks designed to bring about a compromise. But no such compromise was reached and, on June 11th, 1861, Brigadier General Nathaniel Lyon declared war upon all secessionists within the state of Missouri. Governor Jackson, along with those elements of the Missouri State Guard that held Southern sympathies, was forced to leave town.

Two days later General Lyon moved his army in pursuit of Jackson. He clashed with Jackson's forces at Booneville, Missouri on June 17th and again drove them out of town. On July 5th, Colonel Franz Sigel, in an effort to block Jackson's retreat southward, engaged his troops at Carthage, Missouri, a small town just to the west of Springfield. This time it was Jackson's turn. Sigel was soundly defeated and forced to withdraw to Springfield. Jackson was now free to link his forces with the regular Confederate troops under the command of Brigadier Generals Benjamin McCulloch and N. Bart Pierce near Cassville, and those units of the Missouri State Guard under the command of Major General Sterling Price at Cowskin Prairie in the southwestern corner of the state; Governor Jackson had retreated just about as far as he could go without leaving the state. On July 25th, General Price began to move his command toward Cassville in an effort to link his force with that of General McCulloch. By the 29th, the two armies had joined and Price was technically, if not actually, in command of both armies.

Price was a sterling figure, both in name and disposition. He had served his state as both governor and congressman, and he'd fought with distinction in the Mexican War.

Brigadier General McCulloch, on the other hand, had little use for Missourians in general, and for Price in particular. *"They are,"* he was heard to say *"splendid roasting-ear foragers, but poor soldiers."* Price, however, now had more than 7,000 soldiers at his command;

McCulloch, a former Texas Ranger, had a force of about 5,000 Confederate troops from Arkansas, Louisiana, and Texas. The combined force, then, numbered close to 12,000 officers and men. Price and McCulloch, determined to bring Lyon to battle, moved northeast out of Cassville on July 31st.

Meanwhile, Union General Nathaniel Lyon had not been idle, and on July 13th, 1861, he arrived in Springfield and took command of a force, including that of Franz Sigel, of almost 6,000 men supported by cavalry and three batteries of artillery which included 18 guns. Even so, Lyon knew that he was badly outnumbered and sent a strong request for reinforcements to Major General Fremont, the commander of the Federal Department of the West in St. Louis. Then, on August 1st, after learning of the Confederate troop movements in and around Cassville, he moved his army southwest out of Springfield to meet them.

By the afternoon of the next day, the 2nd of August, Lyon's advance units were already encountering those of Confederate Brigadier General James Rains. At 5 o'clock that afternoon at Dug's Gap, the two advance units clashed and Rains' division, under heavy fire, was driven back in disorder. Lyon, though encouraged by his success, now knew without a doubt that he was heavily outnumbered and withdrew his army back toward Springfield to await the reinforcements he was sure were on the way from General Fremont.

General Price, too, was sure that they had Lyon outnumbered. He was also sure that Federal reinforcements must already be on the way to Lyon from St. Louis, and he was impatient to get to Lyon before his advantage was reversed. So, on the evening of August 4th, he went to General McCulloch and tried to persuade him to follow Lyon and bring him immediately to battle. Price's assistant adjutant general, Colonel Thomas Sneed, later described the main points of the conversation between the two as follows:

"Do you mean to march on and attack Lyon, General McCulloch" Price demanded.

"I have not yet received orders to do so, sir," answered McCulloch, *"my instructions leave me in doubt whether I will be justified in doing so."*

"Now, sir," said Price, in his still loud, imperious tone, *"I have commanded in more battles than you ever saw, General McCulloch. I*

Maj. General John C. Fremont.

have three time as many troops as you. I am of higher rank than you are, and I am twenty years your senior in age and experience. I waive all these considerations, General McCulloch, and if you will march on the enemy I will obey your orders, and give you the whole command and all the glory to be won there!" General McCulloch said he was then expecting a dispatch from President Davis, and would take General Price at his word if it should be favorable.

McCulloch received his dispatch which, in fact, ordered him to do exactly what Price wanted, and so the Confederate army set off in pursuit of General Lyon. By August 6th, much to Price's disgust, they were encamped once again, this time near Wilson's Creek.

Lyon, by now back in Springfield, once again sent a courier to General Fremont urgently requesting reinforcements. He was not the only one to urge Fremont to send men and supplies to his aid. John Phelps, on his way to Washington to attend an extraordinary session of Congress called by President Lincoln, visited with General Fremont and urged him to reinforce Lyon. Fremont, however, was unmoved, saying that he didn't believe Lyon was in the desperate straits he claimed, and that Price could not have a strong force because southwestern Missouri was too poor to support a large army. Fremont also said that he had no troops to spare and that, in his opinion, Lyon could take care of himself.

And so it was that, on August 9th, General Lyon received a dispatch from General Fremont telling him that his situation was not critical, that he had overestimated the Confederate Army's strength, that he was not to fall back without good cause, and that he would not be receiving reinforcements.

There's no doubt that Lyon must have been devastated by the dispatch. He was, however, a soldier of great strength and fortitude, not given to complaining. He accepted his situation and made ready to carry out Fremont's orders. The following letter was written by Lyon to Fremont in his own hand; it would be the last letter he ever wrote:

Springfield, Mo., Aug. 9th, 1861
General, I have just received your note of the 6th inst., by special messenger. I retired to this place, as I have before informed you, reaching here on the 5th. The enemy followed to within ten miles of here. He has taken a strong position, and is recruiting supplies of horses, mules, and provisions by forages into the surrounding country. His large force of mounted men enables him to do this without much annoyance from me. I find my position extremely embarrassing, and am at present unable to determine whether I shall be able to maintain my ground or be forced to retire. I shall hold my ground as long as possible, though I may without knowing how far, endanger the safety of my entire force with its valuable material, being induced, by the important considerations involved, to take this step. The enemy yesterday made a show of force about five miles distant, and has doubtless a full purpose of making an attack on me. Very respectfully, your obedient servant,
N. Lyon
Brig. Gen. Vols., Commanding
To Major Gen. J.C. Fremont, Commanding Western Department, St. Louis, Mo.

In the meantime, Confederate General Price had lost all patience with what he saw as General McCulloch's dithering. At sunrise on the 9th of August he sent his assistant adjutant general to McCulloch with instructions to tell him that if McCulloch did not immediately advance upon the enemy he, Price, would resume command of the Missouri State Guard and, no matter what the consequences might be, advance on his own. The result of the message was a council of war between the generals that afternoon and orders were given for a general advance that night to begin at 9 o'clock. Unfortunately, due to a perceived threat of bad weather, and a lack of waterproof ammunition pouches among the troops, McCulloch decided to delay the advance until the following morning.

So, by nightfall on the 9th of August, the situation on both sides was rapidly coming to a head. General Lyon, now resigned to the fact that he was to get no help, decided upon the age-old strategy that the best form of defense is to attack. And with that he too made preparations to move against the enemy encamped at Wilson's Creek. If he could effect a surprise attack at dawn on the 10th he might just be able to overcome his disadvantage in numbers and carry the day.

That afternoon, Friday, the 9th of August, Lyon gathered together his brigade commanders: Brigadier General Sweeny, Colonel Sigel, and Major Sturgis and between them they decided upon a plan for a two-pronged attack on the enemy at first light the following morning. General Lyon, with Sweeny and Sturgis, and two batteries of artillery, would move against Wilson's Creek from the north. Sigel with his brigade, two companies of cavalry, and six pieces of artillery,

Wilson's Creek.

would head south, encircle the enemy encampment and move against it from the rear; thus Lyon would be attacking the Confederate army from two sides at once.

General Lyon and his column moved out toward Wilson's Creek at 6:00 p.m. that evening; Colonel Sigel moved half an hour later at 6:30 p.m. Lyon arrived undetected on the outskirts of the Confederate camp at about 1 a.m. on the morning of the 10th, reconnoitered the area, formed his tiny force into line of battle, and then waited for the first light of dawn. Colonel Sigel and his column of about 1,200 soldiers marched all through the night, arriving within a mile of the sleeping Confederate camp just before daylight and, in accordance with the general plan, deployed his troops to command the Fayetteville Road, thus cutting off a Confederate retreat in front of Lyon's attacking force. He then moved forward up the hill, and placed four of his guns on top in full view of the Confederate camp. Then he settled down to await the sound of Lyon's guns signaling the opening of the battle.

Sigel did not have long to wait. At 5:00 a.m., Lyon's advance units moved forward and immediately encountered pickets of Confederate Brigadier General Rains' division of General Price's Missouri State Guard. Fierce fighting broke out at once and Rains' men began to pull back. For a moment or two the Federal line halted and

General Lyon, seeing what he thought to be an opportunity to outflank the enemy as well as attack him north and south, sent Captain J.B. Plummer's battalion of regulars, along with the Dade County Home Guards, east to cross Wilson's Creek and maintain position with the main advance. Lyon began to move forward again and Captain James Totten's battery of six guns was brought forward and deployed close to the center of the line of battle in support of the main advance, while Lieutenant John DuBois' battery was brought forward and placed 75 yards or so to the left of Totten's guns to deal with Confederate Captain William E. Woodruff's Pulaski Battery which was already in action to the front and left on the far side of Wilson's Creek sweeping the Federal line with a deadly hail of canister and grape shot.

In the meantime, General Price, almost beside himself with impatience, had risen before daybreak and sent for General McCulloch. They were eating breakfast together when, according to Colonel Snead, a courier arrived at the run with news that General Rains was under attack from a Yankee army more than 20,000 strong. McCulloch laughed and said, "*O, pshaw, another of Rains' scares. Tell General Rains I will come to the front myself directly.*" And, with that, the officers continued eating their breakfast.

A minute or so later, a second courier arrived with the story that the Federal army was now less than a mile away and that Rains' men were being driven back. Again McCulloch didn't believe it. At that moment, however, the truth was delivered in the form of Rains' men falling back in confusion, and the first shots from Captain Totten's Federal battery to the north, answered immediately by Colonel Sigel's battery opening fire on General McCulloch's camp to the south. The Federal surprise was complete. The Confederate army, most of it still asleep, some eating an early breakfast, was under attack on two sides. It is a great credit, both to commanders and enlisted men, that there was not panic and confusion among the Confederate units. True, General Rains' division was falling back, but the majority of the army maintained control and were soon putting up an organized resistance.

General Price gathered together his other four divisions under the commands of Generals William Slack, J.H. McBride, John B. Clark, and Mosby Parsons, and moved them quickly into battle in support of General Rains. General Lyon's troops, by this time, were well established on the crest of the ridge that forever after was to be known as Bloody Hill.

In the meantime, at 5:30 a.m., more than two miles away at the southern end of the battlefield, Colonel Sigel heard the first shots fired by Totten's battery in support of the general Union advance and immediately ordered his own battery to open fire on the tents of General McCulloch's camp. McCulloch's troops quickly abandoned their camp and retired in two directions to the northeast and northwest and began forming into line of battle. Sigel, smelling blood, moved his entire line forward across the valley driving the still disorganized Confederate army back even further. Sigel, hearing the sounds of battle raging to the north, and fully convinced that General Lyon was driving the equally disorganized second half of the Confederate army back toward him, continued his advance to the northwest fully intending to attack the retreating Confederate army in the rear. By 8 o'clock his force was established in position across the Wire Road and, certain of General Lyon's success, settled down to await the fleeing Confederate army.

By 6:30 a.m., the battle lines on and around Bloody Hill were fully established. The fighting there escalated to monumental proportions with the two Federal batteries of Totten and DuBois pouring a deadly firestorm of canister and grape into general Price's advancing Missouri State Guard. From the southeast, the Confederate Pulaski Battery was hurling an enfilading hail of fire across the crest of the hill and doing terrible damage to the Federal troops engaged there against those of General Price.

Captain Plummer, now successfully across the creek and advancing southward across Ray's cornfield, saw the damage the Pulaski Battery was doing to Lyon's brigades on Bloody Hill and was determined to take it. Unfortunately for him, however, Confederate Colonel James McIntosh with the 3rd Louisiana and the 2nd Arkansas Mounted Rifles, both of General McCulloch's now organized army, was advancing at great speed toward the cornfield. The two forces smashed together at around 7:00 a.m. Plummer and his 1st United States Infantry Regiment put up a spirited fight, but they were no match for McIntosh's angry troops and, but for Lieutenant John DuBois' Federal Battery of six guns, would probably have been annihilated.

DuBois, seeing Plummer's plight from across the creek, turned his guns on the cornfield and opened a deadly fire that had a devastating effect, not only on McIntosh's troops, but on those of Captain Plummer too. DuBois, however, had given Plummer, now severely wounded, the break he needed, and he was able to withdraw his regiment without further harm.

By now Price and McCulloch knew that Sigel was in control of the road south, and that there was only one way out; they had to fight.

At about 7:30 a.m. there was a lull in the fighting and both sides, each badly mauled by the other, had pulled back only slightly and were regrouping.

On the Federal side, General Lyon was himself directing the battle. DuBois' guns were brought forward in support of Totten's and preparations were being hurriedly made to receive the impending Confederate assault.

Scarcely had Lyon completed his works than General Price's divisions began advancing all along the southern slopes of Bloody Hill. Every available Federal reserve unit was brought quickly into action. The battle raged across the hillside; Federal and Confederate batteries filled the air with a firestorm of canister, grape and shell; the battle lines of infantry, in places three ranks deep, added a hail of minie balls to the deadly hurricane of iron and lead. On they fought, the Confederate firestorm approaching a crescendo as more and more reinforcements were added to the ranks already engaged on the hillside. Gun barrels soon became too hot to handle; company and regimental commanders fell wounded and killed; and still the firestorm swept on until at last, in places, the Federal line began to give way.

Then, at about 9, as Price's divisions surged forward in a determined attack all along Lyon's front, the Federal line seemed to gather new strength, rallied, and then they, too, pressed forward again. The firestorm all along the ridge swelled and continued as first one side, then the other fell back, rallied, surged forward again. The summit of the hill was literally covered with dead and wounded. Both sides were now fighting hand-to-hand, now with volley upon volley of musket fire, and all under a deadly hail of canister and grape from the batteries of both armies. In the midst of this terrible fray, Confederate Generals Price and McCulloch, at great risk to their own persons, urged their men onward and upward. General Price was slightly wounded but refused to leave the field. General McCulloch, in an effort to turn the tide, threw Colonel Greer's and Colonel Carroll's cavalry regiments against the Union left flank, but to no avail. Before the cavalry units could get within effective range, Lieutenant John DuBois' Federal battery devastated their ranks and, within a matter of minutes, they were scattered and had fallen back.

On the Union side, General Lyon and his officers were doing all they could to hold the Confederate advance in check. As he was walking back and forth, leading his horse by the reins, just to the left of Captain Totten's battery, a Confederate shell exploded close to the horse, killing it almost instantly and wounding Lyon in the leg and the head. Lyon stood for a moment, dazed, hat in hand, then turned and walked slowly toward the rear.

There's no doubt that, at this point, Lyon had become very depressed for, as he was receiving medical attention for his wounds, he was heard to say to Major John Schofield, *"It is as I expected; I am afraid the day is lost."* Moments later, mounted on an orderly's horse, blood dripping from his wounded leg, Lyon was once more directing the Federal efforts of Major Sturgis and General Sweeney. Then, waving his hat in the air and calling out to the 2nd Kansas Regiment, *"Come on my brave boys, I will lead you; FORWARD!"* he wheeled his horse, surged forward a few yards, and then was hit in the chest by a Confederate minie ball. He swayed for a moment in the saddle before being gently lowered to the ground by one of his orderlies, a private of Company B, 1st U.S. Cavalry, Edward Lehman, to whom he whispered, *"Lehman, I am killed."* His body was immediately carried to the rear and Major Sturgis took command of the wavering Federal forces.

In the meantime, the Federal forces on the crest of the hill had rallied, reformed, and were once again fighting like demons and General Price's divisions were steadily being driven back down the hill.

While all this was going on the question among the Federal commanders on Bloody Hill was, *"Where is Colonel Sigel?"* If Sigel should suddenly come up on Price's right and rear flank as the original plan called for, then there was no doubt that the Federal army could still carry the day. Sturgis knew, however, that unless Sigel made an appearance, and soon, he would have nothing left to do but retreat and save as much of his beleaguered force as possible. And, by all accounts, Lyon's plan should have worked, would have worked, but for an unforeseen and deadly twist of fate.

Sigel was, as you will recall, under the mistaken impression that General Lyon's initial attack on the sleeping Confederates had been successful. He had established his own line across the Wire Road at about 8 a.m. and was waiting for the fleeing thousands of Confederate soldiers he assumed would soon be coming his way. At about 8:30, skirmishers from Sigel's brigade spotted the gray-clad ranks of the Federal 1st Iowa Regiment moving quickly toward them. At least that's what they thought, but in reality the advancing column was the Confederate 3rd Louisiana Regiment with General McCulloch at its head.

Sigel, unable to see the colors of the advancing column, gave orders to his color-bearer to advance the colors and wave them three times – this so that his own troops would not be mistaken for the enemy. This was done, and the 3rd Louisiana continued its advance. The commanders of Sigel's 3rd and 5th Missouri Regiments and Backoff's Missouri Light Artillery Battalion were given orders "not to fire" on the approaching friendly troops. The approach of the gray-clad supposed 1st Iowa only seemed to confirm that Lyon had, indeed, been successful. Sigel's German troops were delighted.

The 3rd Louisiana had advanced to within 40 yards when a suspicious Corporal Todd of the Federal 3rd Missouri decided to challenge the approaching soldiers. He ordered the column to stop and demanded to know who they were. McCulloch replied in kind by asking Todd the same question. Todd replied that he belonged to Sigel's Regiment and, as he did so, realized what was happening and raised his rifle to shoot McCulloch. Before he could, however, he was cut down by a Confederate minie ball and the 3rd Louisiana surged forward as McCulloch yelled to Captain John P. Vigiline of the Pelican Rifles, *"Captain, take your company up and give them hell."* At the same time the guns of the Confederate Fort Smith Battery opened fire on Sigel from a hidden position at the mouth of Skegg's Branch Creek, causing great injury and confusion in the ranks of the already panicking Federal soldiers. Then Bledsoe's Confederate Battery, located on the lower southern slopes of Bloody Hill, delivered a long-range frontal barrage that did little damage but made a lot of noise and sent the panicking Germans diving for cover.

McCulloch's charge against Sigel's totally surprised and horrified regiments was swift, devastating, and decisive. In minutes the decimated ranks of German soldiers were fleeing panic stricken in every direction. Sigel did his best to contain the situation but it was hopeless. First he directed the six guns of Backoff's battery to return fire against those of the Confederate Fort Smith Battery, then he tried in vain to rally the fleeing Germans; it was no use. Of the six Federal guns only four were brought into action before the drivers of three of the teams had panicked and bolted for the rear, dragging the caissons behind them. The rest of Sigel's brigade soon followed, leaving weapons, cannon, limbers, and caissons to the charging Confederate forces.

Sigel himself left the field and headed overland through the fields toward Springfield with only two of his orderlies in attendance. General McCulloch turned northward and took his victorious force to the aid of General Price's beleaguered troops on Bloody Hill.

By 11 a.m. along the main line of battle on Bloody Hill the end was in sight. General McCulloch's cavalry had been dispersed by a determined effort from John DuBois' Federal Battery, and General Price had pulled back down the hill to regroup and replenish ammunition. On the crest of the hill, the Federal forces too had pulled back, Totten's battery had been moved to the rear and Colonel Sturgis, after a quick consultation with the other commanders, decided to take advantage of the lull in the fighting and ordered a general retreat back the way they'd came.

General Price moved his divisions back up the slopes and, finding the top of the hill deserted, ordered his men forward. By the time Price's skirmishers reached the position where Totten's battery had only minutes before been pouring a deadly barrage of canister and grape into the Confederate ranks, it had become obvious that the battle was at an end and that Price and McCulloch had emerged victorious. Had they then decided to put McCulloch's more than 6,000 Confederate cavalry, as yet fresh, rested, and uncommitted, in pursuit of the retreating Federal army they might well have destroyed it. The two Confederate Generals, however, had had enough. They were content to let the defeated Federal column escape and the Battle of Wilson's Creek was over.

Of the 5,400 Federal soldiers involved in the battle, 258, including General Lyon, were killed, 873 wounded, and 186 were missing, for a total of 1,317 casualties – almost 25% of the entire army. On the Confederate side, 277 soldiers were killed and 945 wounded, for a total of 1,222 – nearly 12% of the army.

The dead of both sides were not treated kindly. Many of the bodies remained unburied or were put into hastily dug, shallow graves. Fourteen Federal bodies were thrown down an old well, 34 more were discovered tumbled haphazardly into a sink-hole, others were buried in mass graves without ceremony or, in many cases, without identification. Several days after the battle had ended, bits and pieces of body parts, torn and chewed by scavenging dogs and buzzards, were found strewn all along the road where many of Colonel Sigel's men had fallen. In 1867, however, when the National Cemetery at Springfield was established, the bodies of the Union soldiers were removed from the shallow graves, the old well, and the sink-hole, then reburied with honor.

Of the Union officers that served at Wilson's Creek, 30 rose to the rank of brigadier or major general.

Confederate General Benjamin McCulloch was killed by a Federal sharpshooter some seven months after Wilson's Creek, while reconnoitering enemy positions at the Battle of Pea Ridge.

General Sterling Price, ever the popular commander – he was affectionately nicknamed "Old Pap" by his troops – continued the war in Missouri, leading his Missouri State Guard northward after Wilson's Creek to capture the Union garrison at Lexington. From there he continued his campaign until driven out of the state into Arkansas early in 1862. There he once again teamed up with General McCulloch at the Battle of Pea Ridge. He didn't return again to Missouri until September, 1864, when he marched his army of 12,000 men more than 1,500 miles, fought 43 battles, and destroyed an estimated $10 million in property. His campaign came to an abrupt end, however, when he was soundly defeated at the Battle of Westport on October 23. Once again he was forced to leave the state with the remains of his defeated army. After the war Price went to Mexico, where he remained until he returned to St. Louis in January, 1867, a broken man, impoverished and in poor health. He died there some eight months later on September 29th, 1867. Major General Sterling Price was one of the South's most steadfast soldiers: dedicated to his cause, his state, and to the men who served under him through four years of toil, devastation and, in the end, defeat.

A footnote to Wilson's Creek is that the misidentification of the 3rd Louisiana Regiment by Colonel Sigel and his subordinates was not an isolated incident. A similar incident at the Battle of 1st Manassas only the day before had been almost as costly when the 33rd Virginia Infantry Regiment, dressed in blue uniforms, approached the Union forces on Henry Hill to a point where they were able to open fire upon them at point-blank range.

Touring the Battlefield

Before you begin your tour of the battlefield, you might like to view the exhibits in the Visitors Center museum. There's a large-scale map of the battlefield and a short film interpreting Wilson's Creek and its significance in the Civil War.

The auto tour of Wilson's Creek National Battlefield Park will take you on a five-mile loop around eight stops, hitting all the major historic points along the way. At each stop you will find wayside exhibits with maps, artwork, and historical information about the battle. At many of the stops you will find walking trails to historic spots and overlooks. The tour road is one-way only. The left lane is for vehicles; the right-hand, narrow lane is set aside for walking, jogging or bicycling. Observe the speed limit and drive carefully. Begin your tour at the Visitors Center and drive to Stop 1.

Stop 1: Gibson's Mill

The area here marks the northern end of the battlefield and the location of some of the Confederate camps, including that of General Rains and 2,500 men, which was established here, close to the mill. At 5:30 on the morning of August 10th, 1861, General Lyon's troops attacked General Rains' position and drove him southward. A walking trail leads from here to the Gibson House and the mill sites. When you return to your vehicle proceed along the trail to Stop 2.

Stop 2: The Ray House and Cornfield

During and after the battle, the Ray House, constructed in 1852, was used as a Confederate hospital. Confederate Colonel Richard Weightman died in the front room of the house and the body of General Lyon was brought here, under flag-of-truce and under escort by Confederate General Rains, after the fighting had ended. It is said that Lyon was still dressed in his old single-breasted captain's uniform coat; his hat was missing, but was later recov-

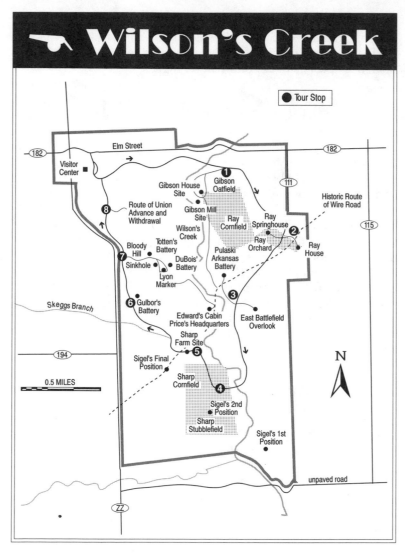

ered from the battlefield and was eventually presented, along with the general's sword, to the Connecticut Historical Society.

The small stone building at the foot of the hill is the Ray springhouse, the Ray's source of water and the only other surviving structure from the time of the battle. Major fighting took place to the northwest of the Ray House in the cornfield when Union Captain J.B. Plummer crossed Wilson's Creek in his effort to outflank the Confederate right. The wooded hilltop you see to the west is Bloody Hill, the ridge where Lyon's brigades fought for several hours against superior forces under the command of Confederate General Sterling Price. From here, proceed on along the road to Stop 3.

Stop 3: The Pulaski Arkansas Battery and General Price's Headquarters

Park your vehicle and take the short walk along the trail to the position held by the guns of Captain William Woodruff's Pulaski Arkansas Battery. It was from here that Woodruff's guns opened fire upon General Lyon's troops advancing over the crest of Bloody Hill, halting the Union attack and causing a great number of casualties. Woodruff's battery bought time, during which General Price was able to form his divisions into line of battle and begin his attack on the Federal positions on the crest of the hill. General Price's headquarters were located a short distance away to the west in the yard of what was at that time William Edward's home, located at the center of the Confederate army's camp.

From here you can return along the trail, cross the road, and take another short walk to the battlefield overlook, or you can return to your vehicle and continue on to Stop 4.

Stop 4: Sigel's Second Position

It was on the ridge across Wilson's Creek to your left that Colonel Franz Sigel heard General Lyon's artillery open fire on the Confederate camp to the north. Sigel immediately ordered Captain Backoff's Missouri Light Artillery Battalion to open fire upon the more than 2,000 sleeping Confederate cavalrymen camped here in this field. The Confederates were taken by surprise and driven off into the woods to the north and west of here. Sigel then crossed to this side of the creek and halted his men about a quarter-mile away in front of you and formed his brigade into line of battle opposing a large Confederate cavalry regiment holding a position at the north end of this field. There followed a heavy artillery engagement and the Confederate cavalry withdrew, leaving Sigel to continue his advance to his final position in line of battle across what was once the Wire Road at Stop 5.

Stop 5: Sigel's Final Position

Following his bombardment of the Confederate cavalry, Colonel Sigel advanced his brigade to this position and deployed into line of battle across the Wire Road. It was here he made his fatal error and wrongly identified the 3rd Louisiana Regiment as the 1st Iowa – a mistake that cost him his brigade and, ultimately, General Lyon the battle. From here continue on along the road to Stop 6.

Stop 6: Guibor's Battery

It was not far from this position that Confederate Artillery Captain Henry Guibor placed his guns into battery in support of the main Confederate line of battle. From its position here, the battery hammered at the Federal troops on the crest of Bloody Hill. On three separate occasions General Price's infantry divisions hurled themselves through these fields against the Federal positions; and three times they were repulsed. When Price and his men assaulted the hill for the fourth time, they found the Federal positions abandoned and the Union army retreating. Proceed along the road to Stop 7.

Stop 7: Bloody Hill

Leave your vehicle at the roadside and take the short walk up the hill, past the positions of Captain Totten's and Lieutenant John DuBois' Federal batteries, to the memorial that marks the spot where General Lyon died. For more than five hours General Lyon's brigades held the ground here at the top of what is today known as Bloody Hill. Time after time, under a devastating firestorm of artillery and musket fire, the Federal line held off General Price's charging Confederate infantry divisions. At the peak of the fighting the south slope of the hill and the crest where you are now standing was literally covered with the bodies of the wounded and the dying. More than 1,700 men lost their lives or fell wounded on the slopes and crest of this hill, among them General Lyon whose granite marker locates roughly the position where he fell at around 9:30 that terrible morning. The two batteries, Totten's and DuBois', kept up a devastating hail of canister and grape shot against the attacking Confederate divisions on the southern slopes of Bloody Hill and against Captain Woodruff's Pulaski Battery away to the east. When you have returned to your vehicle, continue on along the road to Stop 8.

Stop 8: The Historic Overlook

From here you will have a good view of the battlefield. In the distance, away to the southeast, you can see the John Ray House; Bloody Hill is behind you to the south. General Lyon's Union army passed through this position during both the early morning advance on the Confederate positions and its retreat just after eleven o'clock.

What to See, Where to Stay

Springfield

What to See

Museum of the Ozarks. 603 E. Calhoun Street. Located in the historic Bentley House, a restored Queen Anne-style mansion with stained glass windows, seven fireplaces, and period furnishings. Open Tuesday through Saturday.

Springfield National Cemetery. One of only a few national cemeteries where Union and Confederate soldiers are buried side-by-side.

Dickerson Park Zoo. 3043 N. Fort. Elephant herd, elephant rides, playground. Open daily but closed Thanksgiving and Christmas Day.

Bass Pro Shops Outdoor World. 1935 S. Campbell. One of the world's largest sporting goods stores, featuring indoor displays, including a two-story log cabin, a cascading waterfall, and five aquariums with trophy-sized fish. Open daily, but closed Christmas Day.

Annual Event

Ozark Empire Fair. Late July through mid-August.

Hotels

Best Western Coach House Inn. 2535 N. Glenstone Avenue, Springfield, MO 65803. Telephone 417-862-0701. Children under 12 stay free, crib free, cable TV, two pools, playground, cafe, bar. Accepts credit cards.

Econo Lodge. 2808 N. Kansas, Springfield, MO 65803. Telephone 417-869-5600. Children under 12 stay free, crib free, cable TV, free coffee in the lobby, cafe, bar. Accepts credit cards.

Holiday Inn. 2720 N. Glenstone Avenue, Springfield, MO 65803. Telephone 417-865-8600. Children under 18 stay free, crib free, cable TV, two pools, cafe, bar, free airport transportation, meeting rooms. Accepts credit cards.

Howard Johnson. 2610 N. Glenstone Avenue, Springfield, MO 65803. Telephone 417-862-0701. Children under 18 stay free, crib free, cable TV, four pools, playground, cafe, bar, free airport transportation, meeting rooms. Accepts credit cards.

Quality Inn North. 3050 N. Kentwood, Springfield, MO 65803. Telephone 417-833-0477. Crib free, cable TV, two pools, cafe, bar, free airport transportation, meeting rooms. Accepts credit cards.

Residence Inn by Marriott. 1550 E. Raynell Place, Springfield, MO 65804. Telephone 417-883-7300. Crib free, cable TV, pool, cafe nearby, meeting rooms. Accepts credit cards.

Sheraton Inn & Conference Center. 3333 S. Glenstone Avenue, Springfield, MO 65804. Telephone 417-883-6550. Children under 17 stay free, crib free, cable TV, two pools, cafe, bar, free airport transportation, meeting rooms. Accepts credit cards.

Holiday Inn University Plaza & Convention Center. 333 John Q. Hammons Parkway, Springfield, MO 65806. Telephone 417-864-7333. Children under 19 stay free, crib free, cable TV, two pools, cafe, bar, free airport transportation, convention facilities, meeting rooms. Accepts credit cards.

Mansion at Elfindale. 1701 S. Fort Street, Springfield, MO 65807. Telephone 417-831-5400. A Victorian mansion with 13 suites, free full breakfast, complimentary tea, cable TV, cafe nearby, NON-SMOKING. Accepts credit cards.

Chapter 5

Pea Ridge

March 7th & 8th, 1862

Pea Ridge National Military Park is 10 miles north of Rogers, Arkansas on State Highway 62. Or, from Fayetteville you can take U.S. Highway 71 and go 20 miles north to Bentonville, then follow Arkansas Highway 72 east to the junction of U.S. 62, turn east and follow U.S. 62 to the park entrance.

The Story of the Battle

The battle of Pea Ridge was the culmination of the early struggles for control of the State of Missouri. Missouri was strategically important to both sides for a couple of reasons: first there were the two great waterways, the Missouri and the Mississippi Rivers, and secondly she was blessed with an abundance of natural resources and manpower.

For many years Missouri had been a slave state and wanted the situation, not only to continue, but to spread into neighboring states as well. In 1854 the question of slavery flared into bloodshed when Missourians tried to force it onto the free Kansas settlers. The "Bloody Kansas Affair" brought raiding, looting, burning, and murder to Kansas and Missouri. Then the national political situation began to turn sour, and the politicians in Missouri turned their attentions to matters of greater importance.

After the fall of Fort Sumter in 1861 it become obvious that Missouri would not be allowed to remain neutral. When President Lincoln called for troops to put down the rebellion, Missouri's Governor Claiborne F. Jackson, a staunch Confederate, refused the request saying, *"Your request is illegal, unconstitutional, revolutionary, inhuman, diabolical, and cannot be complied with."* The result was General Nathaniel Lyon's ill-fated campaign of July and August, 1861, culminating in a Confederate victory at the Battle of Wilson's Creek south of Springfield, Missouri, on August 10th. It was in that battle that General Lyon lost his life.

Maj. General Earl Van Dorn.

After the battle, the victors of Wilson's Creek, Confederate Generals Benjamin McCulloch and Sterling Price, never the best of friends and able to agree upon almost nothing, each went their separate ways, with General Price leading his Missouri State Guard northward where, on September 20th, 1861, he scored a stunning victory at the Battle of Lexington. Unfortunately, his triumph was short-lived, for on December 25th, 1861, General Henry Halleck, commander of the newly formed Federal Department of the Missouri, charged Brigadier General Samuel Curtis with the task of driving all Confederate forces out of Missouri.

On February 10th, 1862, Curtis embarked upon his campaign with an army numbering almost 11,000 effectives. Confederate Major General Sterling Price and his Missouri State Guard, now more than 8,000-strong, offered little resistance and withdrew his army from Missouri into northwestern Arkansas. There, once again, he joined with Brigadier General Benjamin McCulloch and his force of some 6,000 regulars. The two generals, bickering as usual, retreated still further to a position south of Fayetteville, Arkansas.

The Confederate authorities in Richmond knew the tense situation between McCulloch and Price could not be allowed to continue and appointed Major General Earl Van Dorn, a man of proven military stature, to take command of the Confederate forces in northwest Arkansas.

Van Dorn, a vain, aggressive commander, had graduated 52nd in the class of 1842 from West Point and from that time served with distinction, including a stint during the Mexican War under General Winfield Scott. Van Dorn resigned his commission in the United States Army in January, 1861, and was appointed a Colonel in the Army of the Confederacy. On June 5th, 1861, he was promoted to the rank of brigadier general. Four months later, in September, he was promoted again, this time to major general, and given command of the Confederate Trans-Mississippi Department. And so it was that, on March 3rd, 1862, Van Dorn arrived at the Confederate headquarters located at Cove Creek deep in the Boston Mountains of northwest Arkansas.

Upon taking command of the combined Confederate army, Van Dorn let it be known that he intended to take the offensive, wage an all-out war against General Curtis' Federal army, drive it out of Arkansas, and then move northward, capture the City of St. Louis, and thus take control of the entire state of Missouri for the Confederacy.

Within hours of his arrival at Cove Creek, the Confederate army, now augmented by the addition of

Brig. General Albert Pike.

three Cherokee Indian regiments under the command of Brigadier General Albert Pike and Cherokee Indian Colonel Stand Watie, numbered more than 17,000 effectives, including five batteries of artillery. It was moving northward through the Boston Mountains. By the evening of the 5th, Van Dorn's army, exhausted from its long forced march, had passed through Fayetteville and was within striking distance of the Federal army.

In the meantime, General Curtis' forces were scattered across northwestern Arkansas from Little Sugar Creek to Cross Hollow: Brigadier General Franz Sigel with two divisions of infantry was four miles south of Bentonville, Colonel Jefferson Davis's division was on the bluffs above Sugar Creek, and Colonel Eugene Carr with a fourth division was at Cross Hollow.

Upon learning of the Confederate troop movements, General Curtis ordered his forces to concentrate on a position where the Little Sugar Creek crossed the Telegraph Road. Curtis arrived there himself around 2 in the morning and immediately ordered the Telegraph Road closed and earthworks built in preparation for the battle he was sure must take place there; the earthworks were supposed to command the bluffs on the side of the Little Sugar Creek, and the approaches from the south and southwest. All through the early morning and most of the day of March 6th, the Federals labored at their work, felling trees and constructing a network of trenches. Van Dorn, by now, was only 14 miles to the southwest and moving quickly toward Curtis' positions.

By the evening of March 6th, Van Dorn had reached a position some five miles to the west of Curtis' positions and had gone into camp on the banks of the Little Sugar Creek at the junction of the Bentonville Detour, a road that ran side-by-side with the Little Sugar Creek, eventually connecting with the Telegraph Road at Elkhorn Tavern, close to, and to the north of, the now strongly fortified Federal positions.

Van Dorn's scouts reported in with news of the strong Federal positions and Van Dorn realized that a frontal attack on Curtis would be futile at best, and possibly disastrous. After a lengthy consultation with his generals, Van Dorn devised a plan that relied greatly on deception and surprise. First he would have his men pitch tents and build fires where the army now lay as if for an extended stay, in the hope that such an action would deceive Curtis. Then, later that same evening of the 6th, he would move his army northeast along the Bentonville Detour, past the Federal right flank, and early the following morning make a two-pronged attack on Curtis' positions from the rear.

At 8 on the evening of March 6th, General Van Dorn's forces moved out of camp along the Bentonville Detour. General Price with his Missouri State Guard would go to the junction of the Telegraph Road at Elkhorn Tavern, move south along the road, and attack Curtis on his right rear flank. General McCulloch with Colonel Herbert's infantry brigade, Brigadier General James McIntosh's cavalry brigade, Brigadier General Albert Pike's three regiments of Indians, and five batteries of artillery, would, after reaching a position about two miles short of the Telegraph Road, turn south, skirt the western edge of Pea Ridge, and attack the Federal left in a classic pincer formation. Van Dorn's plan was for both wings of his army to be in position to begin the attack at daybreak. Unfortunately, because the weather was extremely cold and wet, the troops cold and exhausted after two days of forced marching through the wind and snow on the mountains, and because Van Dorn's forces were held up by the icy waters of the Little Sugar Creek, it was almost daylight when the last of the Confederate army passed over the creek, and almost 8 before General Price arrived at the junction of Telegraph Road. In the meantime, General Curtis, as early as 5 a.m., had learned of the Confederate troop movements, and by 6 a.m. was well aware of Van Dorn's intention to attack him from the rear.

Curtis now was faced with something of a dilemma: he must quickly decide how to face this new situation or be overwhelmed. Realizing that what had been a strong position when facing an attack from the south was now a liability, Curtis decided that, as always, the best form of defense is to attack. He, therefore, decided to send a part of General Sigel's command under Colonel Osterhaus, along with two batteries of artillery, to deliver a strike against what he thought would be the center of Van Dorn's line of battle. It was at about this time that he learned that General Price was just to

Elkhorn Tavern.

the north of Elkhorn Tavern, that he, Price, had captured the outpost there commanded by Major Eli Weston. Weston was now in retreat southward toward the Tavern, and was already moving against his, Curtis', new right flank.

It was now imperative that Curtis take major corrective action and quickly; he ordered Colonel Eugene Carr, now commanding the Federal right, to send a brigade of infantry under the command of Colonel Grenville Dodge to the aid of Major Weston. Dodge quickly assessed the situation, and found General Price already moving quickly to the Federal right. Major Weston had already been pushed back a considerable distance by the Confederate cavalry under the command of Colonel Cearnal. On learning this, Carr, now headquartered at Elkhorn Tavern, realizing the gravity of the situation, and that General Price had him considerably outnumbered, established Colonel Dodge in position to the south of Williams Hollow and sent for Colonel William Vandever's brigade to reinforce him. Dodge was soon under heavy fire from General Price's advancing columns.

In the meantime, Colonel Vandever had set off up the Telegraph Road toward Elkhorn Tavern at full speed. Just as he was nearing the tavern, however, he encountered a large concentration of Confederate infantry under the command of Colonel Henry Little, who was just beginning his thrust toward the Federal center. Before he knew what was happening, Vandever had run slap into the Confederate vanguard and was immediately involved in a fierce, hand-to-hand struggle against vastly superior odds. Vandever, however, pressed forward with fierce determination and, for a moment, seemed to be making ground, pushing the Confederate forces under Colonel Little steadily backward. Inevitably, Little's superior numbers began to tell. Yard by yard, Vandever, under a devastating barrage of Confederate cannon and rifle fire, had no alternative but to give way.

Meanwhile, General Price's right wing under the command of Confederate Brigadier General William Slack was driving the Federal forces from the crest of Pea Ridge. During the struggle for Pea Ridge, the Confederate army suffered the loss of the first of three generals who would die as a result of the battle. Confederate General William Y. Slack received a mortal wound and had to be carried from the field; Colonel Thomas H. Rosser assumed command of Slack's brigade.

By 3 that afternoon, the Confederate assault on General Curtis' right flank had been successful. Elkhorn Tavern was in Confederate hands. Colonel Little had driven Colonel Vandever back down the Telegraph Road, and Colonel Rosser had driven the Federals from the crest of Pea Ridge. All that saved the Federal right from being completely turned was the timely arrival of General Alexander Asboth, a magnificently bewhiskered Hungarian with a full division of infantry and a battery of seven guns. Asboth's force, too, was outnumbered and could do little but stem the advancing Confederate tide. Asboth deployed his seven guns on either side of the Telegraph Road and began to pour a deadly barrage of canister and grape shot into the advancing Confederate ranks. Tenuously, Asboth held his position under overwhelming odds until, with the winter sky darkening in the east, General Van Dorn called a halt to the battle and established new headquarters at Elkhorn Tavern. The day had brought victory to General Price's forces on the left side of the field. On the right wing, however, where General McCulloch was moving southward into the vicinity of Leetown, things had not gone quite so well.

On learning that General Van Dorn's Confederate army was moving northeast by way of the Bentonville Detour, but not realizing that Van Dorn had decided on a two-pronged attack to his left and right rear, General Curtis had sent a strong task force under the command of Colonel Osterhaus to attack Van Dorn's center. Soon Osterhaus's pickets encountered a large Confederate force moving in tight formation along the Bentonville Detour. Without waiting, Osterhaus opened fire with three cannon of the 1st Missouri Flying Battery, causing great confusion among the ranks of the marching Confederate soldiers.

Confederate General McCulloch, in command of the right wing of Van Dorn's army, detached Brigadier General McIntosh's cavalry brigade and the three regiments of Indians under the command of Brigadier General Albert Pike to deal with the guns. McIntosh moved west toward the Federal position held by Colonel Cyrus Bussey of Osterhaus' force, while Pike's Indian regiments moved forward on McIntosh's left behind a rail fence that ran east and west on the north side of the field where the three Federal guns had gone into battery. The Federals were overwhelmed and driven back; the three guns of the Missouri Flying Battery were captured and their carriages burned.

At this point Colonel Osterhaus advanced three more cannon and began pounding the victorious and excited Indians. The Indians, not used to this sort of action, panicked and scampered off into the woods away from "the wagons that shoot," and there they remained, pinned down, for most of the rest of the day.

Confederate General McIntosh now deployed his dismounted cavalry in line of battle along the northern edge of the field in opposition to Colonel Osterhaus' Federal infantry. Time after time McIntosh tried to drive the persistent Federals from their positions, only to be repulsed. Then, shortly after 2 o'clock that afternoon, General Benjamin McCulloch decided to make a reconnaissance in person and, dressed in his customary black velvet coat and plumed hat, he rode forward. Private Peter Pelican, a sharpshooter with the 36th Illinois Infantry Regiment was waiting for just such an opportunity and, with a single shot, killed the second Confederate general of the day. McCulloch was replaced in command by General McIntosh, but not for long; within minutes of McCulloch's death he, too, fell under the impact of a sharpshooter's bullet, shot through the heart. The count of dead Confederate generals had risen to three. Things were not going well on the Confederate right.

One last hope remained for a Confederate victory on the right flank; Colonel Louis Hebert's Confederate infantry brigade had moved to the east of Round Top Mountain and, at first, had become lost. Finally, they found themselves confronted by Union forces under the command of Brigadier General Jefferson C. Davis in a position just to the left of Osterhaus. Hebert pushed forward and smashed Davis' troops backward. Davis, however, managed to detach Colonel Thomas Pattison with a strong force and send him to attack Hebert in the rear. Hebert was taken by surprise at the renewed, combined attack by Davis and Pattison on two fronts. It was a situation he couldn't handle. For awhile the Confederates managed to hold their ground, but the outcome was inevitable; Hebert's brigade collapsed. Colonel Hebert and Colonel M.C. Mitchell of the 14th Arkansas were among the Confederate officers captured that afternoon.

Van Dorn was now in serious trouble. Although the fighting of the 7th of March was now at an end, three of his most able generals had been killed and many of his best subordinate officers had been captured. He now had two options: he could withdraw and leave the field to General Curtis, or he could try a magnificent bluff and remain on the field in the hopes that Curtis would succumb to his superior numbers and leave the field during the night. He chose the latter; unfortunately, Curtis stayed put.

During the night the remnants of Van Dorn's right wing, now virtually leaderless, joined him at Elkhorn Tavern. As daylight approached the following morning, March 8th, with ammunition running low, moral among his exhausted troops even lower, and with a growing realization that General Pike's Indian regiments were virtually worthless, Van Dorn prepared once more to do battle.

All through the night the Federals made preparations for the final showdown. General Curtis replenished his depleted supplies of ammunition, gathered together his widely dispersed units and deployed them in strategic positions to the south of Van Dorn's positions across the Telegraph Road; by dawn Curtis had established a formidable array of men and firepower. General Sigel's two divisions were deployed to the left of the road, Brigadier General Asboth was on the extreme left with six cannon, Colonel Osterhaus was to his right with five cannon, and Colonel Jefferson Davis was put into position just to the left of the road with four

more guns. Colonel Carr's division was deployed to the right of the
road with three guns.

Van Dorn's Confederate divisions were deployed in line of battle
just to the south of Elkhorn Tavern from the base of Pea Ridge on
his right flank, across the Telegraph Road, to a point close to Cross
Timber Hollow where the remains of Pike's Indian regiments were
deployed in the hills on the extreme left.

The Federals opened the battle with a devastating barrage of artillery fire all along the line of battle. Van Dorn, in reply, pushed
forward his batteries and the now uneven duel recommenced. Van
Dorn had begun the battle on the morning of the 7th with some 62
cannon, a third more than the Federal army. But now those superior numbers were of little use to him. With ammunition running
low, and thus unable to maintain any sort of sustained fire, Van
Dorn's artillery was systematically destroyed by the devastating
and concentrated fire from the Federal batteries. In a very short
time it became obvious to Van Dorn that he was not going to win
the contest.

By 9, General Sigel had advanced four of General Asboth's guns to
cover the southeastern slopes of Pea Ridge. The Confederate batteries were by now almost out of ammunition. By 10, with most of
his guns disabled, Van Dorn had accepted the inevitable and had
begun to withdraw his troops, first to Williams Hollow northeast
of Elkhorn Tavern, then back to the southeast where he gained the
Huntsville Road and an open line of retreat toward Keetsville,
Missouri.

In the meantime, General Sigel had advanced his divisions beyond
Pea Ridge in the hopes of cutting off a Confederate retreat in that
direction; he was disappointed. All that remained of the once
mighty Confederate army were a few stragglers who were quickly
rounded up and taken prisoner. The Battle of Pea Ridge, or Elkhorn
Tavern, was over. It was a decided victory for General Curtis and
his Federal army. General Sigel was ecstatic; he now felt more than
vindicated for his disastrous mistake that had cost the Union Army
the Battle of Wilson's Creek some seven months earlier on August
10th, 1861.

The battle had been a costly one for General Curtis. Of the Federal
10,500 troops involved, almost 1,400, more than 13%, were killed,
wounded, or missing. On the other hand, with an effective force in

excess of 16,500, Van Dorn had sustained only a thousand casualties, about 6%. Unfortunately, that 6% included three generals and several of his brigade commanders.

General Van Dorn never quite lived up to his potential, or to the expectations of his superiors in Richmond. Following the Battle of Pea Ridge, he moved southward toward Shiloh, arriving there too late to be a part of the battle. On October 3rd and 4th, 1862, with a force of 22,000 soldiers, including General Sterling Price's Missouri State Guard, he fought the Battle of Corinth, Mississippi, a bloody and futile struggle Van Dorn lost at a cost of more than 4,200 casualties. Following the Battle of Corinth, Van Dorn was ordered to face a court of inquiry on charges of misconduct and drunkenness on the battlefield. He was exonerated of all charges, but was never given command of an army again. Van Dorn was a handsome man, vain, well dressed, and popular with the ladies. It came as no surprise to those who knew him well when he died at the hands of a jealous husband at his headquarters in Spring Hill, Tennessee, on May 7th, 1863.

Following the Battle of Corinth the ever-popular General Sterling Price, "Old Pap," continued the war and eventually returned to Missouri in September, 1864. During his famous campaign there, forever to be known as "Price's Missouri Raid," he led his army of 12,000 men through more than 1,500 miles of enemy territory, 43 battles, and caused the destruction of an estimated $10 million in property. His spectacular campaign came to an end when he was soundly defeated at the Battle of Westport on October 23, 1864. Once again he was forced to leave the state with the remains of his defeated army. He returned to St. Louis in January, 1867, a broken man, impoverished and in poor health, and died there some eight months later on September 29th, 1867.

General Curtis' success at Pea Ridge brought him a promotion to major general. He too continued his service throughout the war, eventually retiring to serve as commissioner for the Union Pacific Railroad, a post he held until his death on December 26th, 1866.

Brigadier General Franz Sigel too received a promotion to major general after his success at Pea Ridge. His career thereafter was one of mediocrity, culminating in his defeat on May 15th, 1864, at the Battle of New Market, Virginia; a battle made famous by the charge of the cadets from The Virginia Military Institute. Sigel was relived of field command shortly after and resigned his commission on May 4th, 1865. He died in New York on August 21st, 1902.

Colonel Eugene Carr was wounded three times during the Battle of Pea Ridge, but refused to leave the field. For his efforts there, and for gallantry above and beyond the call of duty, he was awarded the Medal of Honor and promoted to the rank of brigadier general. Following Pea Ridge he fought in the Second Vicksburg Campaign, and again at the Siege of Mobile in 1865. After the war he served on the frontier with the 5th and 6th Cavalry, earning a reputation as "perhaps the most famous and experienced Indian fighter since the Civil War." He retired from military service after a long and distinguished career on February 15th, 1893. He died in Washington, DC, on December 2nd, 1910, and was buried with honor at West Point.

Touring the Battlefield

The seven-mile, self-guided auto tour of Pea Ridge National Battlefield includes 11 stops with interpretive maps, text, and four push-button taped messages to explain the battle action at each site. Artillery is deployed across the battlefield to identify lines of attack and defense. There are also approximately 10 miles of hiking trails and an 11-mile horse trail – please bring your own horse. Bicycles are permitted only on the tour road. After stopping in at the visitor center, follow the arrows from the parking area to the old Telegraph Road, turn left and proceed to Stop 1.

Stop 1: General Curtis' Headquarters Site

It was in this vicinity that General Curtis established his field headquarters just before the Battle of Pea Ridge began on March 7th, 1862. Curtis believed that the Confederate offensive would come from south of Little Sugar Creek, some two miles to the south of here. Consequently, his troops were strongly entrenched across the Telegraph Road there and on the bluffs along the Little Sugar Creek. His wrongly held belief almost cost him the battle. From here, continue on along the road to Stop 2.

Stop 2: Winton Springs

Winton Spring was an important source of water for the Union soldiers during and after the battle. At the time of the battle, the

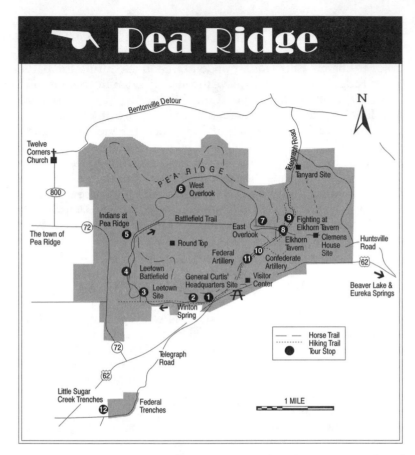

Ruddick family, at one time the owners of Elkhorn Tavern, lived on the hill above the spring. Stop 3 is about a half-mile further on along the road.

Stop 3: The Leetown Site

In 1862, the site where you now stand was the location of the tiny but thriving community of Leetown. The village has long since disappeared, leaving little evidence that it ever existed. At the time of the battle, however, the villagers had to endure almost two days of dreadful horrors as the fighting raged back and forth around them. From here, continue on along the road for a short distance to Stop 4.

Stop 4: Leetown Battlefield

As you stand and look out across the battlefield, try to imagine the carnage that must have taken place here and across the fields to the left, right, and front of you. General McCulloch's Confederate troops attacked in force through the woods to the north of the field and across Round Top to your right and front.

Brigadier General McIntosh's cavalry brigade and three regiments of Indians under the command of Brigadier General Albert Pike moved west toward the Federal positions held by Colonel Cyrus Bussey of Osterhaus' division. At first the Federal position was overwhelmed and driven back, leaving three guns of the Missouri Flying Battery behind them.

Colonel Osterhaus, however, advanced three more cannon, opened fire on the victorious Indians, causing great panic and confusion, and a general retreat commenced as the Indians ran from the field and into the woods away from "the wagons that shoot."

General McIntosh deployed his dismounted cavalry in line of battle along the northern edge of the field in an effort to deal with Colonel Osterhaus' infantry. Time and again McIntosh attacked the Federal position, only to be repulsed.

Shortly after 2 that afternoon, General Benjamin McCulloch decided to make a reconnaissance of the area. A sharpshooter with the 36th Illinois, with a single shot, killed the flamboyant Confederate general. General McIntosh took over in command of McCulloch's forces, but within minutes of McCulloch's death he, too, was shot through the heart. The action on this section of the battlefield continued to rage for most of the rest of the day. The air here was filled with the constant thunder of the great guns, the crackle of musket fire, and the howl of flying lead and iron. Stop 5 is about two-thirds of a mile further on along the road.

Stop 5: The Indians at Pea Ridge

The Battle of Pea Ridge was the only Civil War battle where Indians were used. At first, General Pike's Cherokees were successful. They had much to do with the taking of the three Federal guns that had fired on them from the field over to your left. It wasn't long, however, before they succumbed to the concentrated artillery fire delivered by the three-gun Federal battery brought forward by Colonel Osterhaus. In great panic and confusion they ran from the field, took cover in the woods, and didn't participate in the battle for the rest of the day. Continue on along the road to Stop 6.

Stop 6: The West Overlook

As you look out over the fields and woods to the south you should be able to see the Boston Mountains away on the horizon. Bentonville is 14 miles away to your right. Stop 7, The East Overlook, is a little more than a mile away along the road to your left.

Stop 7: The East Overlook

Leave your vehicle at the roadside and take the short walk along the trail to the overlook; the view is well worth the time and effort. Once there you will find a shelter, interpretive maps, and a recorded commentary that describes in detail the action that took place in the fields below. When you've finished here, return to your vehicle and proceed on along the road to the Telegraph Road. Turn left onto Telegraph Road and proceed to Stop 8.

Stop 8: Elkhorn Tavern

The Elkhorn Tavern you see here is not the original building that stood on the same spot during the Battle of Pea Ridge. That building burned to the ground a short time after the battle. The present building is a faithful reconstruction built upon the original foundations not long after the fire. Today, the Elkhorn Tavern is a museum. You should allow about 15 minutes for a tour of the tavern; there are restrooms and a drinking fountain inside. The museum is closed during the winter months, and is open from 10 a.m. until 4 p.m., May through October. Stop 9 is only a short distance away along the road to the north.

Stop 9: The Fighting at Elkhorn Tavern

From here, in the early morning of March 7th, 1862, the Confederate forces under the command of Major General Earl Van Dorn made their first assaults on the Federal forces on the Telegraph Road to the north of Elkhorn Tavern and drove them steadily back to a position about one-half mile behind you. On the second day of the battle, the 8th, things did not go quite so well for Van Dorn.

General Sigel's batteries opened up a massive bombardment that systematically smashed one Confederate battery after another. By 10:30 that morning, Van Dorn's troops were almost out of ammunition, most of his 62 guns had been silenced, and he was already withdrawing his beleaguered army away through Williams Hollow to the northeast of Elkhorn Tavern, and then back to the southeast and the Huntsville Road, where he had an open line of retreat toward Keetsville, Missouri. The Battle of Pea Ridge began and ended close to the position where you are now standing. When you have finished here you will need to turn around and proceed back the way you came, past Elkhorn Tavern, and on along the Telegraph Road to Stop 10.

Stop 10: The Confederate Artillery

The guns you see here mark the position held by Tull's Confederate Missouri Battery on the morning of the second day of battle, the 8th. This battery and others in the Confederate line of battle, low on ammunition, returned the fire from the Federal batteries about a quarter-mile away to the south as best they could. Stop 11 is about a quarter-mile further on along the road.

Stop 11: The Federal Artillery

It was the massed Federal guns in position here that drove General Van Dorn's Confederate army into retreat southeast along the Huntsville Road. The Federal line extended from the guns in position on the right to a point almost directly behind the visitor center.

This concludes your tour of the battlefield. If you have not already done so, you will enjoy a tour of the museum located in the Visitor Center. There you will find an assortment of exhibits, artifacts, maps and photographs that will help you understand the Battle of Pea Ridge and its implications more fully. There's also a 12-minute slide presentation shown every 30 minutes providing an excellent interpretation of the battle. A complete tour of the museum, the bookstore and the slide show will take a little more than 30 minutes, but is well worth your time and effort.

The park and Visitor Center is open seven days a week from 8 a.m. until 5 p.m., but closed on Thanksgiving, Christmas, and New Years. For more information, contact The Pea Ridge National Military Park, PO Box 700, Pea Ridge, AR 72751. Telephone 501-451-8122.

What to See, Where to Stay

Rogers, Arkansas

What to See

Rogers Historical Museum (The Hawkins House). 322 S. 2nd Street. Exhibits describe the history of the Rogers area from almost every period of American history.

Beaver Lake. A 30,000-acre lake four miles east of Rogers on AR 12. Water sports and outdoor recreation of all types along a 483-mile shoreline. Boating facilities, campgrounds, playgrounds, etc.

War Eagle Mill. A picturesque community on AR 12 and the site of one of Arkansas' largest and most popular arts & crafts shows. Activities include a tour of a working water-powered grist mill. Telephone for information: 501-789-2909.

Hotels

Beaver Lake Lodge. 100 Dutchman Drive, four miles east of Rogers on AR 12. Telephone 501-925-2313. Children under 12 stay free, free crib, pool, free coffee, golf packages, golf privileges, picnic tables and grill. Accepts credit cards.

Ramada Inn. Two miles south of Rogers on US 71. Telephone 501-636-5850. Children under 18 stay free, free crib, pool, cafe, private club, meeting rooms. Accepts credit cards.

Rocky Branch Resort. Box 277, Route 6, 72756. Located 10 miles east of Rogers on AR 12E, then four miles north on AR 303. Telephone 501-925-1688. Children under 6 stay free, pool, golf privileges. Accepts credit cards.

Chapter 6

Fort Pulaski

April 10-11, 1862

Fort Pulaski National Monument is located on Cockspur Island at the mouth of the Savannah River about 15 miles east of the city of Savannah, and may be reached by way of U.S. Highway 80 (the Tybee Highway). The entrance to the fort is located on McQueen's Island at U.S. 80. Cockspur Island is connected by a short road and a bridge across the South Channel of the Savannah River.

The Story of the Fort

Cockspur Island is a natural defensive position upon which fortifications of one sort or another have been located since Fort George, a palisade log blockhouse, was built in 1761. Fort George was dismantled in 1776 by American Patriots who knew the wooden structure could not stand against the guns of a strong British fleet.

In 1794 a new fort was begun on Cockspur Island. This one was named Fort Greene in honor of the Revolutionary War hero, General Nathaniel Greene. The fort was a small one, constructed of earth and timber with a complement of six guns. Unfortunately, Fort Greene was, some nine years after construction was completed, the victim of a hurricane that destroyed the fort and drowned most of the garrison. It wasn't until 1829 that construction of a new fort began on the island.

During the War of 1812 the coastal settlements and cities of the new American nation suffered dreadfully at the hands of the British Navy. The coastline for a 1,000 miles was virtually defenseless. The city of Washington was burned, and settlements along the mid-Atlantic coast were laid waste. Things might have been even worse were it not for the fact that England was fighting the war with Napoleon and that most of her forces were engaged there.

After the Treaty of Ghent in 1814 that ended the war with Britain, President James Madison pursuaded Congress to appropriate the necessary funds for building a chain of forts to protect the vulnerable American coastline. The job of designing this complicated defensive ring was given to a French military engineer, an expert in the field, General Simon Bernard. Bernard was commissioned into the newly formed Corps of Engineers with the brevet rank of brigadier general.

By 1821 the surveys had been completed, the sites for the new forts chosen, and the necessary funds for construction appropriated; Cockspur Island at the mouth of the Savannah River in Georgia was chosen as one of the sites. Work on the new fort, however, did not begin until 1829.

In 1827 Bernard's plans for a massive structure some two stories high and mounting three tiers of guns were determined to be unsuitable due to the fact that the island's geology could not provide a suitable foundation; new plans were drawn and work began in 1829 under the direction of Major Samuel Babcock. Later that year he was joined by a newly graduated West Point engineer with the title *"Acting Assistant Commissary of Subsistence."* That man's name was Lieutenant Robert E. Lee. Babcock was replaced due to ill health a year later by Joseph Mansfield, to whom the credit for the construction of the fort must go.

In 1833, the new fort on Cockspur Island was named Fort Pulaski in honor of the Polish hero, Count Casimir Pulaski, who fought in the American Revolution and was killed in the Battle of Savannah on October 9th, 1779. The actual construction was completed in 1847 but the arming and garrisoning of the fort still had not been completed by the time of Lincoln's election as President of the United States in 1860.

The fort's armament was supposed to consist of 145 seacoast guns, but by 1860 only 20 of those guns had been mounted, and the entire garrison consisted of a caretaker and an ordnance sergeant. An interesting footnote to the years of Fort Pulaski's construction is that every engineering officer employed during the works, with the exception of Major Babcock who died in 1831, eventually became a general, either in the Confederate or Union armies.

As the relationship between North and South deteriorated, Governor Joseph Brown of Georgia with remarkable foresight began to

Fort Pulaski.

prepare his state for the coming conflict. The state's volunteer forces were reorganized and strengthened, a million dollars was appropriated from state government funds for defense purposes, and orders were placed in the North for all sorts of weapons and munitions. Large quantities of cannon and rifles were ordered, and a bonus of $10,000 was offered by the state to anyone who would set up an ordnance factory in Georgia that could cast large cannon and produce as many as three guns a week.

As Governor Brown's preparations for war proceeded at full speed, the situation between North and South was rapidly coming to a head. On December 20, 1860, South Carolina seceded from the Union. The news was received in Georgia with wild excitement and enthusiasm. That same evening Union Major Robert Anderson took possession of Fort Sumter, effectively blocking Charleston Harbor to commerce from Europe; the news stunned the people of Georgia.

Military leaders in Georgia realized that it was only a matter of time before what had happened at Fort Sumter would happen at Fort Pulaski; the Federal Government would lose no time in occupying all the forts along the Eastern seaboard. Matters were brought to a head in Georgia on December 31st when the Savannah Republican newspaper received a telegram from United States Senator Robert Toombs of Georgia warning the people of the state that the Federal Government was taking a hard line, and that Joseph Holt, a staunch foe of the south, had been named by President Lincoln as Secretary of War. So, for their own safety, it was determined that Georgia should lose no time and itself occupy the fort at the mouth of the Savannah River. The following morning Governor Brown arrived in Savannah and ordered the state militia to occupy Fort Pulaski.

As there were at the time no Federal troops at Fort Pulaski, it would be a relatively simple job to garrison the fort; even so, it was no small task to transfer the necessary men and equipment to the island. The task, however, was undertaken with enthusiasm and in something of a holiday atmosphere. Detachments of 50 men each were organized from the Oglethorpe Light Infantry and the Savannah Volunteer Guards; 34 more men from the Chatham Artillery completed the first section of the new garrison. Arms, ammunition and equipment were quickly provided, commissary supplies were purchased, and a steamboat was employed. Each man was ordered to pack a knapsack with a change of clothing, mess kit, and toiletries.

The morning of January 3rd, 1861 dawned under a miserable sky. The 134 men assembled in the pouring rain and then marched through the streets lined with cheering citizens to the wharf on West Broad Street and embarked on the side-wheeler steamboat, *Ida*, for Cockspur Island. It seems that the order for the men to take with them a minimum of personal belongings was ignored; the expeditionary force, under the command of Colonel Alexander R. Lawton of the 1st Volunteer Regiment of Georgia, is said to have *"carried enough baggage to have served a division."* Every soldier took with him a cot and a roll of bedding, while for every three men there was a mess chest with enough equipment to provide for the needs of an entire regiment. In addition, the Chatham Artillery had boarded the boat with its full complement of ordnance: two bronze 12-pounder cannon and four bronze six-pounder field pieces.

The garrison reached Cockspur Island at noon. They disembarked in fine spirits and then marched through the rain into the fort with drums beating and flags flying. As they entered the fort the rain stopped, the clouds broke, and the sun shone brightly on the merry band of adventurers; it was a good omen. Or was it?

For several weeks the garrison worked feverishly to ready the fort in case of attack. The men drilled constantly, mounted guns, sorted equipment, and learned how to handle their artillery. A telegraph line between the island and Savannah was installed, more guns were ordered from the Tredegar Iron Works in Richmond and, before long, the erstwhile defenders on the island were joined by elements of the Georgia Navy, a motley collection or river-boats mounted with field pieces, under the command of Commodore Josiah Tattnall. Colonel Lawton said of the assembly, *"The Commodore will take care of the Yankees at sea and we shall manage them on land."* Then on April 13th, 1861 came the news that Fort Sumter in South Carolina had fallen to the Confederacy and so the great fort at the mouth of the Savannah River prepared itself for the inevitable.

In Washington, President Lincoln turned to the venerable General Winfield Scott, a veteran of the Mexican War and the War of 1812, for military direction. Scott's first reaction was that the South should be left to go its own way in peace, a suggestion that was totally unacceptable to Lincoln. Scott then went to work on a plan designed to strangle and starve the fledgling Confederacy. The plan was devised in three parts: first, Scott called for a mighty army to protect Washington and bring the enemy to battle wherever it may find him and destroy him; second, he called for a naval blockade of the entire Eastern seaboard to isolate the Confederacy from European support; and third, he called for combined army and naval operations in the west to control the Mississippi River and cut the Confederacy in half. The plan was called "The Anaconda" after the South American snake that subdued its prey by squeezing the life out of it.

Scott's plan for a naval blockade was quickly put into effect. At first the Union had only a few ships with which to police the vast coastline. Within a matter of weeks, however, the fleet began to grow to a point where the Union was able to take the initiative. On October 29th, a great Union fleet of some 51 ships under the command of Samuel F. Du Pont, with an army of 12,500 men on board under the command of Brigadier General Thomas W. Sherman, sailed from Hampton Roads. On November 7th, the fleet had reached the entrance to Port Royal Sound, South Carolina, and the two Confederate forts on Hilton Head and Bay Point. Du Pont formed the fleet into two squadrons, each ship following the one in front in line-a-stern. Ship after ship they passed in front of the forts, fired their broadsides, then moved on. Within hours the Confederate garrisons, unable to withstand the constant naval bombardment, were forced to abandon the two forts, leaving Port Royal open to Sherman's expeditionary force. The Union now was able to turn its attention to Cockspur Island and Fort Pulaski.

The news that Port Royal had fallen brought panic to the streets of Savannah. People fled into the surrounding countryside or to towns located further inland away from the fury they were sure was about to fall upon them. It was at this time that Robert E. Lee, charged with the defense of the city, returned to Savannah.

Lee already knew by what had happened at Port Royal that without proper naval support it would impossible to defend and hold the tiny forts located along the many miles of off-shore islands against the mighty guns of the Federal fleet. He determined, therefore, to abandon the sea-island forts, remove the guns, and withdraw the troops stationed there to an inner line of defenses further inland. The decision was a fateful one for Fort Pulaski and its defenders; on November 10th, the defenses on Tybee Island were abandoned, the batteries leveled, and the heavy seacoast guns removed to Fort Pulaski on Cockspur Island. On November 13th, the British blockade runner, *Fingal*, arrived in Savannah with guns and munitions; it was the last blockade runner to make it through the ever-tightening Federal stranglehold. But things at Fort Pulaski were not so bad. Their share of the *Fingal's* cargo was two 24-pounder Blakely rifles and a number of Enfields. They, it was decided, would defend the mouth of the Savannah River, while the responsibility for denying the Federal gunboats access via the side channels was given to Admiral Tattnall's rag-tag flotilla. Early in December, Du Pont tightened his grip on Savannah by sinking boats loaded with stone in the main channel, and by stationing gunboats in the Warsaw and Ossabaw Sounds. Meanwhile General Sherman established a permanent garrison on Tybee Island less than a mile and a half across the South Pass of the Savannah River from the gates of Fort Pulaski.

Christmas came to the great fort. The garrison, snug and safe behind their mighty walls, had a fine old time. After all, General Lee had declared the great walls impervious to artillery fire and the defenders could hold against any sort of attack by infantry. All was well on Cockspur Island, or so they thought.

On the morning of February 13th, as the Confederate steamship, *Ida*, made her usual supply run to the fort, she came under heavy fire from a Federal seacoast battery on the north shore of the river at Venus Point. Steaming full ahead, with shells falling all around her, she ran the gauntlet and made it safely to the dock on Cockspur Island; it was her last run. Two days later she quietly slipped her mooring and made her way back to Savannah via a series of backwaters and creeks.

The following week the Federal Navy closed the sea gates and the channels to Fort Pulaski. Batteries were built on Tybee Island, the telegraph line between Cockspur Island and Savannah was cut, and a boom was thrown across Tybee Creek; Fort Pulaski was isolated.

Inside the fort, the garrison, some 385 officers and men under the command of Colonel Charles Olmstead, prepared for action.

The fort's armament consisted of 48 guns, the bulk of which were brought to bear on Tybee Island. High on the ramparts was mounted a formidable battery of five eight-inch and four 10-inch Columbiads, one 24-pounder Blakely rifle, and two 10-inch sea-coast mortars. In the casemates were four 32-pounder seacoast guns and one eight-inch Columbiad. Outside the fort itself was a battery of two 12-inch and one 10-inch seacoast mortars. In all, 20 of the fort's complement of 48 heavy guns were aimed at the Federal positions on Tybee Island. The rest of the guns were mounted so as to command the river to the north and the marshes to the west.

Sherman now had a choice to make. He could settle down and starve the garrison out of the fort, a strategy that would take at least six months to fulfill, or he could attack the fort and attempt to take it by force. The decision, however, was taken out of his hands when, on February 14th, he received orders to concentrate all his efforts on the reduction of the fort.

On February 19th Sherman sent his Chief Engineer, Captain Quincy Gillmore, to take command of the forces on Tybee Island and prepare to bombard the fort – a somewhat futile procedure, so it was thought at the time, for the mighty walls, seven and a half feet thick and built of solid brick, were considered to be invincible. Furthermore, the fort was surrounded by swamps and marshes, and the nearest heavy guns were more than a mile away – in some cases, more than two miles away. Further, it was a known fact that beyond a distance of 700 yards smoothbore guns were ineffective against such a solid structure as Fort Pulaski. Of

Colonel Quincy Gillmore after his promotion to Brigadier General.

the chosen strategy the United States Chief of Engineers, Brigadier General Joseph Totten, said, "*You might as well bombard the Rocky Mountains.*" Robert E. Lee had expressed a similar opinion to Colonel Olmstead when he said, "*Colonel, they will make it pretty warm for you here with shells, but they cannot breach your walls at that distance.*" Quincy Gillmore, however, had another opinion.

Gillmore was familiar with the test reports of the new rifled guns supplied to the army in 1859 and, after a careful survey, he declared, much to the amusement of all who heard, that he could reduce the fort with rifle guns located on Tybee Island. With that in mind, he drew up a plan and submitted it to General Sherman who, more than a little skeptical of its success, nonetheless gave it his seal of approval.

For more than six weeks Gillmore and his men toiled in preparation for the bombardment: materials, supplies, and munitions had to be off-loaded through the surf and transported through the marshes to Tybee Island; gun emplacements and bomb-proof shelters had to be constructed out in the open, at night, under the guns of the fort only a little more than a mile away to the north. Each morning, before daylight, the works had to be hidden from the eyes of the ever-watchful sentries on the ramparts of the fort. By the time Gillmore had finished, 11 batteries of guns and mortars, seven of them within a mile of the fort and well within the range of its guns, had been constructed. It was a formidable array of firepower consisting of 12 13-inch mortars, two 10-inch siege mortars, six 10-inch Columbiads, and four eight-inch Columbiads, along with the weapons upon which Gillmore had staked his career and reputation: five 30-pounder Parrott rifles, one 48-pounder James, two 64-pounder James, and two 84-pounder James.

By the end of March the preparations for the Federal bombardment of Fort Pulaski were almost complete. General Sherman, however, would not be there to see it. He was relieved of his command on March 31st, and responsibility for the reduction of the fort was passed to Major General David Hunter. Would this change of command affect Gillmore and his proposed plan? Evidently not, for on April 9th general orders were issued, the navy was put on alert, and the bombardment was set to begin the following morning.

Meanwhile, at Fort Pulaski, the Confederates too, though not particularly worried about the Federal activity on the north shore of

Tybee Island, had been making preparations for the defense of the fort. Following General Lee's instructions, they tore down the verandah over the officer's quarters, replaced it with a covered passage-way constructed of earth and timber, and piled sandbags around the guns on the ramparts.

The morning of April 10th dawned clear and cold. Spring had come to the marshes of Eastern Georgia, although an off-shore breeze cut through the clothing of the gunners waiting in the shore-batteries for the order to open fire.

Fort Pulaski was a hive of activity. Changes to the landscape on Tybee Island had been noticed soon after sunrise. The top of the ridge had been leveled, bushes and trees had been removed, and guns could be seen ranged against the fort in a line that stretched along the coastline for more than a mile.

As Colonel Olmstead and his officers watched, they saw a small boat leave Tybee Island and head in the direction of the fort under a white flag. The boat made fast to the dock and Lieutenant J.H. Wilson handed over a formal demand for the surrender of the fort.

The demand was duly considered by Colonel Olmstead and a reply was written as follows:

"Sir, I have to acknowledge receipt of your communication of this date, demanding the unconditional surrender of Fort Pulaski.

"In reply I can only say, that I am here to defend the Fort, not to surrender it."

The die, then, was cast. At 10 minutes past 8 on the morning of the 10th of April, 1862, a single shell from Federal Battery Halleck arced into the air, over the fort, to explode in the marshes beyond. Within minutes every battery on Tybee Island was engaged. Then the heavy guns of the fort opened fire against the shore batteries at King's Landing; first the casemate guns, and then those on the ramparts. The first shots on both sides went wide of their targets; guns on both sides became dismounted from their chassis under the heavy recoil of their mighty charges. Soon, however, the gunners found a rhythm and the fire from both sides increased in tempo and accuracy.

Walls breached, Fort Pulaski.

As the Federal bombardment continued, the Confederate defenders soon realized they had little to fear from the mortars and smoothbore Columbiads; the huge rifle guns, however, were a different story.

All day long the exchange of fire continued. By noon the Federal gunners had scored hundred of hits on the south-facing walls of the fort and, by nightfall, hundreds more. The fort, however, as far as Gillmore and his Union gunners could tell from the extreme distance, was still very much intact. The general feeling among the Federal officers was that the situation was very little different than it had been when the bombardment had begun. Had they been able to get a closer look, however, they would have been greatly encouraged, for the interior of the fort was in chaos. Almost all of the guns on the ramparts had been dismounted and only two of her casemate guns were in action. At the southeast angle of the fort the walls had been smashed down, almost to the moat. The rifle guns on Tybee Island were having the desired effect. Again and again solid shot slammed into the same spot, slowly tearing away the fabric of the structure until there was nothing left. Of the 32 Federal guns ranged against the fort, three did most of the damage: two 84-pounder and one 64-pounder James rifles. These three guns, from a distance of slightly under a mile, hurled solid shot against the walls of the fort with devastating effect. The spinning projectiles were able to penetrate the brickwork for a distance of up to 24 inches, sending terrific shock waves through the structure that cracked and weakened it even further.

By dawn on Friday the 11th of April, after a long night during which the garrison inside the fort had repaired and re-mounted many of her guns, the exchange of fire between the fort and Tybee Island was renewed with a will. Before long the damage the great rifles were doing to Fort Pulaski was evident for all to see; the walls had been breached in several places and fire from the fort was beginning to slacken. By noon the guns on the rampart had been silenced and the interior of the fort could be seen through two huge breaches in the south wall; it was time for a direct assault on the fort. Federal Brigadier General Henry W. Benham gave orders to his men to prepare for an attack.

In the fort things had deteriorated to the point where its commander, Colonel Olmstead, was left with only two choices as to what to do next: he could fight on against overwhelming odds, or he could admit defeat. Unwilling to subject his men to further suffering, he chose the latter and gave orders for surrender. The Confederate flag was struck from the rampart and a white sheet took its place.

On Tybee Island there were scenes of great rejoicing. Men cheered, threw their hats into the air, and danced with one another as Gillmore embarked for Cockspur Island to take the Confederate surrender. By nightfall the Stars and Stripes was flying from the shattered ramparts of Fort Pulaski; the new rifle guns had brought an end to the age-old style of coastal fortifications.

During the bombardment the Federal guns had fired 5,275 shots against the fort. Incredibly there were only two casualties, one Federal and one Confederate.

That, however, was not the end of the part Fort Pulaski would play in the Civil War. When hostilities finally ended, Fort Pulaski became the prison to which many of the Confederate leaders were taken while the victors tried to decide what to do with them. The prisoners included Secretary of State Robert Hunter, Secretary of the Treasury George Trenholm, and Secretary of War James Seddon, as well as several Assistant Secretaries, and three State Governors.

In 1933 the fort was transferred to the jurisdiction of the Department of the Interior, and the National Park Service went to work on its restoration. Today, the fort is open to the public.

Touring the Fort

As you tour the fort you will find a series of numbered markers, each at a significant point of interest.

To enter the fort you must first cross the outer drawbridge and walk across the demilune to the second drawbridge and the sally port, the only entrance into the main structure.

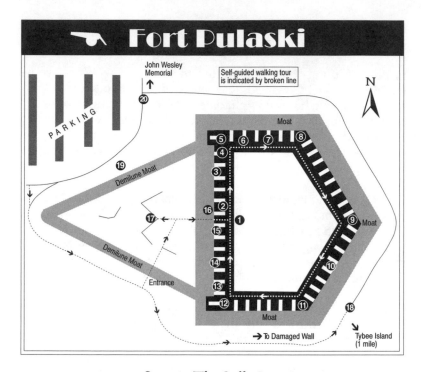

Stop 1: The Sally Port

The sally port is a structure very similar in design to those found on the medieval castles in Europe. The massive drawbridge is counterbalanced by a series of great counterweights; you can see them in the rooms on either side of the entrance. The great portcullis drops down through a slot as the drawbridge is raised. Finally, the inner doors could be closed, making the fort secure against all outsiders.

Stop 2: The Gorge

The Gorge, located along the western, or rear section of the fort, contains the sally port, the only entrance. The living quarters are also located in the gorge. The enlisted men occupied the quarters to the north of the sally port, the officers those to the south.

Stop 3: The Barrack Rooms

These rooms located in the casemates – the word casemate means bomb-proof shelter – were lit by oil lamps or candles. Each has a large fireplace with cooking equipment, and the rear walls are pierced by loopholes angled to provide the fort's defenders with a wide field of fire.

Stop 4: The North Magazine

The walls of the magazine are 12 to 15 feet thick. On the second day of the Federal bombardment, shells exploding near the magazine threatened to blow it up.

Stop 5: The Northwest Bastion

A bastion is a section of a fort or castle that extends beyond the main walls of the structure, usually at its corners, to provide a field of fire in all directions, but especially along the walls to the left and right. Fort Pulaski has two half-bastions, one at the north end of the west wall and one at the south. They are called half-bastions because they extend out in only one direction and give protection only to the west wall. The rectangular openings in the bastion wall are gun ports situated to provide protecting cannon crossfire toward the main drawbridge and the point of the demilune. The openings in the ceiling are smoke vents, and the circular grooves in the floor originally held iron tracks that carried the wheels of the gun carriages.

Stop 6: The Gun Galleries

The bomb-proof gun galleries surround the fort on four sides, giving the structure the galleried look of a great cathedral or monastery. The galleries at Fort Pulaski are fine examples of arched casemates. The arches were built over wooden forms. The bricks, each one hand-cut to fit, were carefully placed and then mortared in position. When the mortar was dry the forms were removed, leaving the beautiful arches you see in front of you.

Stop 7: The Water System

There are 10 water cisterns, or storage tanks, within the walls of the fort beneath the brick pavements of the two center casemates of each galley. Each cistern holds 20,000 gallons of fresh water and is filled by a system of pipes that carry rainwater down from the roof.

Stop 8: The Terraplein

The flat surface along the top of the rampart that carries the gun platforms is called the terraplein. The guns mounted here on the ramparts, because of their elevated position, had a far greater range than those mounted in the casemates below; they were, however, extremely vulnerable to the new rifled guns in the Federal batteries on Tybee Island. The parapet of the terraplein was supposed to provide protection for the guns and their crews. The rifled guns, however, made short work of them, leaving both guns and crews exposed to the enemy.

Stop 9: The Terraplein at the East Angle

From here you will have a fine view of the north shore of Tybee Island. The two Federal batteries containing the three great rifled guns that did most of the damage to the walls of the fort were located just to the north of the present highway bridge. The nine other Federal batteries were located along the shoreline toward the lighthouse for a distance of about two miles.

Stop 10: The Prison

From October, 1864, to March, 1865, the southeast, the northeast, and a section of the south casemates were used as a military prison.

Stop 11: The Breach

The Federal batteries just to the north of the modern highway bridge were able to batter the walls here at the southeast angle to such an extent that they were breached, leaving the interior of the fort open to explosive shellfire. These walls were reconstructed by engineers of the 48th New York Volunteers in 1862 after the surrender of the fort.

Stop 12: The Southwest Bastion

The interior of this section of the fort was destroyed by a fire in 1893. The restoration of the bastion was left incomplete in order to show details of the foundation construction.

Stop 13: Headquarters

It was here, on April 11, 1862, that Colonel Olmstead executed the terms for the surrender of the fort. The officer's quarters were destroyed by a lightning fire in 1925. This room was restored in 1935.

Stop 14: The Cistern

This room, too, was destroyed by the fire of 1925. It was left unrestored in order to show details of its construction. The cylindrical brick structure you see below floor level is the top of a water cistern.

Stop 15: The Bottle Collection

In 1935, the men dredging the mud from the moat found more than 1,000 bottles thrown into the waters by workmen during the construction of the fort and later by Confederate and Union soldiers. A part of the collection is on display in this room.

Stop 16: The Moat

The moat completely surrounds the fort and, as in the European castles of old, was designed to protect the walls from intruders. It varies in width from 30 to 48 feet and has an average depth of about seven feet. Water enters the moat from the South Channel of the Savannah River and is controlled through a series of tide gates. A variety of marine life makes its home in the waters of the moat: turtles, crabs, shrimp, and fish, etc.

Stop 17: The Demilune

The great triangular structure to the rear of the fort is called the demilune. Most of the work here was completed in 1869, after the Civil War. The structure hides a series of passageways connecting four powder magazines to the gun emplacements.

Stop 18: The Damaged Wall

Here it is still possible to see evidence of the damage done to the walls of the fort by the great rifled guns in the Federal batteries. The breach was repaired in 1862 using red brick that contrasts with the original structure of brown brick. The pockmarks along the entire southeast wall facing Tybee Island is evidence that the walls were struck hundreds of times by a variety of projectiles, many of which are still embedded in the brickwork.

Stop 19: The Cemetery

This small cemetery was established during the years of the construction of the fort and was the site where, during the Civil War, soldiers, Union and Confederate, were temporarily buried. The eight-inch Confederate gun that marks the site was damaged during the Federal bombardment.

Stop 20: The Waving Girl

Florence Martus, the daughter of an ordnance sergeant on Cockspur Island, was born in the Officer's Quarters just after the Civil War. As a small child she was fascinated by the great ships that sailed passed the fort on their way to destinations all around the world. So she would stand and wave a white handkerchief at the departing ships; the sailors waved back. As a teenager, Florence went to live with her brother in a small white cottage on the riverbank about five miles upriver from the fort. From that time on, for more than 44 years, she waved at *every ship* that passed her home – a table cloth or sheet by day and a lantern by night. Each ship, as it passed, would return her salute with three blasts of the whistle. The legend of the Waving Girl of Savannah is known by sailors all over the world.

Fort Pulaski is open daily from 8:30 a.m. until 5:15 p.m., and from Memorial Day to Labor Day until 6:46 p.m. The Fort is closed on Christmas day.

For more information, contact Fort Pulaski National Monument, PO Box 30757, Savannah, GA 31410. Telephone 912-786-5787.

What to See, Where to Stay

Tybee Island

Tybee Island has become a popular, year-round resort fronting more than four miles of the Atlantic Ocean and the Savannah River for almost two miles. The beach runs the entire length of the island, with the old coastal defenses and a lighthouse located at the north end. The beach has a boardwalk, fishing pier, amusements, hotels, motels, and vacation cottages.

Tybee Museum and Lighthouse

The museum is located at the north end of the island in a coastal battery built in 1898 – one of the seven batteries that comprised Fort Scraven. The museum traces the history of the island from colonial times to 1945. There are exhibits featuring Martello Tower, the Civil War, and Fort Scraven, doll collections, gun collections, and a large assortment of artifacts of all shapes and sizes.

The lighthouse is the oldest active lighthouse in the United States. Visitors may climb to the top for a view of the island.

Motels

Econo Lodge. 404 Butler Ave, Tybee Island. Telephone 912-786-4535. Children under 18 stay free, pool, cafe. Located on the beach. Accepts credit cards.

Dining

Macelwee's Seafood House. 101 Lovell Ave (US 80), Tybee Island. Telephone 912-786-4259. Bar, semi-à la carte menu, lunch, dinner, children's meals. Specializes in seafood and steak.

For Further Information: Hotels, motels, camping and additional visitor information, contact the Savannah Area Convention and Visitors Bureau, 222 W. Oglethorpe Avenue, PO Box 1628, Savannah, GA 31402-1628. Telephone 912-944-0456.

Chapter 7

McClellan's Peninsula Campaign

Richmond: The Seven Days

June 25th to July 1st, 1862

The Visitor Center at the Richmond National Battlefield Park is located at 3215 East Broad Street in Richmond.

There are 10 separate battlefields and historic sites which comprise the Richmond National Battlefield Park in Virginia. Six of them relate to General George McClellan's Peninsula Campaign of 1862, and four to the final defense of Richmond from March 1864 until the city fell to General Grant in April, 1865. This section of the book deals with the campaign of 1862, the events leading to the Battles of the Seven Days, and the battles themselves.

The auto tour of the battlefields of the Peninsula Campaign and the Seven Days will take you on a drive around Richmond of about 80 miles and will require at least a full day to complete.

The first section of this chapter deals with McClellan's campaign from the landings at Fort Monroe at the end of March, 1862, through May and June, to the eve of the Battle of Beaver Dam Creek on June 26th, the first of the Battles of the Seven Days. At that point we will begin the auto tour and take in each of the battlefields in turn, with the exception of Drewry's Bluff and the engagement fought there on May 15th.

The battles that became known as "The Seven Days" were the culmination of Union Major General George Brinton McClellan's Peninsula Campaign against Richmond in the spring and early summer of 1862. During the Seven Days, six major battles were fought producing a combined total of more than 36,000 casualties.

Maj. General George McClellan.

McClellan's campaign really began as far back as July 27th, 1861, when he arrived in Washington to take command of the Army of the Potomac following the debacle that was the Battle of 1st Manassas, or Bull Run, on July 21st. For the rest of that year and the early months of 1862, McClellan set about turning the badly demoralized Army of the Potomac into a confident and efficient fighting force capable of dealing with anything that the Confederacy might send against it. He thus earned his troops' undying devotion and the unofficial title, "The Young Napoleon."

McClellan lived to become one of the most controversial figures in American history. He graduated from West Point in 1846, second in a class of 50 that produced no fewer than 20 generals, Union and Confederate. In 1857 he resigned his commission as captain in the 1st United States Cavalry to take up a post as chief engineer of the Illinois Central Railroad. When war broke out in April, 1861, however, he was appointed major general of Ohio Volunteers in command of all forces in that state. Only three weeks later, his organizational skills and personal magnetism had brought him to the attention of President Lincoln who, sight unseen, appointed him a major general in the regular army, outranked only by the aging Winfield Scott. Upon Scott's retirement, only three months after taking command of the Army of the Potomac, McClellan replaced him as General-in-Chief of the Armies of the United States – heady stuff for a man as yet only 35 years old. It's no wonder, then, that he thought himself somewhat superior to all men, even to his commander-in-chief, President Lincoln.

Lincoln, however, was willing to forgive McClellan his eccentricities so long as he fulfilled his potential and moved quickly against the Confederate forces in Virginia under the command of General Joseph E. Johnston. But it was not to be. McClellan dawdled and procrastinated throughout the closing months of 1861 under the pretext of devising a master plan that would deliver a conquered

Richmond into his victorious hands until, finally, Lincoln had had enough. Although he was not completely happy with McClellan's plan for an invasion of the Virginia Peninsula, he needed action in general, and a major victory in particular. And if McClellan could deliver Richmond, he would have all that and more; the war could be over in a matter of months.

Thus it was that he bowed to McClellan's professional judgment and gave grudging consent to the expedition into the Virginian peninsula, but with two conditions: McClellan must leave behind a force strong enough to contain the Confederate forces near Manassas, and he must provide forces capable of defending Washington should the need arise. Never again would Lincoln allow a threat to the nation's capital such as the one that followed the army's defeat at Bull Run.

McClellan, though he reluctantly agreed to Lincoln's conditions, had no intention of fulfilling them and set off by sea with 100,000 men for Fort Monroe. By the end of March the Army of the Potomac was established on the Peninsula and, on April 1st, set out to do battle with the Confederate forces defending Richmond to the northwest. Lincoln, however, discovered McClellan's duplicity and ordered Secretary of War, Edwin Stanton, to retain a full army corps under the command of General Irvin McDowell; McClellan was furious.

As McClellan began his campaign in earnest, the Confederate General Joseph Johnston had only 10,000 men deployed in a thin defensive line across the Peninsula from Yorktown on the York River to the Warwick River at its junction with the James. McClellan, however, was convinced that he faced a foe more than 100,000 strong and deeply resented what he perceived to be Lincoln's lack of perception and support. And so, instead of making an all-out attack on the tenuous Confederate line, he decided to invest it and conduct siege operations. For a month he continued in this fashion until, on May 3rd, the Confederate defenders withdrew up the Peninsula toward Williamsburg. The following morning five divisions of the Army of the Potomac, bogged down in deep mud, followed after them. They caught the Confederate rearguard on May 5th. The battle of Williamsburg was the first real conflict of McClellan's campaign. The result was inconclusive and cost the Union army more than 2,200 casualties; the Confederates lost perhaps 1,700. General Johnston continued his retreat up the Peninsula, and both commanders were happy with the way things were going: McClellan with his capture of Yorktown and Johnston with his narrow escape and the fact that he and his army would live to fight another day. Unfortunately for both generals, their presidents were not so happy. Lincoln was irritated by McClellan's refusal to pursue the retreating enemy and Davis was thoroughly alarmed by Johnston's continued retreat toward the Confederate capital. Johnston and his beleaguered army arrived in Richmond dispirited, demoralized, bedraggled and seemingly unfit to cope with the Federal hordes now rapidly approaching the city from the southeast.

President Lincoln, with Secretary Stanton, arrived at Fort Monroe on May 6th to take stock of the situation and to talk to General McClellan in the hopes of spurring him on to Richmond. McClellan, however, was busy in Williamsburg and "*it was impossible to go to the rear.*" President Lincoln had no option but to spend his time talking to what few high ranking army and naval officers were available. Then, in a fit of pique and frustration, he ordered the capture of the Confederate port of Norfolk; not a terribly difficult task considering it was, by this time, virtually abandoned following General Johnston's retreat toward Richmond. Norfolk was duly taken, leaving the way open up the James River all the way into the heart of Richmond. President Lincoln, somewhat mollified, returned to Washington. General McClellan complained about the weather; it was, after all, the rainiest spring in recorded history.

Norfolk, up until the time of its fall, had been the home port of the Confederate ironclad *Virginia*. On May 9th, unable to take the ship and escape into the open sea, the crew scuttled the ship and made good their escape up-river to Fort Darling at Drewry's Bluff; they arrived there a few days later.

With the way now open up the James to Richmond, a fleet of two Union ironsides, the *Monitor* and the *Galena*, along with three wooden warships, headed up-river toward the Confederate capital.

President Davis and his adviser, General Robert E. Lee, were of the opinion that Fort Darling on Drewry's Bluff was just the place to put a stop to the Federal fleet. Consequently the fort was strengthened, heavy guns were installed, and weighted hulks were sunk in the river to obstruct the gunboats. The *Virginia*'s now homeless crew under the command of Captain John Taylor Wood, CSN, was given charge of the mighty guns on the bluff.

At 5 o'clock on the afternoon of May 15th the citizens of Richmond heard the distant booming of the great guns some seven miles to the southeast and realized that the Federal ships had reached Drewry's Bluff. Virginia's governor, John Letcher, declared that he would see the city destroyed before he would abandon it. Richmond's mayor, of a like mind, also declared his defiance, saying that some other mayor would have to give up the city. Both men were relieved at the outcome of the battle at Drewry's Bluff.

It was pretty much a one-sided affair. The sunken hulks in the river did their job and blocked the heavy-draft ironclads; the wooden ships stayed down-river out of range. On the bluff above the river, Captain Wood's great guns pounded the *Monitor* and the *Galena*, both unable to elevate their guns high enough to return fire on the Confederate batteries, to the point where they were forced to break off the engagement and retreat to safety down-river. The *Virginia's* crew, veterans of the famous naval battle with the *Monitor*, were ecstatic over their victory. A somewhat more prudent Captain Wood, however, declared that they were lucky and that if the Federal ships had had the support of ground-based infantry, the battle might well have turned out differently.

After Drewry's Bluff, Confederate President Davis realized that it was his army that would keep the Confederate cause alive, not its capital city. Together, Davis and Johnston agreed, an unusual situation in itself, that the Federal army must be beaten outside of Richmond. It was therefore decided that Johnston should carry the battle to McClellan. And Davis was anxious that he do so as quickly as possible. Johnston, on the other hand, was concerned that wherever and whenever the attack took place it would be successful. But Johnston had had problems in his dealings with Davis before, and he resented the President's constant questions, his pushing, and his very presence at his headquarters. For a while, at least, it seemed that matters would come to a head and the two men would fall out completely. Fortunately, there was another, more soothing presence available to mediate between these two strong and demanding personalities. General Robert E. Lee was always there to offer advice when it was needed, and in such a manner as to make both men feel that each idea was his own. But the situation in the Confederate camp was almost congenial, compared to that between Lincoln and McClellan.

After the Battle of Drewry's Bluff, McClellan, still convinced that he was vastly outnumbered, once again called on his President for reinforcements. He received none, and so was convinced that his government in general, and Secretary Stanton in particular, was conspiring against him. Still, McClellan was nothing if not persistent, and he renewed his pleas. This time Lincoln obliged and sent a full corps under the command of General Irvin McDowell to McClellan's aid.

Three days later, however, much to "Little Mac's" displeasure, McDowell's march was diverted and he remained in Fredericksburg ready to answer a new challenge offered in the Shenandoah Valley by one Thomas "Stonewall" Jackson. McClellan was forced to continue his campaign without him.

By the end of May the Federal army was deployed over a long line that extended from a point south of the Chickahominy and Beaver Dam Creek, then north across the river, and east to White Oak Swamp, with his main supply base at the White House Plantation on the Pamunkey River east of Richmond. General Erasmus Keyes with the IV Union Army Corps was at the village of Seven Pines across the Williamsburg Road and the Richmond & York River railroad. Also, heavy rains had turned the peaceful Chickahominy into a raging torrent that swept away the bridges connecting the Federal army deployed on both sides of the river. This presented General Johnston with an opportunity he couldn't refuse.

The Battle of Seven Pines was a bloody affair fought over the two days of May 31st and June 1st. It was bungled by the Confederates from start to finish and resulted in a decided victory for the Federal army, costing Johnston more than 6,100 casualties, against Union losses of 5,000. During the battle Johnston was twice wounded, once by a minie ball in the shoulder, and again by a shell fragment to the chest. He was carried from the field with subordinates fearing that his wounds were mortal. Many of the Confederate units sustained losses of almost 50%. General Johnston had failed miserably.

Victory or not, the affair at Seven Pines only further convinced McClellan that he was severely outnumbered and that General Johnston could carry the war to him at any time he might choose. This, and erroneous intelligence supplied to him by Alan Pinkerton's agents, continued to feed his need for caution.

With General Johnston down, if not out, President Davis needed a strong hand to steer the fortunes of his beleaguered Army of Northern Virginia. General Robert E. Lee took command on June 1st, 1862, and so was brought together with the two men who were soon to be his most trusted lieutenants: Major General Thomas. "Stonewall" Jackson and Major General James Longstreet.

Lee's first priority on taking command of the Confederate forces around Richmond was to take the war to McClellan. He knew that to defend a Richmond under siege would take more than 100,000 men, and he didn't have them. His second priority was to gather intelligence, find out exactly what McClellan's strength was and how his army was deployed. He knew that Union General Fitz John Porter's V Army Corps, with General George McCall's division, a force of more than 30,000 men, was north of the Chickahominy near Mechanicsville, separated from the main Federal army by the swollen waters of the river. Porter's task was to protect McClellan's lines of communication and to wait for General Irvin McDowell's corps of 40,000 men to join him from Fredericksburg. To Lee it seemed to be a heaven-sent opportunity. If

Maj. General James Longstreet.

he were to cross the river with a strong enough force and take Porter by surprise he could destroy an entire army corps and deliver McClellan a staggering blow.

Lee's plan was to bring Stonewall Jackson from the Shenandoah Valley to Ashland and from there, down the north shore of the Chickahominy, where he would attack Porter on his right flank. At the same time Lee would cross the Chickahominy at Beaver Dam Creek with three divisions under the commands of Generals James Longstreet, A.P. Hill and D.H. Hill, and attack him from the front. It was a bold plan, but a dangerous one, for it depended, first, on split-second timing and, second, on taking the Federal army by surprise.

Lee used the days while Jackson was winding up his affairs in the Valley for gathering information and preparing his army for the march to Mechanicsville.

On June 12th, at 2 o'clock in the morning, General James Ewell Brown "Jeb" Stuart ordered his command of 1,200 cavalry troopers into the saddle for what was to become famous as "Stuart's Ride Around McClellan." Unfortunately, that was not what General

Maj. General A.P. Hill

Lee had ordered or desired. Stuart's orders were, first, to maintain secrecy at all costs and, second, to move to the right of the Federal right flank north of the Chickahominy, determine the enemy's strength and disposition, and then return. Stuart, however, got carried away. He managed to maintain secrecy only during the day

of June 12th. The following day, the 13th, Stuart clashed with Federal pickets at Hanover Court House, then he turned south and encountered Federal cavalry at Haw's Shop, then again at Old Church, where his men destroyed a Federal camp. By now Stuart had the information Lee needed, but the Federals also were well aware of Lee's interest in the north side of the Chickahominy and of Stuart's whereabouts. Stuart had a decision to make: should he retrace his steps and return to Lee the way he'd come, thus risking his command should the Federals decide to cut him off? Or should he continue on and ride completely around the Army of the Potomac, returning to Lee from the south? He chose the

General J.E.B. Stuart

latter. Stuart re-entered Richmond on the morning of the 15th. His main force followed a day later after a ride of more than 150 miles. Lee had the information he needed, but the element of surprise had gone. McClellan, however, responded to Stuart's ride with his usual indecision.

On the afternoon of June 23rd, General Lee convened a council of war. In attendance were Generals Longstreet, A.P. Hill, D.H. Hill, and a travel-weary Stonewall Jackson whose army, though on the move, was still several days away.

Lee's plan called for him to leave a force of 25,000 men under the command of Major Generals Benjamin Huger and John B. Magruder to hold the ground between Richmond and the Army of the Potomac. The three divisions under the commands of Longstreet and the two Hills, some 47,000 men, would cross the Chickahominy, form into line of battle near Mechanicsville and attack Fitz John Porter's V Corps on the left flank; Jackson's force of 18,500 men would attack Porter on the right flank. It was an ambitious plan that depended very much on perfect timing and four generals that were unused to working with each other. And it was a risky plan. If McClellan were

Maj. General Benjamin Huger.

to realize just how thin the Confederate line between the main Army of the Potomac and Richmond was, he could drive forward with a force that would outnumber Magruder and Huger by almost four-to-one and the fall of the city would be inevitable. Lee, however, didn't believe McClellan would make such a move and decided to continue with his plan. Thus, by June 25th, the stage was set for the first of the Battles of the Seven Days; it came later that day when McClellan, still in a state of indecision, sent two divisions under the commands of Generals Philip Kearny and Joseph Hooker to conduct a limited assault on the Confederate lines east of Richmond. The result was a short, sharp altercation that became known as the Battle of Oak Grove and which cost McClellan some 516 casualties, against a loss of only 316 for the Confederates.

Auto Tour of the Seven Days

To begin your auto tour, leave the parking lot at the Visitor Center at 3251 East Broad Street in Richmond, turn left onto Broad Street and go for about one mile, then turn right onto 18th Street, Route 360, and continue for another mile. Next, turn right onto Fairfield Avenue and get into the left-hand lane. You can see the old White House of the Confederacy to your left (a three-story building with a red roof near the smokestacks). From Fairfield Avenue, turn left onto the Mechanicsville Turnpike (Route 360), and follow the road to Chickahominy Bluffs, the first stop on your tour, a distance of about two and a half miles from your turn onto the Mechanicsville Turnpike. The entrance to the park is on the right and is identified by a brown and white sign a few hundred yards before the turn. Leave your vehicle in the parking lot and go to the interpretive marker adjacent to the parking area.

Stop 1: Chickahominy Bluffs

The Mechanicsville Road in 1862 was not the major highway it is today. Back then it was an unpaved dirt road along which, at 2 in the morning, the divisions of James Longstreet and D.H. Hill marched out of Richmond toward Mechanicsville. The head of the column halted here at Chickahominy Bluffs some six hours later at 8 a.m. to await the signal to cross the bridge and begin the assault on General Porter's Federal right. The column of soldiers stretched back from here for several miles and must have been an impressive sight. A.P. Hill headed out from Richmond along the Meadow Bridge Road about a mile and a half upstream to the left of where you are now at Chickahominy Bluffs. General Lawrence O'Bryan Branch's division was detached from A.P. Hill's force and sent six miles further upstream to cross the river at Half Sink, join with General Jackson's corps. Together they would assail Porter's right rear and flank, at which point A.P. Hill was to cross the river and, with Jackson, "sweep" General Porter and his V Corps down the Chickahominy. Generals Longstreet and D.H. Hill were to move across the river in support of Jackson and A.P. Hill. That was the plan, an ambitious series of actions that depended entirely upon precise timing and the perfect coordination of all four infantry divisions. Alas, it was not to be.

The earthworks you see around you are a part of the Confederate outer defenses around Richmond, a huge system of rifle pits,

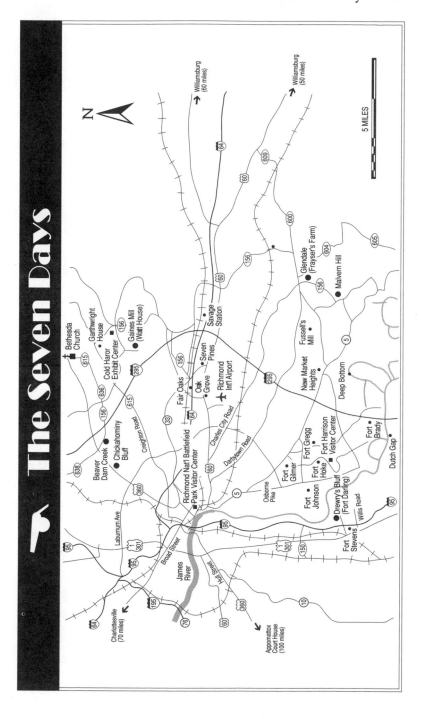

The Seven Days

N

Bethesda Church
615
636
156
Cold Harbor Exhibit Center
Garthwright House
Gaines Mill (Watt House)
156
295
615
156
Fair Oaks
Oak Grove
Seven Pines
156
Savage Station
64
Richmond Int'l Airport
33
156
Charles City Road
60
Darbytown Road
Creighton Road
5
Richmond Nat'l Battlefield Park Visitor Center
Chickahominy Bluff
638
Beaver Dam Creek
360
Laburnum Ave
295
New Market Heights
Fussell's Mill
5
Deep Bottom
Glendale (Frayser's Farm)
156
Malvern Hill
600
604
605
156
60
609
64
Williamsburg (60 miles)
Williamsburg (50 miles)
60
Fort Gregg
Fort Harrison Visitor Center
Fort Gilmer
Fort Hoke
Osborne Pike
Fort Johnson
Drewry's Bluff (Fort Darling)
Willis Road
Fort Brady
Dutch Gap
95
10
360
60
76
Appomattox Court House (100 miles)
Hill Street
James River
Broad Street
301
95
95
64
Charlottesville (70 miles)
95
301
150
1
Fort Stevens
95

5 MILES

trenches, and dirt forts that provided for both heavy fixed artillery and light mobile artillery batteries. The outer defensive line, begun in early 1862 in response to the threat of McClellan's Army of the Potomac, and of which these earthworks are but a small part, ran in one long continuous line from the banks of the James River north of the city to the banks of the James River south of the city. The earthworks you see in front of you are but half the size they were in 1862. More than a century of erosion by wind, rain and the feet of more than a million clambering visitors have worn them down to their present condition.

From here you should make the short walk along the trail to the shelter and from there to the interpretive marker on the overlook.

Federal General George McCall's division was entrenched along a two-mile front on the eastern side of Beaver Dam Creek, but his right flank was dangerously exposed. It was here, to McCall's right and rear, that General Jackson was supposed to make his assault, thus giving the signal for the other three Confederate divisions to move in and join the battle, driving Porter's corps before them.

Jackson's attack was supposed to begin at 9 on the morning of June 26th, 1862, and by that time General Lee was here at Chickahominy Bluffs, waiting impatiently for the battle to begin. Nine o'clock came and went, then 10, noon, and still Lee had heard nothing from Jackson.

Try to imagine the scene that morning as thousands upon thousands of men on the Mechanicsville Road beside the bluff waited under the hot sun, sweating and itching in thick woolen clothing that gathered the dust and sand like some sort of diabolical trap, transferring it from the surface to the skin with each movement of its unfortunate wearer. Thousands of men waited for the signal to cross the bridge; no one knew that Jackson was running more than six hours late.

By 3 that afternoon, with Jackson still not in sight, A.P. Hill, waiting at the Meadow Bridge, decided that he could wait no longer. Feeling sure that Jackson must by this time be well within striking distance, moved his division out across the Meadow Bridge and turned right toward Mechanicsville and the Federal right flank, never knowing that Jackson was still miles away and would not be in position to support him that day. At first Hill encountered little resistance, but on clearing Mechanicsville he ran into the heavily defended Federal positions at Beaver Dam Creek.

Lee, waiting here on Chickahominy Bluffs, at first thought Jackson had arrived and that the battle was proceeding as planned. It soon become obvious, however, that this was not the case, and that A.P. Hill had exceeded his orders and had moved across the river without the support of General Jackson. As Lee rode off to find Hill, Generals Longstreet and D.H. Hill immediately went into action and prepared to move across the Mechanicsville Bridge and take their place on the Confederate right. Unfortunately they were delayed at the river crossing; the Federals had destroyed the bridge and it had to be rebuilt before the two Confederate divisions could make the crossing.

When you've finished here at Chickahominy Bluffs, return to your vehicle and proceed to Stop 2 on your tour, Beaver Dam Creek. Turn right out of the parking area onto Route 360, proceed across the bridge and follow the road for about a mile and a half to the exit for Route 156. Turn onto 156 and follow the road for a little more than a half-mile and turn right into the Beaver Dam Creek unit of the park, leave your vehicle in the parking area provided, and walk over to the signs at the overlook.

Stop 2: Beaver Dam Creek

You are now standing on the west bank of Beaver Dam Creek facing east toward the Federal positions on the other side of the creek. Look at the map on page 108 and locate your position on the battlefield; it's marked by a Maltese cross to the north of Ellerson's Mill where the old road crossed the creek. The mill and the bridge across the creek are gone now, but you can see where the road continues on the other side to your right. The mill would have been about 100 feet away on the other side of the creek to the left of the road. The mill was driven by water diverted from the creek into a millrace, a deep trench that provided a ready-made defensive position for General McCall's Federal units. The position was further strengthened by felling the trees that grew in front of the millrace. For almost two miles, from a position beginning some 600 yards to your right and to the south of Ellerson's Mill, and extending northward to your left and beyond the Bethesda Church Road, the crest of the ridge in front of you bristled with Federal artillery commanding the approaches from the west. The Federal infantry was well-entrenched in line of battle along the front of the ridge.

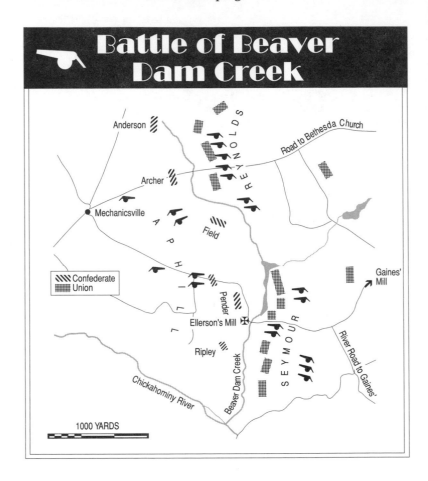

A.P. Hill's Confederate brigades had to approach the Federal Line at Beaver Dam Creek from the west across the open fields behind you. To assault the Federal line here at its center about a half-mile to your left, Hill's men, not only had to advance under heavy fire across the fields, they also had to make it through swampy ground to the west, cross the creek, and then deal with more swampy ground on the east side of the creek. Hill began his advance with three of his six brigades in line of battle, with two batteries of artillery in support. As the Confederate brigades advanced across the open fields, the Federal artillery opened up a devastating barrage of shot and shell that soon put Hill's batteries out of commission. The Confederate advance continued and soon the leading regiments were heading into a hail of musket fire from the Federal trenches and a veritable firestorm of canister from the artillery. Only one Confederate regiment made it across the creek

Ellerson's Mill on the battlefield at Mechanicsville.

before being turned back by the intensity of the concentrated Federal fire.

Slowly the Confederate advance began to falter, then, still under a withering fire from the Federal positions, Hill's brigades began to fall back. Hill now knew that any further assault on the center of the Union line was doomed to failure. So he decided to try for the Federal left flank near the mouth of Beaver Dam Creek where it enters the Chickahominy. Confederate General Dorsey Pender's brigade, fresh on the field, was diverted southward to make the attack. Unfortunately, the Federals had anticipated just such an attack and had strengthened their positions in readiness. Those positions were on the ridge in front of you to the east of Beaver Dam Creek. General Pender's brigade commenced its attack toward you, across the open fields to the west behind you. The Federal batteries opened up a deadly firestorm of canister and case-shot, causing great confusion in the Confederate ranks. One regiment, under heavy fire, strayed away to the right, another to the left, leaving only the center regiment, the 38th Carolina, unsupported, to make the attack on the strong Federal positions here at Ellerson's Mill. Unbelievably, they made it across the creek in front of you and succeeded in advancing to within 100 yards of the Federal positions. The 12th Pennsylvania Reserves poured volley after volley of deadly musket fire into the advancing Carolinians; the Federal artillery hit them with barrage after barrage of double-loaded canister. Finally, unable to withstand the hail of death and destruction flying in upon them, the 38th Carolina began to withdraw once again across the open fields behind you, suffering further casualties as they went. But it was not over yet.

General Lee, frustrated and upset by the sad turn of events, was determined to make one last attempt on the Federal left flank south of Ellerson's Mill. By this time the first of General D.H. Hill's brigades under the command of General Robert S. Ripley had crossed the river and had moved east from Mechanicsville. Lee ordered Ripley into battle in support of General Pender. Unfortunately, Ripley miscalculated and failed to go far enough south; his assault came over the same open fields behind you that had been so costly to General Pender. The Federals again opened fire on the advancing Confederates with results much the same as before. Ripley's brigade was decimated, suffering some 575 casualties before being forced to withdraw. By 9 that evening the battle of Beaver Dam Creek was over, a decided victory for the Federal army. General Lee had lost more than 1,500 men against a Federal loss of fewer than 400 men. Only the arrival of Jackson's corps in the early hours of the following morning rendered the Federal position untenable; they moved out along the road across the creek to your right and pulled back four miles, with the intention of taking up new positions behind Boatswain's Swamp.

In the early hours of the morning of the 27th, the Confederates of General A.P. Hill's division, seeing the Union columns retreating along the road, forced a crossing here at the Mill and gave chase. They lost time rebuilding the bridge and clearing the way of felled trees and debris so that the wagons and artillery would be able to pass. The Union rearguard was, by now, making a fighting withdrawal.

The morning of the 27th dawned into brilliant sunshine and quickly the air turned hot and sticky. The men on both sides sweated in their heavy clothing and choked in the swirling dust and smoke of battle as slowly but surely, under heavy fire from the Confederate artillery, Porter's Federal rearguard drew back, buying time for the main body of the army to establish new positions behind Boatswain's Swamp. The Seven Days had not begun well for General Lee.

Lee's failure to destroy Porter's V Corps at Beaver Dam Creek caused a serious problem. His army was now dangerously divided and on the wrong side of the Chickahominy. Because New Bridge, some three or four miles downstream to the east, was still behind Union lines, he would be unable to return quickly to the defense of Richmond should the need arise. If McClellan were to realize that only Magruder and Huger's small army of 25,000 men was all that stood between him and the capture of the Confederate capital, he would surely take the initiative and Richmond would be in his hands within a matter of hours. If Lee were forced to return with his army to the defense of Richmond, he would be faced with a march of at least eight hours, back through Mechanicsville, over the river, and along the turnpike. If, on the other hand, New Bridge could be taken, he would be able to cross there and go quickly to Magruder's and Huger's aid. Lee knew, then, that it was imperative he push Porter's V Corps back beyond New Bridge and thus open the way across the Chickahominy into Richmond should a need for it arise.

So, on the evening of the 26th, with Lee stranded on the north side of the Chickahominy, McClellan was, for the first and only time during his Peninsula Campaign, in a position where he would be able to capture the Confederate capital with little cost to his army. McClellan, of course, still believing that his army was outnumbered by more than two-to-one, did nothing.

When you have finished your visit to Beaver Dam Creek, return to your vehicle and proceed to Stop 3 at Gaines' Mill. Leave the parking area the same way you entered, turn right onto Route 156 and go about one and a half miles to Cold Harbor Road (still Route 156). Then go three miles more to a point where the road turns sharply to the left. There, take the smaller road, Route 718, and drive straight ahead to the Watt House. Leave your vehicle in the parking area and walk to the interpretive signs in front of the Watt House. Look at the map on page 112 and locate your position on the battlefield; it's marked by a Maltese cross close to the left center.

Stop 3: Gaines Mill Battlefield

On June 27th, 1862, the Watt House was behind Union lines and was occupied by 78-year-old Sarah Watt and several servants and field hands. Sarah, a widow, had lived in the house for almost all of her married life. At the time of the battle she was sick and confined to her bed; one of her granddaughters was here looking after her. Her grandsons, Confederate soldiers, were serving with the 15th Virginia Infantry Regiment just beyond the Chickahominy.

For almost two days the members of the Watt household listened to the sounds of battle away to the west. Now, as the retreating Federal army came closer, the sounds grew louder. As Porter's

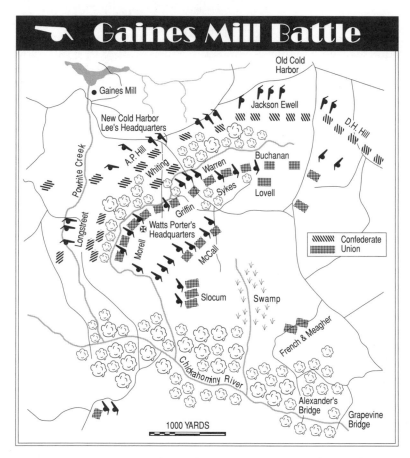

men came streaming in from the west, a Federal officer informed the Watt family that the Union army was going to make a stand here at Gaines Mill and that they would have to be evacuated. Sarah Watt was placed in a bed in a wagon and taken to her daughter's home a few miles away. There she stayed until her death a few months later; she never saw her home again. During the battle, General Porter used the house as his field headquarters. After the battle it was used as a field hospital for the wounded Confederate soldiers. When you've finished here at the Watt House return to the interpretive signs in the parking area.

By 2 o'clock on the afternoon of the 27th the situation was as follows: General Porter's V Corps was deployed in strong positions on a plateau behind Boatswain's Swamp; Confederate Generals A.P. Hill and Longstreet had deployed their divisions in line of battle in front of him – A.P. Hill on the Confederate left flank and

Longstreet on the right flank. New Bridge, although still well within range of the Federal guns on the plateau, was in Longstreet's hands, but a crossing in force still could not be made until Porter's army could be driven off the ridge. Confederate Generals Stonewall Jackson and D.H. Hill were still several hours away but moving quickly to join Longstreet and A.P. Hill. Jackson was expected to reach the field first, but Lee could not afford to wait, and so, in the meantime, he ordered A.P. Hill to attack the Federal center and Longstreet to threaten the Federal left flank. Thus, when Jackson and Hill arrived to threaten the Federal right General Porter would be forced to move troops in that direction, enabling Longstreet to smash through the weakened Federal left. The four combined Confederate divisions could then mop up the remains of Porter's decimated V Corps.

Unfortunately, Jackson's advance was held up by massive obstructions left by the enemy to delay him; Federal sharpshooters harassed his men as they labored to clear the way, thus delaying his advance even further. General D.H. Hill, then, would arrive before him on the extreme Confederate left and could do little until Jackson did finally arrive to take his place between him and A.P. Hill.

So, once again, Lee's plans were frustrated. Instead of a coordinated Confederate effort against Porter's strong positions as intended, the four divisions of Generals Longstreet, Jackson and the two Hills assaulted the Federal positions in a series of disconnected engagements that did little to further Lee's cause and, just as at Beaver Dam Creek, his artillery was deployed in such a fashion as to be of little use to the attacking Confederate forces. Indeed, it was with very little effort that the Federal guns, once again, put most of the Confederate artillery out of commission before they had any real chance to go into action.

A.P. Hill, unsupported on Longstreet's left, went into action against Porter's center and within minutes was systematically being cut to pieces by the Federal artillery on the ridge. By 2:30 that afternoon General D.H. Hill was in position on the extreme Confederate left flank to the east of the Old Cold Harbor Road facing Federal Brigadier General George Sykes' brigade of regulars about a mile away to your right. General Jackson's corps began arriving piecemeal to D.H. Hill's right and A.P. Hill's left at around 3 o'clock, but it would be at least another two hours before all of his troops were in position and ready to begin the assault. General

Richard "Old Baldy" Ewell of Jackson's corps, after first marching off in the wrong direction, arrived first and was ordered into position on D.H. Hill's immediate left and to the west of the Old Cold Harbor Road. General William Whiting, also of Jackson's corps, arrived a short while later and was ordered into position on Ewell's right in support of General A.P. Hill's beleaguered division; by 5:30 in the afternoon, all of the Confederate forces were at last present and in position on the battlefield.

Although Generals Longstreet and A.P. Hill had been unsuccessful in driving through Porter's lines, they had inflicted heavy casualties upon him. By 5 that afternoon he was in a vary precarious position with all of his brigades committed to the fight, including General Henry Slocum's division of the Federal VI Army Corps.

For General Lee, however, time was running out. If he were to be successful he had to do something to break Porter's line, and quickly. He decided that only a single, tightly coordinated attack by the combined Confederate divisions of Longstreet, Jackson and the two Hills could do the job.

At this point, because the Confederate breakthrough came just to the south of the Watt House, you might like to take the walking trail that begins beyond the interpretive signs in front of you. The walk is a strenuous one past the field, into the woods, and up the slope for about a quarter-mile. If you are unused to strenuous walking you might find that the climb up the steep trail will leave you quite breathless, so be warned and take it easy.

As you walk the trail through the woods and up the hill to the top of the ridge, you will be passing through the Federal positions. Take your time and look around. Try to imagine the thousands of Union infantrymen deployed in three long lines behind hastily thrown up breastworks of felled trees and limbs facing General A.P. Hill's Confederate line of battle to the west just beyond the creek. For almost five hours the men here fought off one assault after another. They were exhausted, hot, filthy, but still determined to hold onto their tenuous positions. All afternoon the fighting continued. The air here where you are walking was filled with the constant howl of thousands upon thousands of minie balls, canister, and case shot. The trees around you were stripped of their branches by the firestorm of lead and iron. All around you the screams and groans of the wounded and the dying echoed through the ranks of beleaguered Federal soldiers. And everywhere a pall of dirty, gray gunsmoke hung over the woods like a blanket. As the hours passed the Federal lines continued to hold. The rifled muskets of the men in the breastworks around you grew hot from constant use and then, because the soldiers had no time to clean them, useless, as residue in the barrels made them impossible to load.

Next, try to put yourself on the Confederate side. Try to imagine charging through the woods, up the hill, clambering over the fallen trees, and the limbs and branches stripped away by the hail of fire from your comrades. Picture the firestorm of minie balls howling around you, tearing into the bodies of the friends at your side. You blunder onward through the trees and the smoke, your eyes streaming. You yell at the top of your lungs, and then you find yourself swept backward by your companions in front as they turn, forced back down the hill by the awesome firepower of the well-entrenched Federal infantry in front of you. And, if you can, try to imagine how men could find the courage to fight under such conditions.

When you reach the crest of the ridge you will find a stone marker that roughly indicates the position where the Confederates finally broke the Federal line.

As you will recall, General Lee had decided upon a single, massive assault all along the Federal line. At a little after 5:30 that afternoon, General Longstreet was already attacking the extreme Federal right flank, and General D.H. Hill was hammering hard against the extreme Federal left. Lee, therefore, ordered General A.P. Hill's already badly used division, along with General Whiting's division, to hit the Federal center with everything they had. Brigadier General John Bell Hood's and Colonel Evander Law's brigades of Whiting's division were to lead the attack upon the Federal positions held by Brigadier General George Morell. For some reason, just as Hood and Law were about to move forward, Whiting gave them an unusual order: the regiments were to advance across the open fields, ford the creek, and move quickly against the Federal lines in the woods on the slopes of the ridge, *they were not, however, to open fire until they reached the first line of the enemy's works.* It was this order that made the difference. As the Confederate brigades moved forward they soon came under heavy fire from the Union lines. But, instead of stopping to return fire, they continued onward and upward, men falling in the ranks under the hail of fire, only to be replaced by the ones behind. Onward, across the open

Maj. General John Bell Hood.

fields into barrage after barrage of canister from the Federal artillery on the crest of the ridge, over the creek, into the woods, past the bodies of A.P. Hill's soldiers that had fallen during the futile charges of the previous hours until, at last, they reached the Federal lines.

As General Hood led his brigade up the hill he observed a gap in the Union line that had opened up on the other side of Colonel Law. Without stopping to think, he took two of his regiments, the 4th Texas and the 18th Georgia, and moved to the right behind Law and into the gap between Law and General George Pickett, who was fighting hard on Longstreet's left. By some strange quirk of circumstance, Hood had found the weak spot in the Federal line.

Finally, as the Confederate brigades began to reach the first Union defensive line, the Federals in the breastworks delivered a withering volley of musket fire; and with it they expected the enemy to stop, return fire, and reload, thus giving them time to reload and meet the renewed advance. That didn't happen. The Federals discharged their weapons, dozens of Confederate soldiers fell dead and wounded, but the charge never faltered. On they came without firing a single shot, and then they were upon them. In one mighty volley they delivered a storm of minie balls into the Federal ranks and, without stopping, hurled themselves upon them with fixed bayonets. The result was inevitable. The Union front line collapsed and the defenders ran back up the hill in confusion. The second rank, unable to fire for fear of hitting their fleeing comrades, also broke, and so did the third rank. Then the entire Union center collapsed and the panicking soldiers ran for the bridges over the Chickahominy south of the Watt House.

Within minutes, under heavy pressure all along the line, the Union positions began to collapse; the Federal line was broken. The breach in the Union line where you are standing began to widen as the Federal regiments, in fear of being flanked, pulled back. Along the Union line to the right and left of this position, the Federals managed to retreat in good order. But here, at the point of General Hood's breakthrough, the panic was widespread and complete.

When you've finished your visit here at the stone marker, you can continue on along the trail until you eventually arrive back at the Watt House.

General Porter, you will recall, was using the Watt House as his field headquarters and was holding several batteries of artillery here in reserve. With the Confederates advancing rapidly in this direction his main concern was to remove the batteries to the rear and save them from falling into enemy hands. Federal Brigadier General Philip St. George Cooke (Confederate Cavalry General J.E.B. Stuart's father-in-law), with a full brigade of the 5th United States Cavalry, was also deployed here in reserve at the Watt House. And so, with the best of intentions, and in a brave attempt to buy time during which the Federal artillery batteries could be withdrawn, General Cooke ordered a cavalry charge in classic order. The 5th U.S. Cavalry formed in line of battle and charged the advancing Confederate infantry. Unfortunately for Cooke, things at this point went disastrously wrong. First the Confederate infantry, after having braved more than five hours of sustained fighting against the well-entrenched Federal lines, had little to fear from the charging horsemen firing at them from the saddle. Second, Cooke's cavalry very quickly became entangled with the draft horses, limbers and caissons they were trying to save. Cooke's entire effort turned from a magnificent military spectacle into a debacle of the first order. The classic cavalry charge turned into a humiliating stampede to the rear. Of the batteries they were trying to save, 14 guns were captured by the victorious Confederate brigades as they swept on past the Watt House in pursuit of the fleeing Federals. By nightfall, the defeated Union corps had managed to withdraw across the Chickahominy to relative safety on the other side. The exhausted Confederates were in no shape to follow them. The third battle of the Seven Days at Gaines Mill was over – a tactical victory for General Lee.

The cost to both sides at Gaines Mill was horrendous. General Porter's V Corps had lost some 6,837 men killed, wounded and missing and, although he had emerged from the conflict victorious, General Lee had lost even more: 8,750 of his 57,500 soldiers lay dead and wounded on the battlefield. The scene on the hillside and in the fields to the east of the creek was one of total revulsion; everywhere the bodies of the dead and wounded, for as far as the eye could see, littered the countryside. The total losses for the 27th day of June, 1862, were in excess of 15,500. It was the bloodiest of the Battles of the Seven Days.

Take a few minutes here at the Watt House to reflect upon the momentous events of that far off day in 1862, and then return to your vehicle and continue your tour of the battlefields.

As you leave the parking area you will return to Route 156 by the same park road you used when you arrived. Turn right onto Route 156 and go for about three-tenths of a mile, where you will see the entrance to the Cold Harbor Unit of the Richmond National Battlefield Park on your left. Cold Harbor was not one of the Battles of the Seven Days, but a part of the Campaign of 1864. However, because you're here, you might like to take a short diversion and visit the battlefield, where you will find interpretive markers explaining the action and a short driving or walking tour that will take you through the Confederate and Union trenches on the battlefield. If you decide not to tour Cold Harbor you should continue on along Route 156, following the route taken by Generals Stonewall Jackson and D.H. Hill in their pursuit of the retreating Federals, for about three and a half miles to the Grapevine Bridge. After you cross the bridge, move immediately into the left-hand lane and go one fifth of a mile and turn left. Go a fifth of a mile further and turn left again onto Grapevine Road. Continue on along Grapevine Road until it ends at Meadow Road, turn left onto Meadow Road and then pull off the road at the three Savage Station Markers.

That night, the 27th, after the Battle of Gaines Mill, General McClellan, still firmly convinced that he was heavily outnumbered and in dire straights, gathered together all of his corps commanders and explained his plan to move his base of operations from the White House on the Pamunkey River to Harrison's Landing on the James River. It would be a difficult operation. His main concern was for his wagon train, numbering some 5,000 wagons and carrying all his supplies and ammunition, along with a great herd of cattle. The IV Army Corps under the command of General Erasmus D. Keyes was to escort the mighty wagon train to Harrison's Landing while General McCall's division protected the reserve artillery. General John Porter's V Corps was to guard the crossroads at Glendale and the flank of the retreating Federal army against the Confederate forces advancing from the east. The II, III and VI Corps were to fall back about a mile and concentrate their forces to the west of Savage

⤳ Savage Station Battle

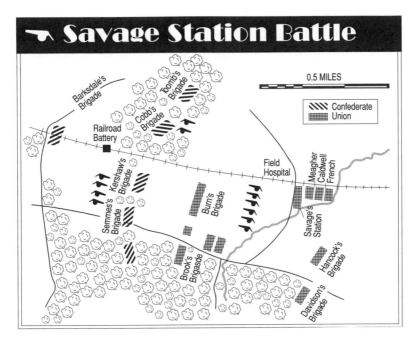

Station on the Richmond and York River Railroad, where the supplies were being loaded onto the wagons, and hold the position there until nightfall on June 29th. At that point the three corps were to pull out and move south, destroying any supplies that had not already been moved out.

For most of the next day, the 28th of June, General Lee and the Army of Northern Virginia stayed on the north side of the Chickahominy, trying to decide what McClellan would do next. Would he re-cross the Chickahominy further down-stream? Or, would he retreat all the way down the Peninsula to Fort Monroe? By late afternoon it became obvious that McClellan would do neither, that he was, in fact, retreating south toward the James and that he had almost a day's start on Lee.

As Lee studied his maps he finally decided that McClellan, slowed by his massive supply train, could be caught as he emerged from White Oak Swamp. So, with that in mind, he ordered Generals Longstreet and A.P. Hill to cross the Chickahominy at New Bridge and follow the Derbytown Road to Long Bridge Road, south of White Oak Swamp; General Huger, who was already south of the swamp, would attack McClellan from the Charles City Road as he marched out of the swamp. As all this was happening, General Magruder, who was on the Williamsburg Road south of the

Chickahominy but north of the swamp, was to pursue McClellan's rear guard heading south from Gaines Mill and attack them as they prepared to cross the swamp. Generals Jackson and D.H. Hill were to rebuild Grapevine Bridge, destroyed by the retreating Federals, and then join General Magruder attacking the Federal rearguard. The great pursuit was to begin at daybreak the following morning, the 29th.

While everything on the Union side was proceeding smoothly and according to plan, things were not going quite so well for General Lee; he couldn't get his generals working together. By midday on the 29th, General Magruder had been on the road for more than eight hours, moving cautiously eastward until he reached the old battlefields at Seven Pines and Fair Oaks. There he stopped, convinced that he was about to be attacked by a superior force to the front and that Jackson and Huger were not in position to support him. First he called for reinforcements, which he received in the form of two divisions from Huger's corps, and then he settled in and began building defenses against the Federal attack which he was sure was imminent. Magruder was right about Jackson. He was still north of the Chickahominy, rebuilding the Grapevine Bridge, a task that should have taken less than 12 hours, but in fact took more than 36. Generals Longstreet and A.P. Hill were hurrying south, trying to reach White Oak Swamp before McClellan's army emerged. Time was quickly slipping away.

At last, after much prodding and persuading from General Lee, Magruder ordered a general assault on the enemy at Savage Station; not too general though. Of the six brigades available to him, Magruder committed only two and a half.

As you stand in front of the Savage Station Markers you will be facing what was, on the 29th of June, 1862, the battlefield of Savage Station. The topography of today bears little resemblance to that of 1862. The tracks of the Richmond and York River Railroad, McClellan's supply line from the White House, are about a half-mile to the south, running under the highway bridges. The markers you see in front of you have been moved and are somewhat misleading. The road referred to is not the Meadow Road upon which you are standing, but the old Williamsburg Road about a mile to the south of here.

As you look southward across the battlefield and to your left, you will see from the map on page 119 that the Federal army had established a field hospital to the north of the railroad. The II and VI Corps of the Federal army under the commands of Generals Edwin Sumner and William B. Franklin were in line of battle extending southward across the railroad and the Williamsburg Road, from a point close to where you are now standing, for about a mile and a half, waiting for the Confederate attack from the west. In the meantime the III Federal Army Corps under the command of General Samuel P. Heintzelman had moved out of Savage Station and had begun crossing the White Oak Swamp.

Finally, at about 5 o'clock in the afternoon, General Magruder ordered his brigades forward into battle. They advanced with the same lack of coordination that had plagued the Confederate army during the three previous battles of the Seven Days. General Toombs' brigade in position near here where you are standing never made contact with the enemy. Neither did Cobb's brigade, in line of battle just to the south of Toombs. Brigadier General Joseph Kershaw's brigade working to the south of the railroad, however, did make contact. Kershaw's South Carolinians smashed into the center ranks of General William W. Burns brigade of General Sedgewick's division and immediately became engaged in fierce, hand-to-hand combat. General Burns' line broke and, for a time, Kershaw's brigade continued to hammer the beleaguered Federal regiments. Unfortunately, Kershaw's success was short lived and, due to lack of support, he was forced to withdraw. The fighting at Savage Station, such as it was, finally ended at nightfall under a terrifying thunderstorm. The Federal army slunk away across White Oak Swamp under cover of darkness, leaving behind them millions of dollars worth of burning supplies and more than 2,500 of their wounded in the field hospital. The fourth of the Battles of the Seven Days was over, and it too had not gone well for General Lee.

At 3 o'clock that morning, the 30th of June, General Jackson finally arrived with the news that his men would all be across the Grapevine Bridge by dawn; he was given the task of pursuing the Federal rearguard.

Return to your vehicle and continue on to the site of the fifth Battle of the Seven Days at Glendale Crossroads. When you leave the parking area, turn right onto Meadow Road and drive on for two and a half miles until you reach the Williamsburg Road. Cross the road very carefully and rejoin Route 156. Continue on along Route 156 for six miles, following Jackson's route as he pursued the

Federal rearguard, and turn left, still on Route 156, onto the Willis Church Road at Glendale. Stop when you reach Frayser's Farm at Glendale.

On the morning of June 30th, things seemed to take a turn for the better for General Lee. Jackson was in hot pursuit of McClellan's rearguard, General Huger was in position on the Charles City Road ready to hit the Federal flank at Glendale south of White Oak Swamp, and Generals Longstreet and A.P. Hill were moving quickly to intercept the Federal column south of the Swamp and were only two miles away on the Darbytown Road. Confederate General Theophilus Holmes with a full division of infantry was moving east on the Newmarket Road and nearing the junction with the Willis Church Road ahead of McClellan's columns.

In the meantime, General McClellan's retreating army was in real trouble. The head of the Federal column had reached Glendale and the wagons had become bogged down and were blocking the road. With Confederate troops less than two miles away to the west and converging on them from three different directions, as well as from the rear, something had to be done and quickly. Fortunately, they found a small dirt road leading away from the Willis Church Road to the east and they diverted the wagons along it and away from the impending battle.

As the last of the Federal troops crossed the White Oak Swamp Bridge they destroyed it, leaving Jackson stranded on the far side. Then they deployed artillery on the bluffs facing Jackson to keep him from rebuilding it. Jackson, under orders to cross the swamp via that bridge, and carrying them out to the letter, ignored the several fords available to the east and west of the bridge, brought up artillery of his own, and began shelling the Federal positions on the bluffs in front of him. His lack of initiative was fortuitous for McClellan, for Jackson's delay north of the White Oak Swamp Bridge meant that he would be unable to support Generals Longstreet and Hill in their assault on the Federal positions now building to the west.

Realizing that the arrival of Longstreet and Hill was imminent, the Federal forces deployed west of the Willis Church Road and prepared to meet them as they turned onto the Long Bridge Road. It was at this point that, once again, Lee's generals failed to carry out his orders, and another opportunity to destroy the Federal army was lost.

While General Jackson was fiddling around to the north of White
Oak Swamp Bridge, General Huger allowed his advancing column
to become bogged down by felled trees across the Charles City
Road; General Magruder, advancing cautiously, had also fallen
behind schedule. Thus, when Longstreet and Hill attacked the
Federal positions on the bluffs west of the Willis Church Road, they
did so alone.

The Confederate attack began at around 4 o'clock on the afternoon
of June 30th, with Longstreet and Hill assaulting the strongly
defended positions of General George McCall's Federal division.
At first the attack was successful. The Federal line was broken and
General McCall captured. Unfortunately for them, Hill and Longstreet had attacked at the very center of the Federal line and
reinforcements were quickly brought in to seal the breach. Generals Sedgewick's, Kearny's and Hooker's divisions were thrown
into the gap and closed it, forcing Longstreet and Hill into a savage
hand-to-hand battle that raged on into the darkness. The Battle of
Glendale ended when, under cover of darkness, the Federals left to
join again with the main body of the Army of the Potomac retreating southward to take up defensive positions on Malvern Hill.
When you've finished at Frayser's Farm continue on along Route
156 for two and a half miles to the Malvern Hill Unit of the
Richmond National Battlefield Park, turn right onto the park road
and proceed to the visitor parking area. Leave your vehicle in the
parking lot and walk to the shelter overlooking the battlefield.

Malvern Hill

Following the Battle of Glendale, or Frayser's Farm, on June 30th,
1862, McClellan's Army of the Potomac continued its withdrawal
southward toward its new base at Harrison's Landing on the banks
of the James River. With General Lee's army in hot pursuit, however, McClellan was more and more concerned that his vulnerable
wagon trains would soon be within reach of one or another of the
fast-moving Confederate columns.

Malvern Hill, a mile-wide plateau, looked to McClellan like a very
strong defensive position. And undoubtedly it was, for Generals
Porter and Keyes had held the position for most of the day of the
30th against repeated assaults from the south by General Holmes.
It was here, then, that he decided to make a stand and thus buy
time for his wagons to reach the relative safety of Harrison's
Landing.

Battle of Malvern Hill

Union
Confederate

Long Bridge Road

Willis Methodist Curch

Willis Church Road

French's Grist Mill

Eppes

Longstreets Division

To Richmond

Early

C. W. Smith's Shop

Garthwright

Law

Trimble

Hood

Armistead

Poindexter

BERDAN'S SHARP SHOOTERS

Morell

Heinzelman's

Sumner's

Greenwood Hospital

LOW MEADOW

MALVERN HILL

River Road

To Harrison's Landing

1 MILE

1st Massachussetts Artillery at Malvern Hill.

As you look at the map of the battlefield, you will see there are steep bluffs to the east and west, but to the north the hill slopes gently away to a wheatfield, beyond which was a dense and swampy forest. The only clear way over the mountain was the Willis Church Road, now completely blocked by four-fifths of the Federal army.

By the morning of July 1st, the Federals had placed a heavy concentration of guns, in line, and as close to each other as efficient working of each piece would allow, all along the top of the hill facing the open ground and the Willis Church Road to the north. The guns you see here facing north are a representation of those batteries.

McClellan also deployed his reserve artillery about a half-mile to the rear and to the west on the top of the bluffs overlooking the New Market Road. Also, believing his right flank to be vulnerable to attack, he placed seven divisions of infantry to the right of the road around the West House facing the Western Run and the woods just beyond to the east. On this side of the road he deployed two divisions between the Willis Church Road and the Crew House. Forward of the artillery and to the front he placed a line of sharpshooters stretching the entire width of the wheatfield from the Western Run to the right and across the road to the Turkey Run on the left. Then the Federal army settled down to wait.

Union artillery moving to the front. Peninsula Campaign, 1862.

On the morning of July 1st, General Lee, concerned about the strength of the Federal positions on the plateau, sent General Longstreet to reconnoiter the situation and determine whether or not it would be feasible to attack them. Longstreet, after skirting the bluffs to the west to a point beyond the Federal left, climbed the hill and surveyed the Union positions. He returned to Lee at noon and, in conference with Jackson and D.H. Hill, told him that the Federal defenses were formidable, but that massed guns placed to the right on a hill near the Crew House and more placed to the left on the Poindexter Farm might catch the enemy artillery in a deadly crossfire. If so, and if the infantry could be raked with canister, case and shell, Confederate infantry might be able to carry the Federal positions with one great charge. D.H. Hill, in possession of vital information from a local farmer, felt that the Federal position was too strong to be taken in such a manner and said so. Lee, however, agreed with Longstreet. He knew he could not let McClellan's army slip away unmolested; Malvern Hill would be his last chance.

Lee's plan was simple. He would use his freshest troops for the attack; consequently General Jackson was to deploy his entire corps to the east of the Willis Church Road, north and east of the Western Run on the heights opposite the Federal positions on Malvern Hill. General Magruder was to advance along the road and deploy his corps on Jackson's right. Brigadier Generals Lewis Armistead and Ambrose Wright, whose brigades had become separated from General Huger's division, were to advance along the Willis Church Road and fall into position on Jackson's right and Magruder's left. The Confederate batteries would rake the Federal positions and break them. Brigadier General Armistead, once in position with his full brigade of infantry to the west of the Willis Church Road, was to observe the effect of the massive bombardment on the Federal artillery positions. Once he had determined that the Confederate artillery had broken the Federal batteries, he was to order his brigade to charge with a great yell, up the open ground in front of where you are now standing, and thus give the signal for a general attack on the Federal positions by all sections of the army.

Unfortunately for Lee, the Federal artillery was equipped, not only with a great many smoothbore Napoleon cannon – devastating when loaded with canister and used at close range against charging infantry – but also with a large number of rifled Parrott guns that far outranged those of the Confederate army. In addition, McClellan had deployed 14 large siege guns about a mile to the rear at the Malvern House, just for good measure. Thus Lee's batteries never were able to deploy close enough to the enemy positions to do any real good. General D.H. Hill described the Confederate artillery fire as "almost farcical."

For almost two hours Armistead and his brigade, under heavy fire from the Federal batteries along the crest of the hill where you are standing, waited and watched. The Federal line remained unbroken; the Confederate guns, outranged and outmatched, were rendered almost ineffective. By 3 o'clock it had become obvious to the Confederate High Command that the plan was not going to work. In the meantime, the Federal sharpshooters in line on the lower slopes of the hill began to move forward and engage Armistead's infantry brigade. Armistead's brigade responded with a yell and charged the Federal sharpshooters, driving them back in confusion. Unfortunately, in doing so, they put themselves in a most dangerous situation. The Federal positions on top of the hill were far too strong for them to attack, and they were now so far forward they were unable to retreat without suffering heavy casualties. They dropped to the ground under the protection of a shallow ravine and waited for help to arrive.

It was at this point that things began to go very wrong for the Confederate army. General Magruder and his division arrived in position behind Armistead and, seeing Armistead deployed in a forward position, concluded that Armistead had made a successful attack on the Federal positions. He sent word to General Lee telling him so. Lee responded by sending orders to Magruder to follow up on Armistead's perceived success and move forward in support of the attack.

Magruder did just as he was told and the forward units of his division charged forward with a yell. Unfortunately, General D.H. Hill, in position between Jackson and Magruder, was waiting and watching for Armistead to do exactly what Magruder was now doing. He mistook Magruder for Armistead and the Rebel yell for the signal initiating the general attack, and he, too, ordered his men forward into the attack. It was a disaster. The charging Confederate infantry was no match for the Federal artillery and the firestorm of canister and case-shot they rained down upon them. Not a single Confederate regiment was able to approach within 200 yards of the Federal positions where you are standing.

Try to imagine the spectacle as it must have been. Thousands of gray-clad infantry men in line of battle on the lower slopes of the hill away to your front; the single continuous line of Federal guns stretching away into the distance on either side of you; and then the noise as the men of the Federal batteries, each one working like a well-oiled machine, firing at will, load after load of deadly canister and case; the hillside disappearing under a great pall of gunsmoke; the air hot from the sun; the men choking in the acrid and overpowering pall of gunsmoke. And, in the distance down the slope, the faint beating of the Confederate drums, the Rebel yell drifting on the wind and, as the smoke cleared a little, the sight of the Federal canister tearing great gaps in the advancing Confederate line; men falling, five and six at a time, all along the line, only to be replaced by the men behind. It was, as we might say today, like shooting fish in a barrel. More than 5,000 Confederate soldiers fell on the slopes of Malvern Hill in front of you; the Army of the Potomac lost only 3,000 men in the battle. By nightfall, when the fighting ended for the day, the two armies were in much the same positions as they had been at the beginning of the battle. All night long the men on both sides did their best for the wounded and the dying. The following morning, however, as mist lifted from the fields, the true horrors of war were revealed for all to see. The fields in front of you were littered with bodies, dead and wounded. A Federal officer was heard to say, *"Our ears had been filled with agonizing cries from thousands before the fog lifted. Our eyes saw an appalling spectacle upon the slopes down to the woodlands a half a mile away. Over 5,000 dead and*

Union staff officers during the Peninsula Campaign, 1862. The man lying with the dog is 22-year-old Captain George Armstrong Custer.

wounded were on the ground in every attitude of distress. A third of them were dead or dying, but enough were alive and moving to give the field a singular crawling effect. The different stages of the ebbing tide are often marked by the lines of flotsam and jetsam left along the seashore. So here could be seen three distinct lines... marking the last front of three Confederate charges of the night before."

McClellan's army withdrew from Malvern Hill during the night of July 1st, leaving only a single brigade of infantry, a brigade of cavalry, and one battery of artillery as a rearguard.

The Battles of the Seven Days were over, as was McClellan's Peninsula Campaign. Of his 118,000 soldiers, the Battles of the Seven Days had cost McClellan more than 16,000 casualties; Lee had lost more than 20,000 of his 88,000 men. The threat to Richmond was gone; the Army of the Potomac was safe. But neither commander was happy.

To President Davis Lee said of McClellan's refuge at Harrison's Landing, "*I fear he is too secure under cover of his boats to be driven from his position. I discover no intention of his either ascending or crossing the river at present.*" To his army he had this to say, "*Today the remains of that confident and threatening host lie upon the banks of the James River, thirty miles from Richmond, seeking cover, under the protection of the gunboats, from the effects of a series of disastrous defeats.*" And to his wife this, "*Our success has not been as great or as complete as I could have desired.*"

General McClellan, secure under the protection of the Federal gunboats on the James River, lay at Harrison's Landing and wondered what to do next. At first he thought he might renew his offensive, but then, still under the impression that he was outnumbered at least two-to-one, decided that such an action was folly and could only result in disaster, and he told President Lincoln so.

On July 8th Lincoln arrived in person to see for himself the exact state of his army. He was not pleased. McClellan took the opportunity to complain in person to Lincoln about the perceived lack of support he and his army had received during his Peninsula Campaign. And then he asked Lincoln for 100,000 reinforcements. Lincoln refused, informing him that there were not more than 75,000 soldiers anywhere in the Eastern Theater.

After Lincoln returned to Washington, McClellan wrote to his wife telling her that, "*I can never regard him with other feelings than those of thorough contempt.*"

When you've finished here at Malvern Hill, leave the parking area and turn right onto Route 156. Follow the road for a little more than a mile, turn right onto Route 5 and drive for eight miles to the Fort Harrison unit of the park system. The earthworks there are a continuation of those you saw at the beginning of your tour at Chickahominy Bluff and are a part of the outer defenses around Richmond. You will find audio stations and interpretive signs at strategic points around the unit. After your visit to the Fort Harrison unit, return to Route 5 and go for five miles more, turn right at the traffic light at 25th Street, drive three more blocks to Broad Street and turn right; the Visitor Center is a half-mile further on along Broad Street.

For more information, contact the Richmond National Battlefield Park, 3215 East Broad Street, Richmond, VA 23223. Telephone 804-226-1981.

What to See, Where to Stay

Annual Events

Historic Garden Week in Virginia. Over 200 private houses and gardens of historic interest are opened to the public during this event held in mid-April. For tours and information, contact 12 E. Franklin Street, Richmond, VA 23219. Telephone 804-644-7776.

The June Jubilee is held downtown and features the performing and visual arts of the region. Telephone 804-643-4993 for more information.

The Virginia State Fair is held in late September and early October and features a carnival, horse shows, and music. For more information, telephone 804-228-3200.

The Christmas Open House Tour is held in the historic Fan District of Richmond during either the 2nd or 3rd week in December. For more information, telephone 804-355-0892.

What to See

The State Capital. 9th and Grace Streets, Capital Square. The capital building is modeled after La Maison Carrée, an ancient Roman temple at Nimes in France, and was designed by Thomas Jefferson. The hall features the first interior dome ever built in this country. Open daily March through October and Sunday afternoons the rest of the year; closed Thanksgiving, Christmas day, and January 1st.

Museum of the Confederacy. 1201 E. Clay Street, North of Capital Square. This museum contains the nation's largest collection of Confederate military and civilian artifacts, including uniforms, equipment, flags, and the personal belongings of Jefferson Davis, Robert E. Lee, and J.E.B. Stuart. Open daily except Thanksgiving, Christmas day, and January 1st.

The White House of the Confederacy. 12th & E. Clay Streets. A classic revival house used by Jefferson Davis as his official residence during the period when Richmond was the capital of the Confederacy. The house has been restored to its wartime appearance and features original furnishings.

The Edgar Allen Poe Museum. 1914 E. Main Street. An old stone house thought to be the oldest structure in Richmond. Four additional buildings house a collection of Poe mementos, including James Carling's illustrations of "The Raven," and a slide presentation depicting Poe's life in Richmond. Open daily except Christmas day.

The Virginia Museum of Fine Arts. Boulevard and Grove Avenue. This museum is America's first state-supported museum of art, and features collections of original paintings, prints, and sculptures from the major cultures of the world. There is also a collection of jewels and jeweled eggs by Faberge. Open daily except Monday and closed during all national holidays.

For more information about the sights and sounds of Richmond, contact the Richmond Convention & Visitor's Bureau, 6th Street Market Place, 550 E. Marshall Street, Richmond, VA 23219. Telephone 804-782-2777.

Where to Stay: The list of major hotels and restaurants located in and around the city of Richmond is far too large to list here. So, for hotel and lodging information in the Richmond area, contact the Richmond Convention & Visitor's Bureau, 6th Street Market Place, 550 E. Marshall Street, Richmond, VA 23219. Telephone 804-782-2777.

Chapter 8

Perryville

October 8th, 1862

Perryville Battlefield State Historic Site is located 45 miles southwest of Lexington, Kentucky and is open daily the year-round. From Lexington, take U.S. Highway 68 to U.S. Highway 150. The Museum and Gift Shop are open daily from April 1st through October 31st from 9 a.m. to 5 p.m.

On October 8, 1862 all the realities of the Civil War were brought home to the people of Kentucky. On that day two mighty armies met in what would be the greatest battle of the war ever to be fought on Kentucky soil.

The early months of the War in the West had not gone well for the Confederacy. True, they had won a marginal battle at Wilson's Creek more than a year earlier on August 10th, 1861, but from then on things had deteriorated to the point where all of Missouri and most of Tennessee had fallen to the Union forces. Confederate forces had suffered major defeats at Forts Henry and Donelson, Nashville was in Union hands, and the South had lost the first great battle of the war at Shiloh. By the beginning of October, 1962, only two Confederate armies remained in Tennessee. Both were convinced that the future good fortunes of the Confederacy lay within the borders of Kentucky, and that Kentuckians would rally to the cause and "rise up en masse against the Union" if that state could ever be brought under the control of the Confederate government.

Confederate Generals Braxton Bragg and E. Kirby Smith met in Chattanooga, Tennessee on July 31, 1862 and, after lengthy discussions, agreed to invade Kentucky. Smith marched from Knoxville on August 14th with a force of 10,000 men and, after a series of quick victories at Cumberland Gap and Richmond, Kentucky, established himself at Frankfort, Kentucky on September 3rd.

Meanwhile, Bragg, with an army of more than 30,000 men, marched northwest from Chattanooga, slipped past the Federal Army of the Ohio at Nashville, and moved quickly toward Louis-

General Braxton Bragg.

ville. After a short siege, the city of Munfordville fell to Bragg on September 17th. At this point, Bragg was undecided on what to do next. His first inclination was to move against the Union forces in Louisville and if he had had Kirby Smith's army with him he might have done so. However, Smith was at Frankfort, and there were rumors that large numbers of Union reinforcements were flowing into Louisville. Bragg, ever cautious, abandoned his plans for Louisville, turned eastward and, on September 21st he occupied the city of Bardstown.

At this point Bragg decided to split his force, and sent Major Generals Leonidas Polk and William J. Hardee to sweep the area to the southeast of Louisville, while he went to Frankfort to supervise the installation of a Confederate State Government.

In the meantime, Union Major General Don Carlos Buell and his Army of the Ohio had left Nashville, Tennessee, and was in hot pursuit of Bragg; by September 25th he was in Louisville.

On October 1st, Buell moved out of Louisville with a force of more than 55,000 men. He divided the army into four columns which fanned out to the east and to the south and, following separate routes, they all headed for Bardstown and a showdown with the Confederate army. Union General Alexander McCook's 1st Army Corps took the Taylorsville Road, General Thomas Crittenden's II Corps headed straight for Bardstown, General Charles Gilbert's III Corps took the

Maj. General E. Kirby Smith.

Shepherdsville Road, and Brigadier General Joshua Sill's division headed for Frankfort.

The scattered Union army pushed on through Bardstown and Harrodsville, engaging the Confederate skirmishers in a series of small actions until Buell ordered his forces to converge on Perryville by October 7th. Unfortunately, because of the unusually dry weather, only 22,000 of his men were on hand for the conflict that was about to begin.

Maj. General Don Carlos Buell.

By October 7th Confederate Generals Polk and Hardee, with a force of only 16,000 men, were centered on Perryville. Bragg arrived on the morning of the 8th and ordered Generals Benjamin F. Cheatham's and Simon Bolivar Buckner's divisions to attack the Union left flank and left center. Cheatham and Buckner, along with two of Anderson's brigades, on the far right of the Confederate army, hit McCook's 1st Corps on the Union left flank hard at around 2 o'clock in the afternoon and, like a great door with its hinge firmly fastened at the southern end, they began to swing in a huge arc to the west around the Union flank, pushing McCook back past the intersection of the Mackville Road. From then on, things would have gone very badly for the Union army had it not been for the gallant action of Colonel John Starkweather's Brigade. Starkweather and his men would make their stand on a small hill to the west of the battlefield.

By late afternoon the battle had escalated and was raging, sometimes hand-to-hand, across a wide area. By the end of the day when the fighting ended, Union General Alexander McCook's corps had been pushed back more than a mile, and General Charles Gilbert was holding only tenuously to his positions at the center of the Union line. Thomas Crittenden's II Corps was spread out in a thin line more than three miles long to the southwest of Perryville and was never fully engaged.

Buell was determined to resume battle on the morning of October 9th, but by then General Bragg had withdrawn his forces and had retired to Harrodsburg, leaving the field to the enemy. The Federal losses during the one-day battle totaled more than 4,200 killed, wounded, or missing in action; the Confederate casualties were fewer than 3,500. The result? The Battle of Perryville was a tactical Confederate victory only because of Bragg's timely withdrawal. Had he stayed, the following morning he would have had to face a Federal army more than 40,000 strong.

General Bragg, ever the hard-luck general, was severely criticized for his failure to hold Kentucky for the Confederacy. He moved on to the Battle of Stones River where, once again, he enjoyed a tactical victory only to abandon the field to the enemy. At Chickamauga he won a magnificent victory against General William Rosecrans and the Federal Army of the Cumberland, but his failure to follow through and destroy his badly defeated foe probably cost the Confederacy the entire war. After his defeat at the Battle of Chattanooga some two months later he was relieved of his command; he died penniless, a broken man, in Galveston, Texas in 1876.

Brig. General Benjamin Franklin Cheatham.

As for General Buell, for allowing the Confederate army to escape, he was relieved of his command on October 24th, 1862 and was never again given command of an army.

Today, the one-time killing fields at Perryville are a memorial to the soldiers of both armies who gave their lives for their countries. The Crawford House, General Bragg's headquarters, and the H.P. Bottom House, both of which were at the center of the battle, are still standing. More than 100 acres of Kentucky park land, a museum, hiking trails, picnic shelters and playgrounds offer visitors to the park a day out with a difference.

The battlefield at Perryville, during the time of the Civil War.

Touring the Battlefield

Perryville Battlefield State Historic Site encompasses only a small part of the original battlefield: the area where General Cheatham's forces were engaged against those of General McCook on the Union left flank. A self-guided walking tour of the park – it's a walk of about a mile – will take you to eight stops along the way, where you will find red and white markers to help you interpret the battle as it took place. Stand facing the markers for correct orientation.

Stop 1:

As you stand in front of the marker, you are facing east looking toward the Confederate line of battle as it was at about 1 o'clock in the early afternoon of October 8th, 1862. Confederate General Benjamin F. Cheatham's division was deployed beyond the far line of trees ahead of you across the Chaplin River. To your right, at about the same time, Confederate Colonel John Austin Wharton's cavalry made a sweep from your left to your right, encountering skirmishers of the 33rd Ohio Volunteers over to your right. Wharton cleared the area and reported to his commanders that the way was now open for them to advance.

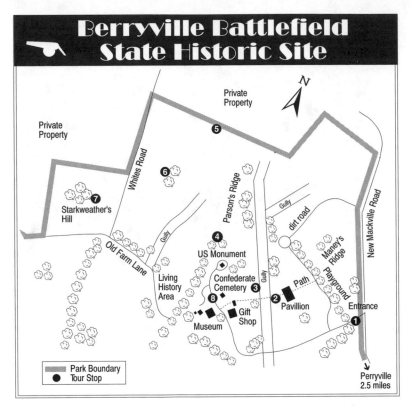

General Cheatham's division, along with that of General Simon Buckner and two brigades of James Anderson's division, crossed the river and assembled in the fields ahead. The attack on the Federal positions began at 2 o'clock, with the Confederate brigades of Generals Donelson and Stewart moving through this position, where you are now standing, toward Union General William Rufus Terrill's artillery battalion of eight guns and a full brigade of infantry in line of battle behind you.

As Donelson's brigade moved forward, it came under a devastating barrage of Federal cannon fire. Double-loaded canister and case shot tore through the air like a hundred swarms of angry hornets. In only a few minutes, on this very spot where you are now, the 16th Tennessee Infantry Regiment lost more than 200 men. As the battle here raged on, Confederate General Maney's Brigade, under orders to clear the area and capture Terrill's guns, assembled in the fields in front of you and to the left. A Confederate brigade at that time numbered perhaps 2,000 men. At least three brigades were engaged in the fields before you and to the left and right of where you are standing. Try to imagine what a magnificent and terrifying sight it must have been to see rank upon rank of gray-clad soldiers, flags flying, drums beating, advancing across the fields toward you; the carnage in the Confederate ranks as the Federal guns opened up behind you; next, the desperate fighting as the blue and gray hoards collided in a hail of shot, shell and minie balls; then the frantic, all-out hand-to-hand struggle as Maney's brigade smashed into General Terrill's positions.

From here walk almost due east, past the picnic area, to a small wooden bridge where you will find Stop 2. In 1862 the area through which you will walk was thickly wooded and covered with heavy undergrowth.

Stop 2:

As you stand in front of the marker here, you are roughly at the center of the position held by the 9th Tennessee Infantry Regiment, a part of General Maney's front line facing General Terrill's positions to the southwest at about 2:30 in the afternoon. In 1862 a split rail fence ran the length of the gully separating the woods that were behind you from the open fields. Maney's line of battle stretched the entire length of the gully, more than 1,500 feet. The 1st and 27th Tennessee Infantry Regiments were positioned in line of battle just to the rear of the 9th Tennessee, behind you and to the right, near what is now the playground area. From here you should cross the footbridge and proceed to Stop 3.

Stop 3:

You have now crossed over from the Confederate line of battle to a point close to the center of the position held by the Federal 123rd Illinois Infantry Regiment. At 2:30 that afternoon, their line of battle extended roughly 400 feet to the left and right of where you are now standing. The 123rd was a rookie regiment; many of its soldiers had never been in battle before. They started off well enough, just beyond the hill behind you. When Maney's Confederate brigade came into view, they charged down the hill toward them until they reached this position, fired a volley at the advancing gray lines, and then they retreated just as quickly back the way they'd come. But minutes later, the 80th Illinois Infantry, in a long line stretching back beyond the point where the park museum stands today, advanced in perfect formation to the crest of the hill behind you and opened fire on the advancing Confederate brigade.

Before long, however, they too had to pull back, leaving this position to the enemy. From here, turn left and walk up the hill past the Union monument to Stop 4.

Stop 4:

You should now be facing northwest at the position from which this eight-gun Federal battery under the command of Captain Charles Parsons devastated the 16th Tennessee Infantry Regiment of General Donelson's Brigade when the battle opened. The eight guns were in position here, in a line that extended for about 100 yards in front of you, and were aimed at the Confederate line of battle to your right. It must have been an awesome sight. Each gun was supported by a limber and caisson. Each limber and each caisson was pulled into position by a team of eight horses and three outriders – 96 heavy draft horses and 48 riders, all milling around to the rear of the battery at your left. At the guns, the crews numbered nine men per piece: 72 cannoneers, all supposed to work together like clockwork firing at a rate of more than two rounds per minute. Combined, they could deliver a devastating barrage of canister and case-shot. Unfortunately, the crews were almost totally inexperienced, regular soldiers, members of the 105th Ohio Infantry Regiment pressed into the artillery unit only a week earlier, and they had little idea of how to handle the big guns. After the initial damage had been done to the 16th Tennessee, things on the Federal side quickly went downhill. Finally, as Maney's Confederate brigade came over the fence at the bottom of the valley and charged up the hill toward where you are now standing, the gun crews abandoned their weapons and ran away. Had they been a fully trained artillery unit, there's no doubt they would have made things very hot for Maney's charging Confederate infantry. As it was, Parsons could do little but try to save his battery. It was an impossible task; he was able to save only a single gun, and that only because it had never been unhitched from its limber. Parsons, unwilling to leave his command, had to be forcibly dragged away by his men, leaving seven of his guns to the enemy. From here continue straight ahead to Stop 5 at the northern end of the park.

Stop 5:

You are now facing southeast, in a position close to the extreme left flank of Union General McCook's division. It was here that another rookie Union regiment, also untried in battle, was supposed to have been in line of battle facing the Confederate charge. Unfortunately, however, these men were so inexperienced they even had problems forming up in a straight line. Several times they tried to get into formation; each time they became a little more confused. Officers and NCO's screamed and yelled at the milling mass of men to little avail. Finally, at about 2:30 in the afternoon, with General Cheatham's Confederate division rapidly approaching, they were ordered to get down as best they could and fire at will. Some dropped to the ground where they stood, some moved forward to get a better view of the enemy, and some dropped back, not really knowing what to do next. The result was inevitable: the Union line here and to the left collapsed completely and the Federals turned and ran westward in panic and confusion. You will find Stop 6 down the hill to your right near a small clump of cedars.

Stop 6:

At this point you should be facing almost due south. By 3 o'clock that afternoon General Terrill's brigade had been devastated and was streaming back toward the top of the hill across the road to your right and front. The 21st Wisconsin Volunteer Infantry Regiment of Colonel John Starkweather's Union Brigade was deployed in the cornfield along White's Road to your right. The rest of Starkweather's veteran brigade was in position further back on the hill across the road in front of you. At 3 o'clock General Cheatham's Confederate division smashed through into the cornfield to your left. The 21st Wisconsin stood and delivered a devastating hail of musket fire into the advancing Confederate line of battle. It was soon obvious, however, that they would not be able to hold their positions. As the Confederate line continued to advance across the cornfield, the 21st Wisconsin conducted a fighting withdrawal and pulled back to where the rest of Starkweather's brigade was waiting in line of battle on top of the hill. To reach Stop 7 on top of the hill, you will need to cross the road. Please use the designated crossing area, watch out for traffic, and proceed with caution.

Stop 7:

At this point you are facing north toward the advancing Confederate forces of Major General Benjamin F. Cheatham's division, with General Maney's brigade leading. Try to imagine the pageant as it must have been seen by the Union brigade in position where you're standing. Thousands of gray-clad soldiers, bayonets fixed, flags flying and drums beating as they advanced across the cornfield in a great crescent-shaped formation centered on this hill: a solid mass of men in line upon line, each one following the one in front in perfect order. Then turn and look around you; try to imagine the scene as it must have been here on the top of the hill. Twelve Federal cannon were in position in a line 150 yards long along the top of the ridge. Thousands of soldiers, many of them the remnants of the broken regiments that had fled in panic only 30 minutes or so earlier, were milling around in confusion. There were horses everywhere, 144 of them, heavy draft horses that had pulled the 12 limbers, guns, and caissons into position. The entire area was seething like a giant anthill. Then, all hell broke loose.

As the Confederate brigades moved out into the cornfield, the Union batteries here on the hill opened a devastating barrage of double-loaded canister and case-shot, tearing huge holes in the Confederate line of battle. As the Confederate line drew closer, the infantry opened fire, a deadly hail of minie balls that, when combined with the firestorm of canister from the Federal cannon, tore the Confederate ranks to shreds. And still the great gray line moved forward. Soon they were so close the cannon were unable to depress sufficiently to fire down the hill; for a moment they fell silent, but the terrific noise of musket fire from both sides continued unabated. Hundreds of men on both sides fell under a withering hail of minie balls. More than half the 144 artillery horses were killed, and then the Confederate attack faltered, broke, and the gray lines fell back. Quickly, they regrouped and pressed forward again. For an hour the battle swayed to and fro. Twice, the Confederate brigades captured the Union battery here on the hill, and twice they lost it again. At about 4 o'clock the 1st Wisconsin captured the 1st Tennessee Infantry Regiment's battle flag and the Confederates withdrew once more. The battle here, however, was almost over. About to be outflanked both right and left, Starkweather's brigade had no other option but to withdraw. At a little after 4 o'clock, his magnificent stand having saved the entire left flank of the Union Army, Starkweather retreated down the road behind you. To reach Stop 8, walk on down the hill to your right, through the gate, and on down the old farm lane. Then, at the bottom of the hill, turn left into the meadow and walk to the Confederate Cemetery.

Stop 8:

It was here that some of the Confederate dead, most of them left for days unburied on the battlefield, are interred close to the position where the initial Confederate attack on General McCook's Union division took place. At the end of the battle, this field was literally covered with the bodies of dead Confederate soldiers. Squire H.P. Bottom gathered more than 300 of them together. Some he was able to identify, most he was not. He buried them here where you now stand. The Union dead were buried along the Springfield Pike the day after the battle. There they rested until they were disinterred and carried to Camp Nelson to be re-buried with honor in the National Cemetery.

The Battle of Perryville was a tactical Confederate victory that was not followed up on. During the battle the Union army suffered 854 killed, 2,851 wounded, with 515 missing or captured; Brigadier General Terrill was among the fatalities. The Confederate losses are listed as 510 killed, 2,635 wounded, and 251 missing in action. The combined casualties numbered more than 7,600. Perryville was, indeed, Kentucky's bloodiest day.

For more information, contact the Perryville Battlefield State Historic Site, PO Box 296, Perryville, KY 40468-9999. Telephone 606-332-8631.

What to See, Where to Stay

Danville, Kentucky

What to See

Constitution Square State Shrine. Located on U.S. Highway 127 in the center of the town, the shrine is an authentic reproduction of Kentucky's first state courthouse on the exact site where the first State Constitution was drafted and adopted in 1792.

The McDowell House and Apothecary Shop at 125 S. 2nd Street is the residence and shop of Dr. Ephraim McDowell, a noted surgeon of the early 19th century. The house is maintained by the Kentucky Medical Association.

The Isaac Shelby State Shrine is located six miles south, off U.S. Highway 127 and is the site of Traveler's Rest, Shelby's Stone House (no longer standing) and the burial place of Kentucky's first and fifth governors.

Pioneer Playhouse Village-of-the-Arts, located one mile south on Stanford Avenue, U.S. Highway 150, is a reproduction of an 18th-century Kentucky village set on a 200-acre site featuring an art gallery, a museum, and a drama school.

Seasonal Event

The Pioneer Playhouse presents Summer Stock, a season of Broadway comedies and musicals from mid-June to late August.

Hotels

Holiday Inn. 4th Street, at the junction of U.S. 127S. Telephone 606-236-8600. Children under 19 stay free, free crib, pool, cafe, room service, meeting rooms. Accepts credit cards.

Super 8. 3663 U.S. 150 at U.S. 127 Bypass. Telephone 606-236-8881. Children under 12 stay free, free crib, free coffee, cafe nearby, meeting rooms. Accepts credit cards.

Chapter 9

Pickett's Mill

May 27, 1864

Pickett's Mill is claimed to be "one of the best preserved Civil War battlefields in the nation" and may well be the best kept secret in Georgia. It was at Pickett's Mill that on May 27th, 1864 a full corps of General Sherman's Union army under the command of Major General Oliver O. Howard suffered a major defeat on its march toward Atlanta.

Pickett's Mill State Historic Site is located five miles northeast of Dallas just off Georgia Highway 381. From Interstate 75 take Exit 123 (the Red Top Mountain Exit), turn right and go about 500 yards to the junction of Highway 41 and turn left. From there go about eight miles to a red light at the junction of Highway 92 and turn right. Drive four more miles to a four-way stop at the junction of Highway 92 and Highway 381. Go straight through the stop light onto 381 and then go two more miles until you see a Park Service sign on the right and Mt. Tabor Road on the left. Turn left onto Mt. Tabor Road and drive about four-fifths of a mile to the park entrance on your left.

The Road to Pickett's Mill

The road to Pickett's Mill was a long and arduous one. General Sherman and his Army of the Tennessee, after the Union victory at Chattanooga, set out on May 6th, 1864 toward Atlanta with an army of more than 100,000 men, including seven army corps and four divisions of cavalry. Sherman's primary objective was, at that time, not Atlanta but General Joseph E. Johnston's Confederate Army of Tennessee.

Johnston's Army numbered about 75,000 men including three army corps and one cavalry corps, almost all of them veterans of a dozen or so battles and campaigns.

Sherman and his generals. Standing, left to right: Oliver O. Howard, William B. Hazen, Jefferson C. Davis, Joseph A. Mower. Seated, left to right: John A. Logan, Sherman, Henry W. Slocum.

From the very beginning of Sherman's campaign, Johnston set out to frustrate him at every turn. Time and again he was able to anticipate Sherman's next move and, even as Sherman began to move his vast army southward, he found Johnston waiting for him behind the mountains at Tunnel Hill and Rocky Face Ridge in northwest Georgia. The skirmishes there were followed by another at Buzzard's Roost and then by a short but bloody battle at Dug Gap, where Union casualties numbered about 350, against Confederate losses of about 150.

By May 13th, Sherman's army was on the outskirts of Resaca and engaged in heavy skirmishing with Johnston's Confederate defenders. On the 14th, the action broke out into a full-scale battle, with almost all of the vast Union army involved. At first, Sherman's fortunes seemed to be going well. By nightfall on the 14th, however, a determined counter-attack by the Confederate divisions under Lieutenant General John Bell Hood had driven the Federal army back. The following day, the 15th, Sherman pushed his army forward again, and again the Confederate forces were able to hold their own. Johnston, however, realizing a Union threat to his line of supply, moved quietly out of Resaca during the night to take up strong new positions at Cassville. Federal casualties at Resaca were about 6,800, Confederate casualties 5,200.

Allatoona Pass.

The Confederate commanders were, however, unhappy with their positions at Cassville and Johnston again moved his army southeast to a veritable fortress at Allatoona Pass, a position so strong that Sherman had no intention of engaging the enemy in a futile assault that could only cost him heavy casualties. Instead, he turned his army southwest to skirt the strong Confederate positions at Allatoona, take the little community of Dallas, then turn east again and rejoin the railroad at Marietta. But Johnston, ever alert to his adversary's style, anticipated the move and responded by moving westward to meet the threat. The result was the Battle of New Hope Church on May 25th.

Sherman's information led him to believe that he was beyond Johnston's left flank and that reports of a large concentration of enemy forces in front of him, close to the crossroads at New Hope Church, must be incorrect. Accordingly, he ordered an attack to secure the intersection. General Hooker moved his three divisions of the XX Army Corps forward in column of brigade "one brigade behind the other" and was soon heavily engaged with Confederate Major General A.P. Stewart's division of Hood's corps, which was supported by a full battalion of artillery: 16 guns in three batteries. The fighting raged through deep woodlands. Stewart's division devastated the Union front with a solid wall of musket fire; the Confederate artillery did even more damage with barrage after barrage of deadly canister. Union casualties at New Hope Church numbered more than 1,900, against Confederate losses of only 500.

The battlefield of New Hope Church, Georgia.

It was a defeat for Sherman that would have been much worse had it not been for a violent thunderstorm that effectively brought an end to the fighting.

During the night of the 25th, Johnston's army dug in and fortified their positions over a six-mile front that extended all the way to Pickett's Mill.

The following morning Sherman, unable to find a weakness in the enemy line before him, decided to extend his line to the left, attack Johnston's right flank, turn it, then roll up the entire Confederate army. And so it was that on May 27th, 1864 Union Major General Oliver O. Howard, with elements of the IV, XIV and XXIII Army Corps, more than 14,000 men, faced off against Confederate Major General Patrick Cleburne's division, a force of about 10,000.

After a march of more than five hours, Howard arrived at Pickett's Mill, only to find Cleburne ready and waiting for him.

The Battle of Pickett's Mill

Howard's force was comprised of Wood's division, IV Army Corps; General Richard Johnson's division, XIV Army Corps; and General Nathaniel McLean's brigade, XXIII Army Corps. At 10 o'clock on the morning of May 27th, Howard's forces began forming for the assault in deep woodland to the rear of the main body of the Union XXIII Corps in position across the Dallas-Acworth Road.

The Federal troop movements of the 26th, however, and the heightened activity of the 27th had not gone unnoticed by the Confederates. Johnston once again anticipated Sherman's strategy; he, too, determined to extend his lines. On the 26th he ordered General Thomas Hindman's division of Hood's corps to move to the right, and Major General Patrick Cleburne's division of Hardee's corps

General William T. Sherman.

stationed at Dallas, to move to the right of Hindman. This placed Cleburne at Pickett's Mill at about 3 o'clock on the afternoon of the 26th.

Patrick Ronayne Cleburne, an immigrant Irishman late of Her Majesty's Army, and a master tactician with the battle skills of a surgeon was, perhaps, one of the most underestimated generals in the Confederacy. Certainly he never received the credit he deserved.

On the afternoon of the 26th, Cleburne deployed General Lucius Polk's brigade immediately to the right of Hindman's division with the brigades of General Hiram Granbury and Mark P. Lowrey in echelon directly behind. He then deployed the 12-gun artillery battalion of Major T.R. Hotchkiss on Polk's right, with a single regiment of General Daniel C. Govan's brigade to the right of Hotchkiss. All through the night of the 26th and the morning of the 27th, the Confederate forces under Cleburne's command labored at the building of the defensive line in readiness for the battle that was sure to come. The Confederate line, screened by dense woodland, was soon a maze of earthworks and log breastworks. The work done, Cleburne's forces settled down to wait; they would not have to wait for very long.

Maj. General Oliver O. Howard.

At about 11 o'clock on the morning of the 27th, Howard's force moved out in an easterly direction with General William B. Hazen's brigade of Wood's division in the lead. Hazen's orders from Wood were very specific. Hazen was to march in line of battle southeast by compass for a distance of a mile and a half. He was then to wheel to the right and march southwest until the enemy was found. Four other brigades were to follow behind. Hazen was ordered to attack the instant the enemy was found, without waiting for further orders, and whether or not the enemy was in position behind fortifications.

Hazen wheeled his brigade at the prescribed position and marched for a further mile until, upon the crest of a heavily wooded hill, he encountered a large force of Confederate infantry well entrenched and ready for battle. At this point, General Howard ordered his left flank to a position a mile further to the east, bringing him to the vicinity of Cleburne's strongest positions at Pickett's Mill. The strength of Cleburne's positions were not, however, readily apparent. It seemed that Wood's approach might be less well defended. Even so, Howard moved General Johnson's division up to the left of Wood and made ready to begin a general assault on the Confederate line.

Howard's plan was for Wood's division to attack in column of brigade, three brigades one behind the other, very much the same as General Hooker had attacked at New Hope Church with such disastrous results only two days earlier. It was a formation perfected and employed during the Napoleonic wars to great effect. It was designed to bring a heavy concentration of manpower to bear against a small and specific section of the enemy's line of battle; to deliver a massive punch to the enemy's heart. Modern warfare and weapons, however, had rendered such a formation obsolete. A well defended battle line of infantry with the new rifle muskets, fully supported by artillery, as Cleburne's was, could devastate such an attack and inflict horrendous casualties in the process. Confederate General Braxton Bragg had employed the same strategy at Shiloh. The result had been chaos. When the first echelon of Bragg's advance had been stopped, the brigades following on behind had piled in one on top of the other causing terrible confusion.

Even so, things might have gone differently for Howard had he stuck to the plan and advanced Wood's division by column of brigade. At least he would have been able to throw a great number of troops into the battle, and perhaps even overwhelm Cleburne's entrenched forces. But, for some reason still unknown, Wood, with

Pickett's Mill Creek.

Howard's blessing, decided to send Hazen against Cleburne without the support of the following brigades: "*We will put in Hazen and see what success he has.*" Hazen, according to a member of his staff, was present when Wood suggested this new strategy to Howard, and was stricken speechless when Howard agreed. Apparently, though, good soldier that he was, he rode back to the head of his brigade and waited patiently for the order to advance.

Hazen assembled his brigade in two lines. The front line consisted of the 1st, 41st, 93rd, and 124th Ohio regiments. The second was composed of the 5th, 6th and 23rd Kentucky, and the 6th Indiana. General McLean was assigned to the Wheatfield to protect Hazen's right flank and to remain in full view of the enemy works. Colonel Scribner's brigade of Johnson's division was ordered into position along Little Pumpkinvine Creek (now Pickett's Mill Creek), to protect Hazen's left flank. Scribner, however, was under the mistaken impression that his was supposed to be the brigade that was to follow Hazen. So Hazen already was at a disadvantage twice over: no following brigades and support of doubtful quality on his left flank.

At 4 o'clock that afternoon, Wood gave the order to advance and Hazen with his brigade of only 1,500 men moved forward, without support, against the massed defenses and artillery of Patrick Cleburne's Confederate division. Hazen, was totally unaware of, and unprepared for, the carnage that was about to fall upon him.

At 4:30, Howard sent the following message to General George H. Thomas, the commander of the Federal Army of the Cumberland: *"I am on the ridge beyond the hill that we were looking at this morning. No person can appreciate the difficulty in moving over this ground unless he can see it. I am now turning the enemy's right flank... I think."*

On the Confederate side, General Cleburne had not been idle. At about 11 o'clock that morning, just as the Federal march was beginning, Confederate General Govan informed Cleburne that a massive movement of Federal troops to the right was under way toward the east and Cleburne's right flank. Cleburne immediately ordered Govan into position to the right of Polk's brigade and placed two 12-pounder howitzers from Hotchkiss' artillery battalion on Govan's right. These two guns commanded the deep ravine to Govan's front and the area across which Cleburne expected the main Federal attack to come.

At around 4 o'clock Cleburne ordered Hiram Granbury's Texas brigade into the Confederate line of battle to Govan's right; a position along a spur ridge that ran northeast from Granbury's right. Between this ridge and another running north from the Confederate line at Granbury's left was a deep ravine, its walls steep and rocky, covered with trees and dense undergrowth. To Granbury's right, some 1,000 dismounted Confederate cavalrymen of Brigadier General John H. Kelly's cavalry division held the ground to the banks of what is now called Pickett's Mill Creek. Granbury's position, then, on top of the ridge, with the ravine between him and the Federal force, was almost impregnable.

By 4:35 p.m. Hazen's brigade had moved forward to a point where they were within range of Cleburne's guns. Federal Lieutenant Ambrose Bierce of General Hazen's staff describes the action as follows: *"We moved forward. In less than one minute the trim battalions had become simply a swarm of men struggling through the undergrowth of the forest, pushing and crowding. The front was irregularly serrated, the strongest and the bravest in advance, the others following in fan-like formations, variable and inconstant....*

"Suddenly there was a ringing rattle of musketry, the familiar hissing of bullets, and before us the interspaces of the forest were all blue with smoke.... The uproar was deafening; the air was sibilant with streams and sheets of missiles. In the steady, unvarying roar of small-arms the frequent shock of the cannon was rather felt than heard, but the gusts of grape which they blew into that populous wood were audible enough,

The bottom of the ravine.

*screaming among the trees and cracking against their stems and branches.
We had, of course, no artillery to reply."*

Somehow, during the heat of battle, Hazen's second line, consisting of the 5th, 6th and 23rd Kentucky, and the 6th Indiana, became separated from the first, changed direction to the left, went forward again into the cornfield toward the Confederate right, and rejoined the first rank of Hazen's brigade on its left flank. By accident Hazen's left flank was now in a position to threaten Granbury's now exposed right flank.

Granbury, however, was no slouch. Recognizing his fragile position to the right, he immediately sent a message to General Govan requesting reinforcements. Govan was at this point still uncommitted because General McLean and his men, contrary to General Howard's order to keep Govan busy while Hazen carried out his attack, were still hidden in the dense woodland beyond the Wheatfield. Govan responded to Granbury's request by rushing Colonel G.F. Baucum's Arkansas regiment to the extreme Confederate right where they took the brunt of the Federal charge, slowing it down, but not stopping it. Baucum, too, was now in grave danger of being flanked.

Cleburne, well aware of what was happening on his right flank, moved his last brigade under the command of Colonel Mark P. Lowrey quickly to the right. Lowrey arrived in the nick of time, just as Hazen's left flank was beginning to overwhelm Baucum's right flank. It was the closest Howard's assault at Pickett's Mill would come to victory. The tables were quickly turned and Hazen's men were soon engaged in a wild and disorderly retreat back across the cornfield from whence they'd came.

In the meantime, the Confederates, under fire from the Union left in the cornfield, had pulled back, creating the impression that the line had been broken. Far from it, when General William Quarles' brigade arrived to mend the supposed break in the line he found it to be intact and the men in fine spirits. Quarles was then repositioned to Lowrey's rear in reserve.

Colonel Scribner's Federal brigade, following on behind Hazen, too, had fallen upon hard times. That movement had commenced some minutes after Hazen's force had split. Scribner's brigade advanced with its left flank hugging the west bank of the Little Pumpkinvine Creek. They moved through the wheatfield toward the Mill, and then on into the steep ravine. Waiting for them in a forward position atop two hills on either side of the creek was Confederate Brigadier General Kelly and his cavalry division, dismounted, and raring for a fight. As Scribner's men moved toward the mill, Kelly's men began to pour a deadly curtain of fire down upon them. Scribner, unaware of Hazen's plight and desperate need of support, stopped his advance and engaged Kelly and his dismounted cavalry. Kelly, now under fire from almost an entire Federal brigade, was quickly driven from the hill-top, but not before valuable time had been lost; Hazen's brigade, totally without support and assailed on three sides, was fighting a desperate action in the ravine in front of Baucum and Lowrey. Time and again Hazen sent couriers back with pleas for help; almost all were shot down before they cleared the cornfield. Those that did make it through were unable to locate any significant source of support. Hazen now had no option but to order his brigade to withdraw. Those that could, began to make their way back through the cornfield. Unfortunately, many of his units were unable to retreat due to the intensity of the Confederate fire. Lieutenant Bierce described the retreat as follows: "...*as the wreck of our brigade drifted back through the forest we met the brigade which, had the attack been made in column, as it should have been, would have been on our heels, with another behind its own. As it was, just forty-five minutes had elapsed, during which the enemy had destroyed us and was now ready to perform the same kindly office to our successors.*"

As the remnants of Hazen's brigade staggered back through the wheatfield, General Wood ordered Colonel William Gibson to move his brigade forward (the same one Bierce described) to renew the attack. This proves that the original plan to attack in column of brigade had been abandoned. Why, has never been determined, but it's likely that the heavily wooded and difficult terrain, and the lack of a clear line of sight, made such a massive troop movement difficult in itself, and almost impossible to control. Perhaps the Federal commanders believed the terrain to be just as difficult for the enemy as it was for them. In any event, the lack of Gibson's support made Hazen's forward position untenable.

During the lull between Hazen's retreat and Gibson's attack, Cleburne's defenders strengthened their breastworks, resupplied themselves with ammunition, and moved reinforcements forward into the line of battle; Gibson was about to enter a hornet's nest.

Gibson began his advance at about 6:00 p.m. and at once became entangled in the heavy undergrowth in the forest. And, just as did Hazen's brigade, the second line of his advance lost contact with the first and drifted away to the left. Soon, the advancing Federal line was under the guns of the Confederate line of battle on the ridge. Volley upon volley of musket fire rained in upon them, barrage after barrage of deadly canister from Hotchkiss's cannon filled the air with the howl of flying lead and iron. Trees were stripped of their limbs, the undergrowth was stripped away in front of them, men were killed and injured, not only by the hail of minie balls and grape, but by falling limbs stripped from the trees above them.

Soon the advance units of Gibson's brigade began to encounter the remnants of Hazen's decimated force still pinned down below the crest of the hill. They drove on past them and immediately came under heavy fire from front and right, and still they charged onward. Their objective was in sight, they drove on, some reached the first line of log breastworks only to find the wily Confederate defenders had withdrawn to the second line and were continuing to pour a devastating hail of fire into their dwindling ranks.

Seeing their position was hopeless, Gibson's men began to seek cover on the hillside, expecting reinforcements to arrive at any minute. Like Hazen's men, they would be disappointed. The Confederates, now very much in command of the situation, moved back to their forward line. For them the early evening had become a turkey shoot. Soon, Gibson was under heavy fire from both sides as well as from the front. Realizing his position had become untenable, he ordered his men to withdraw. And, just as had happened to Hazen's brigade, many of his units became pinned down, were unable to move, and had to be left behind on the hillside. By now Federal casualties were mounting. Hazen had lost 487 of his original 1,500 men; Gibson had fared even worse with losses totaling 687.

By 7 o'clock, with darkness falling, Wood ordered his third brigade forward, not to engage the enemy, but to maintain the Federal line and provide protection while the wounded were brought out. Two hours after the battle had begun Colonel Frederick Knefler and his brigade moved forward toward the ravine and they, too, came under heavy fire from Hotchkiss' guns. The Federal wounded would lay where they fell for most of the night.

As night began to fall, the firing on both sides began to subside. The situation at this point was as follows: Knefler's brigade was pinned down, along with remnants of Hazen's and Gibson's brigades, less than 100 yards in front of the Confederate breastworks and Scribner's men, having pushed General Kelly's cavalry off the hill, had advanced to the point where the could join with Knefler's left flank in the cornfield in front of Lowrey, now well dug in behind breastworks to the south of the cornfield. It was a situation Confederate General Granbury was entirely unhappy with.

Granbury went to General Cleburne and explained his position. After a short conference the two men decided upon a night attack. General Edward Walthall's brigade of Hindman's division was ordered into line to replace Granbury whose men were ordered to make ready for an attack. At 10 o'clock that evening, the order to charge was given and the screaming hoard of Confederate infantry plunged down the hill, bayonets fixed, in total darkness, upon Knefler's brigade. They met with little resistance. The Federal line, taken by surprise, disintegrated. Many of the Federals panicked and ran off into the darkness, many more simply stood with their hands in the air and surrendered. To Knefler's left, Colonel Scribner, realizing what was happening and that his right flank was about to become extremely vulnerable, quickly ordered his reserves into position to the left of what had only a few minutes earlier been Knefler's flank, but the Confederate attack was over, an outstanding success. Scribner, his men almost out of ammunition, withdrew his brigade from the field at around midnight; the Battle of Pickett's mill was over. More than 1,600 Federals were killed or wounded. The Confederates lost only 500 men.

The Battle of Pickett's Mill was a shattering defeat for General Sherman. So embarrassed was he by it, he completely ignored it in his memoirs. Even his official photographer, George N. Barnard, seems to have ignored it, jumping from the Battle of New Hope Church on May 25th three days to May 28th when Federal forces enjoyed a somewhat different outcome in an engagement at Dallas. Ignore it though he may have done, Pickett's Mill was an important part of Sherman's Atlanta campaign.

For the Confederates, glorious though it had been, the Battle of Pickett's Mill was little more than a delaying action. Johnston, faced with overwhelming odds, was forced to withdraw from the area on June 4th. General Cleburne went on to a greater glory when, during those five tragic hours that were the Battle of Franklin, he gave his life for the cause that he had loved so long and so well. As always, he was at the head of his division when he died, a terrible loss to the Confederacy.

Today the old mill from which the battlefield takes its name is gone; only a few foundation stones remain on the banks of the creek. The battlefield itself looks much the same as it did in 1864. The Confederate earthworks are still there and visitors may wander the old trails at will, walk through the ravine that became the final resting place for hundreds of Union soldiers, and ponder the momentous events that took place there. Pickett's Mill is a quiet place, very much undeveloped, beautiful as only the Georgia woodlands can be, and now dedicated to the men of both armies that so willingly gave their lives in defense of one cause or the other.

Touring the Battlefield

There are three trails marked out on the battlefield: Red, White, and Blue. The most comprehensive is the Red trail, starting at the Ravine Overlook just to the rear of the Visitor Center. The trail is marked by red blazes on the trunks of the trees, and by a series of numbered stations, each with a red blaze and an arrow pointing in the direction of the next marker. To begin your tour, leave the

Visitor Center by the rear exit, turn left, and follow the trail a few
yards to the Overlook.

The Ravine Overlook:

As you stand and look down into the ravine you are very close to
the positions held by Confederate General Hiram Granbury on the
other side of the road in front of you. Turn right here and proceed
along the trail to Stop 1.

Stop 1:

Across this cornfield, from beyond the small stream which bisects
it, the second line of Brigadier General William B. Hazen's brigade
moved, reaching this point to the right and rear of the Confederate
line. Here they were struck by Baucum's men, quickly followed by
Brigadier General Mark P. Lowrey's Brigade. Hazen's brigade was
driven back to the far edge of the cornfield, where they reformed
and repelled Lowrey's attack. This was the high point of the Federal attack. Had Hazen received the support of Gibson's and Knefler's brigades, as was the original plan, the outcome of the battle
would surely have been different. Continue on along the trail
following the red blazes to Stop 2.

Stop 2:

The trenches here were constructed by Lowrey's brigade after the
battle. As you continue on toward Stop 3, you will see the cleared
cornfield to your left. In 1864 it was larger and extended into the
trees to the stream on your right.

Stop 3:

As you walked the trail to reach this point, you moved forward
toward the ravine in front of you, following the line of attack by
elements of Lowrey's brigade on Hazen's brigade, which was
fighting along the ridge to your right. At this point Hazen's left had
been flanked and only a hasty retreat saved the 23rd Kentucky
regiment from capture. From here, follow the red blazes to Stop 4.

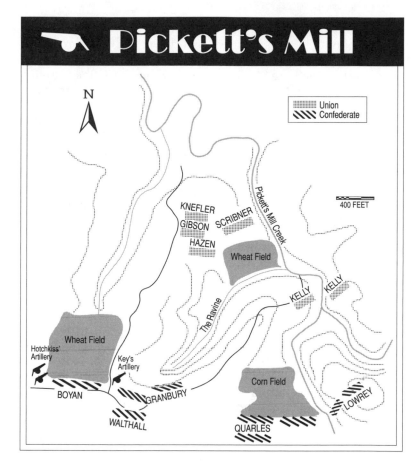

Stop 4:

You are now standing at what was, at the time of the battle, the northern end of the cornfield. It was here that Hazen's brigade, after having been pushed back by Lowrey's Confederate brigade, reformed and repulsed the pursuing Confederates. As night was falling, this section of the battlefield was also held by Knefler's brigade which had joined with elements of Scribner's brigade. You can now proceed along the trail following the red blazes to Stop 5.

Stop 5:

You should now be standing on the west bank of the Little Pumpkinvine Creek (now Pickett's Mill Creek). This position was the scene of intense fighting. As Scribner's brigade advanced along the creek toward you at about 5 p.m. they found Confederate Brigadier General John Kelly's dismounted cavalry waiting for them on the hill to your left and rear. During the action Kelly's men crossed the creek and occupied the hill in front of you, enabling them to fire down the entire length of Scribner's line of battle at the edge of the wheatfield.

The old mill from which the battlefield takes its name was located on the bank of the creek where you are now standing. Only a few stacked foundation stones remain; you can see them at the edge of the water in front of you (please don't walk on them). In 1864 the mill was owned by the Pickett family and was used for grinding corn and wheat into meal.

Now follow the red markers to Stop 6.

Stop 6:

You are now standing at the southern edge of the wheatfield, looking along the line which was held by Scribner's brigade. From here the Federals assaulted Confederate General Kelly's dismounted cavalry on the hill to your left and front. At the same time, three Federal regiments crossed the creek behind you and attacked the Confederates on the hill to your left and rear. General Kelly was forced to abandon his position and withdraw. His efforts had not been in vain, however, for he had bought valuable time, during which General Hazen's brigade, attacking through the woods and the cornfield, suffered heavy casualties. Colonel Scribner and his brigade didn't reach the cornfield until about 7 p.m. Continue along the trail to Stop 7.

Stop 7:

The trenches you see here were constructed by Federal reserve troops. It was from this position at the northern edge of the wheatfield, prior to the construction of the trenches, that Colonel Scribner began his advance. After the battle, Scribner withdrew to this area and was placed in line behind King's brigade of Johnson's division sometime after midnight. As you continue on up the hill toward Stop 8 you will be able to see the line of trenches to your right.

Stop 8:

You are now looking down a line of Federal trenches that was constructed after the battle. The line extends at a right angle to the line you followed as you came up the hill. Its purpose was twofold: first it was to provide protection against Confederate enfilading fire (fire along the line) from across the creek; second, it was to provide a supporting line for Federal troops driven out of the main line by a Confederate attack. You will see more Federal trenches to your left as you continue on along the trail toward Stop 9.

Stop 9:

It was here that Federal Brigadier General William Hazen formed his brigade for his initial attack at about 4:30 p.m. These woods did not exist in 1864. Hazen's brigade moved out into dense woods and undergrowth similar to those where you are now standing. The Federal attack, as originally planned, should have gone forward in column of brigade with the brigades of Colonels William Gibson and Frederick Knefler following Hazen into the attack at roughly five minute intervals. Unfortunately for Hazen, the plan was abandoned and the following brigades advanced piecemeal, one after the other, but some 45 minutes to an hour apart. The consequences for all three brigades were devastating. Without support, all three brigades suffered heavy casualties under heavy, concentrated fire from both Confederate infantry and massed artillery. Follow the trail of red blazes to Stop 10.

Stop 10:

The trenches to your right were constructed after the battle by elements of General William Hazen's brigade and formed a line that was at the time more than three-quarters of a mile long. Unfortunately, weather erosion, farming, and logging have reduced the line to what you see today. Continue on to Stop 11.

Stop 11:

It was here, if you remember the story of the battle, that Hazen's second line composed of the 5th, 6th and 23rd Kentucky, and the 6th Indiana, unable to see the line in front, became separated from the first, changed direction to the left and moved forward again into the cornfield toward the Confederate right. The forward line of Hazen's brigade consisting of the 41st, 93rd, and 124th Ohio regiments moved on in the same general direction as the trail. They were, you will recall, rejoined by the second rank on its left flank when it wandered into the cornfield, outflanking Confederate General Granbury's right flank. From here, follow the red markers along the trail to Station 12.

Stop 12:

At this point in your tour you have reached the end of Granbury's line, which was on the ridge in front of you. As you can see, the terrain over which the Federal troops had to make their attack is extremely difficult. The slope on the other side of the ravine is just as steep as this one. Imagine, then, moving forward up the slope under a hailstorm of musket fire and canister. The odds of reaching the top alive would not be very good. At a little after 4:35 that afternoon, units of Hazen's first line came over the hill behind you, down to the bottom of the ravine, then up the slope, where they engaged Granbury's men at close quarters. The scene was repeated again more than an hour later when Gibson's brigade renewed the attack, and again some 45 minutes after that when Knefler's brigade tried his hand against the almost impregnable breastworks on the ridge in front of you.

All along the ravine, from here to Pickett's Mill and the banks of the Little Pumpkinvine Creek, Federal troops were surging up the hill under a terrible firestorm of minie balls and canister. There was no protection for them on the slopes; only at the bottom of the ravine could they avoid the hail of fire from the Confederate guns. Proceed along the trail to Stop 13.

Stop 13:

This is the final stop on your tour of the battlefield. This position was held successively by all three Federal brigades as they made their assaults on Granbury's Confederate line. Hazen's brigade arrived first and was quickly repulsed. Gibson's brigade followed more than an hour later and was decimated, leaving some 681 casualties lying on the slopes and at the bottom of the ravine. Finally, as dark was falling, Knefler's brigade arrived here and was repulsed by the withering fire from Granbury's guns. To your right and front, Granbury had posted two cannon under the command of Captain Thomas Key. Those two guns poured load after load of deadly canister down upon the charging Federals, inflicting devastating losses. The whole area in front of you was literally carpeted with dead and wounded Federal soldiers. A survivor of the battle claimed he counted more than 200 bullets and canister balls in the trunk of a single tree. That should give you some idea of the intensity of the Confederate blanket of lead and iron that covered the field of fire across the slopes of the ravine before you.

From this position, at around 10 p.m., Granbury mounted his night attack. His brigade charged down the ravine, driving Knefler's men from their position in front of you and capturing more than 250 prisoners. It was the final action of a day that had been very good to the Confederate defenders on the ridge. They had inflicted more than 1,600 casualties on the enemy for a loss of only 500 of their own. It was a devastating defeat for Sherman; one, so it seems, he was very pleased to forget.

The Visitor Center houses a fine museum, with authentic clothing and uniforms of the day, weapons, maps, photographs, and artifacts found on the battlefield. From time to time, the park service offers a variety of living history demonstrations in which authentically uniformed personnel act out the everyday lives of the soldiers of the Civil War era. It's worth a phone call to find out what's going on, and when.

Annual special events include the Battle of Pickett's Mill Commemoration.

The site is open all year round Tuesday through Saturday from 9 a.m. until 5 p.m. and on Sundays from 2 p.m. until 5:30 p.m. It is closed on Mondays except for legal holidays and on Thanksgiving and Christmas Day.

For more information contact Pickett's Mill State Historic Site, 2640 Mt. Tabor Road, Dallas, GA, 30132. Telephone 404-443-7850.

What to See, Where to Stay

Kennesaw Mountain National Battlefield Park

The battle of Kennesaw Mountain saw the first shots fired in the battle for Atlanta; it also saw the worst defeat of General William T. Sherman's career.

Kennesaw Mountain National Battlefield Park is located three miles north of Marietta, GA and is well sign-posted and easily accessible either from U.S. 41 or I-75 at Exit 116 just 20 miles north of Atlanta. There are designated picnic areas in and around the park, and several hiking trails. The trails start at the visitor center and vary in length from two to 16 miles. The trails are steep, strenuous, and there is no water or shelter available along the way, so be prepared. Bring a camera and plenty to drink. The visitor center is open from 8:30 a.m. to 5 p.m. daily and admission is $1. PO Box 1610, Marietta, GA 30061. Telephone 404-427-4686.

The City of Marietta

What to See

White Water. A water theme park located on Marietta Parkway with 40 rides, including a body flume, rapids ride, and wave pool. Telephone 404-424-WAVE.

American Adventures. A children's amusement park with more than a dozen rides and various activities located on the Marietta Parkway. Telephone 404-424-6683.

Big Shanty Museum. The museum is located six miles north of Marietta off US 41 or Interstate 75 at Exit 118, at 2829 Cherokee Street in Kennesaw. The L&N locomotive, *The General*, of Andrew's Raiders fame, is permanently housed at the museum. The exhibit includes an audio visual presentation of the famous raid. Telephone 404-427-2117.

Annual Event. The Bell South Golf Classic, part of the PGA Tour, is held annually in early May at the Atlanta Country Club on Atlanta Country Club Drive in Marietta. Telephone 404-951-8777.

Historic Inns

The Marlow House, Marietta, built in 1866. Telephone 404-426-1887.

The Stanley House, built in 1895, Marietta. Telephone 404-426-1881.

Motels

Best Inns of America, 1255 Franklin Road, Marietta, GA 30067. Telephone 404-955-0004. Under 18 years old stay free, free crib, pool, free coffee in the lobby, meeting rooms. Accepts credit cards.

Hampton Inn, 455 Franklin Street, Marietta, GA 30067. Telephone 404-425-9977. Under 18 years old stay free, free crib, pool, wading pool, free continental breakfast, free coffee in the lobby, meeting rooms. Accepts credit cards.

La Quinta, 2170 Delk Road, I-75 N. Delk Road Exit 111. Telephone 404-951-0026. Under 18 years old stay free, free crib, pool, free coffee in the lobby, meeting rooms. Accepts credit cards.

Hotels

Holiday Inn Northwest, 2255 Delk Road, Marietta, GA 30067. Telephone 404-952-7581. Under 18 years old stay free, pool, bar, room service, dancing, health club privileges, meeting rooms. Accepts credit cards.

Sheraton Atlanta Northwest, 1775 Parkway Place, Marietta, GA 30067. Telephone 404-428-4400. Under 17 years old stay free, free crib, pool, cafe, bar, room service, valet service, meeting rooms. Accepts credit cards.

Restaurants

La Strada, 2930 Johnson Ferry Road NE. Telephone 404-640-7008. Italian menu, bar, semi-à la carte dinner, children's meals, specializes in stuffed shrimp and soft shell crab. Parking. Accepts credit cards.

The Planters, 780 Cobb Drive. Telephone 404-427-4646. Reservations accepted, bar, wine cellar, à la carte entrées, children's meals, specializes in seafood, filet mignon, and rack of lamb. Own baking. Pianist. A Greek-revival plantation house completed in 1848 with 13 landscaped acres. Accepts credit cards.

Shilling's on the Square, 19 North Park Square. Telephone 404-428-9520. Reservations accepted, bar, semi-à la carte menu, specializes in Black Angus beef and fresh seafood. Pianist. Parking. Tavern decor: a century-old wood bar, stained glass. Accepts credit cards.

Chapter 10

Kennesaw Mountain

June 27, 1864

Kennesaw Mountain National Battlefield Park is located three miles north of Marietta, GA and is well sign-posted and easily accessible either from U.S. 41 or I-75 at Exit 116, just 20 miles north of Atlanta. There are designated picnic areas in and around the park, and several hiking trails. The trails start at the visitor center and vary in length from two to 16 miles. The trails are steep, strenuous, and there is no water or shelter available along the way, so be prepared. Bring a camera and plenty to drink. The visitor center is open from 8:30 a.m. to 5 p.m. daily and admission is $1.

On May 4th, 1864, General William Tecumseh Sherman set out into the wilds of northwest Georgia with the intention of finding the Confederate Army of Tennessee under the command of General Joseph Eggleston Johnston, bring him to battle, and destroy him. For almost two months the two armies maneuvered for position. At the beginning of the campaign Johnston's army numbered close to 70,000 men and Sherman's almost 100,000. Time and again Sherman and Johnston faced off, and time and again the wily General Johnston outmaneuvered his Federal opponent, all the time being driven steadily southeast toward Atlanta, the supply center of the Confederacy. Their first confrontation came on May 8th and 9th at Rocky Face Ridge, with fierce engagements at Buzzard's Roost and Dug Gap. They clashed again at the Battle of Resaca on May 14th, and again at Cassville on May 19th. At New Hope Church on May 25th Sherman suffered major defeat and some 1,900 casualties. Two days later at Pickett's Mill on May 27th he suffered a second major defeat, this time with casualties over 1,600. At Dallas on May 28th, he turned the tables on Johnston when he inflicted heavy losses on the dwindling Confederate Army of Tennessee.

Finally, by June 19, 1864, Sherman's army, now numbering well in excess of 100,000, had forced General Joseph Johnston to withdraw almost to the outskirts of Atlanta. Johnston's army, now under 66,000 men, was occupying a well prepared and heavily defended

General Joseph E. Johnston.

position on Kennesaw mountain less than five miles from Marietta. It was here, he decided, that he would make his stand.

Sherman, hampered by bad weather, felt that the Confederate positions might not be as strong as they appeared, and that one mighty thrust could destroy the entire Southern army. He was wrong. On June 27 he launched a bloody, two pronged assault on the mountain that ended with Union losses of more than 3,000 officers and men; Johnston lost only 1,000.

Once again Sherman's plan was to extend his line toward the south, thus putting himself into position to gain the enemy's flank and, once again, the wily Confederate commander anticipated him. Johnston's answer to Sherman's strategy was to shift 11,000 men under the command of General

The Kolb Cabin.

John Bell Hood to Kolb's Farm, where on June 19th Hood struck the Federal line hard. But he was unable to drive them back. He was, however, able to check Sherman's drive southward.

For several days Sherman waited for the weather to change, but the rain continued unabated. For days he plotted and planned what to do next. It seemed he had but two options: he could try to continue his drive southward in the hope of flanking the enemy, or he could attack. The drive south did not appeal. Sherman's scouts were reporting strong Confederate positions at Olley's Creek, and Johnston's cavalry, operating in small groups, was playing havoc with his lines of communication to the rear. So, thinking that Johnston's positions on Kennesaw might not be as strong as they appeared, he decided to do the unexpected and attack. Meanwhile, General Johnston and his army lay in wait in a great semicircle from the Canton Road to the north, along the heights of Kennesaw Mountain, and southward past Kolb's Farm to Austell Road.

On June 24th, Sherman issued orders for his plan of battle. His corps and division commanders would take two days to reconnoiter the area and make preparations to assume the offensive at precisely 8 a.m. on the morning of June 27th. Secrecy was to be maintained at all costs; only subordinate officers with a need to know were to be informed of the plan.

Kennesaw Mountain, 1866.

Maj. General George Thomas.

The main thrust of Sherman's attack was to be made by General George H. Thomas (The Rock of Chickamauga) and his Army of the Cumberland. He was to assault the enemy center, drive on through, and seize the Western and Atlantic Railroad to the south of Marietta. At the same time, General McPherson, commanding the Army of the Tennessee, would attack the Confederate line to the south of Kennesaw. Sherman was hoping that Thomas's attack at the Confederate center would cause Johnston to move troops north to strengthen that position, thus leaving the southern position vulnerable.

To further aid these two main thrusts, Sherman decided to initiate diversionary demonstrations toward Johnston's flanks, north and south.

Sherman established his headquarters on the brow of Signal Hill just to the south of the center of his own line, where he could maintain his view of Thomas's drive toward the enemy's center. He was linked to his subordinates by telegraph wire and could thus maintain control of the battle firsthand.

For two days the area seethed as Sherman's commanders made ready for the onslaught. Skirmishers of both armies clashed again and again. Artillery fire from both sides created spectacular displays of pyrotechnics. And still the Confederate defenders on the mountain waited, secure in the knowledge that their positions were all but impregnable.

Maj. General James McPherson.

On June 26th, the day before Sherman planned for the battle to commence, General Schofield began his demonstrations designed to draw the Confederate troops toward him. Brigadier General Jacob Cox, with a brigade of infantry, became involved in a sharp engagement on the Sandtown Road at a point where it crosses Olley's Creek. Confederate dismounted cavalry, supported by artillery, successfully held the line there. A mile further upstream, however, Cox's second brigade managed to make a crossing and dig in; Sherman's army now had a toehold on the south bank of Olley's Creek. And again, near Kolb's Farm, Federal artillery put on a brave show by firing on the Confederate trenches across the creek valley. It was all to no avail. Once again the artful General Johnston saw through what was happening and, knowing the strength of his own lines, did not move reinforcements south to strengthen his left flank.

The morning of the 27th dawned bright and clear and promised a day of sweltering heat. Troops on both sides would suffer in their heavy woolen uniforms. By the time dawn had broken, General Schofield had already moved a brigade across the creek to reinforce the tenuous Federal hold on the south bank gained by General Cox the day before, and to make demonstrations against the entrenched defenders there in order to draw attention away from the more northern positions where the main action was to take place. Schofield made contact with the enemy at around 6 o'clock in the morning and skirmishing began immediately.

All went well for the Federals at the southern end of the field. By the time the main engagement had begun against the ridges to the north, Cox had established a second crossing at the Sandtown Road Bridge and had pushed the Confederate cavalry out of the creek valley and over the ridge to a point beyond the Austell Road. The day had begun well for General Sherman.

By 8 o'clock, the time Sherman planned for the battle to start, it was already hot and humid. The damp trees, grass, swamps, and undergrowth steamed under the early morning sun. It was going to be a long day; but, after the early success to the south, Sherman's spirits were high.

At the stroke of 8, the Federal artillery opened fire on the Confederate positions all along the ridge and General McPherson began his feint attack against the Confederate right flank. For 15 minutes more than 200 Federal guns blasted the heavily defended positions along the entire mountain range, while Federal Brigadier General Mortimer Leggett moved his division of the XVII Army Corps against the entrenched positions of Featherston's brigade at the extreme Confederate right flank. But he was quickly driven back by heavy musket fire and a withering barrage of canister from four batteries of Confederate artillery.

A little further to the south, Federal brigades of the XVI Army Corps under Sweeny and Gresham continued the feint against Big Kennesaw mountain with more success. Men of the 66th and 64th Illinois Regiments smashed through the trenches on the foothills of the mountain held by the 1st Alabama and the 25th Arkansas and began the difficult climb toward the crest of the mountain; some reached positions only 30 yards or so from the main Confederate line of defense, but nowhere were they able to seriously challenge the Confederate stronghold. It made little difference, though; the feint, if nothing else, had gained the Confederate's attention.

The attack began at 8:15 in two prongs. The main thrust to be made by two divisions of General George H. Thomas' Army of the Cumberland was to move against Cheatham Hill. At the same time, a secondary attack was to be made by the 2nd Division of the XV Army Corps under the command of Brigadier General Morgan Smith further to the north against the strongly held Confederate positions of Generals Samuel French and William Walker on Pigeon Hill, a spur of the ridge attached to Little Kennesaw Mountain. If Smith could carry the Confederate defenses on Pigeon Hill he would cut General Johnston's line in two. It would then be a relatively simple job to pour in troops, move north and south, and roll up the Confederate line in both directions.

General Smith's plan for his assault on Pigeon Hill called for a frontal attack straight up the Burnt Hickory Road and the hill beyond. This was to be carried out by a force of more than 5,500 men in three brigades. The first brigade under the command of Smith's younger brother, Brigadier General Giles Smith, would move straight ahead up the Burnt Hickory Road. The second brigade under the command of Brigadier General Andrew Lightburn would advance on Smith's right, while the third brigade under the command of Colonel Charles Walcutt would advance on his left.

As the 15-minute Federal bombardment died away, Smith's three brigades began to move forward. Almost immediately, they came

Little Kennesaw.

under heavy fire from Confederate musketry, and from six batteries of artillery on Little Kennesaw Mountain and Pigeon Hill. Before long, the Federal advance had reached the banks of a tiny tributary of Noyes Creek. The terrain, after the weeks of heavy rain, had become a swamp, soggy and jungle-like, in the midst of which the Federal advance began to flounder. And to make matters worse, the whole area in front of them was alive with Confederate skirmishers and sharpshooters who were able to pick off the floundering Federals at will. But the Confederates, at this point were not having things all their own way. The rookie 63rd Georgia Regiment, stationed in a forward position in front of Lightburn's advancing brigade, had never before been in a battle. Realizing what was about to happen, their commander called for reinforcements. The companies, not knowing what it was they were supposed to be doing, began running this way and that and, before anyone realized what was happening, six regiments of Lightburn's Federal brigade burst from the swamp and smashed into the confused and befuddled Georgians. There ensued a brief, one-sided, ferocious hand-to-hand battle that ended with the Georgians bolting in panic toward the rear with Lightburn's men in wild pursuit.

But help was only a few hundred yards away on the crest of the mountain. A Confederate Missouri regiment, dug in in a forward position on the slopes of Pigeon Hill, opened a hail of musket fire upon Lightburn's pursuing infantry. Then, a heavy bombardment of shell and case shot from the Confederate batteries on the heights of Little Kennesaw began to inflict heavy casualties in the now clearly exposed Federal ranks. It soon became clear to Lightburn that the Confederate line could not be carried and so, to avoid the destruction of his brigade, he ordered his men to fall back to the cover of the captured Georgian rifle pits. The Confederate defenders were now free to concentrate their fire on the still advancing brigades of General Giles Smith and Colonel Charles Walcutt.

General Smith's brigade was rapidly advancing up an old winding trail onto the slopes of Pigeon Hill, while Walcutt had made it into a gorge to Smith's left between Pigeon Hill and Little Kennesaw and was soon in desperate trouble.

The gorge was a terrible place from which to attack the heights of the mountain. The terrain was littered with fallen trees, dead logs, loose shale and boulders – a treacherous footing that caused the Federals almost as many problems as did the Confederate defenders on the crest of the mountain. In places the slope was so steep that the attacking Federals were forced to advance on hands and knees. Further on, the slopes turned into cliffs, sheer and impassable, from the top of which the defenders were able to hurl massive rocks down upon the hapless Federal infantry.

To Walcutt's right, General Smith was doing little better; he had by now come under heavy musket fire from Confederate Brigadier General Frances Cockrell's brigade, and heavy artillery fire from a battery of four Napoleon guns directly in front of his advance. Undaunted, Smith's brigade, consisting of the 6th Missouri, the 55th Illinois, the 57th Ohio, the 111th and 116th Illinois, pressed on forward. Some Illinois regiments managed to get within 25 yards of Cockrell's trenches before they were hurled back in disorder. The 57th Ohio, too, got almost to the line of trenches, but they encountered such a withering hail of fire they were forced to withdraw, leaving many of their comrades trapped among the boulders and rocky outcrops on the slope of the mountain.

By 10:30 that morning, some two hours after the fighting had started, General Morgan Smith's division had all but withdrawn, having done little damage to the Confederate line of battle on the mountain. Smith's ill-fated attack on Pigeon Hill had cost him more than 850 casualties; the Confederates had suffered fewer than 200.

The combined Federal attack on Pigeon Hill must have been a sight to see. Confederate Major General Samuel French describes it as follows: *"We sat there, perhaps an hour, enjoying a bird's-eye view of one of the most magnificent sights ever allotted to man – to look down upon an hundred and fifty thousand men arrayed in the strife of battle on the plain below.*

"As the infantry closed in, the blue smoke of the musket marked our line for miles, while over it rose in cumuli-like clouds the white smoke of

The 125th Ohio Infantry. They charged up Kennesaw.

artillery. Through the rifts of smoke, or, as it wafted aside the struggle was hard, and there it lasted the longest. So many guns were trained on those by our side, and so incessant was the roar of cannon and sharp the explosion of shells, that naught else could be heard."

Of the action as it played out before him General French had this to say: "...a courier came to me about 9 o'clock and said General Cockrell wanted assistance, and his line had been attacked in force. General Ector was at once directed to send two regiments to support him. Soon again a second courier came and reported the assault on the left of my line. I went immediately with the remainder of Ector's brigade to Cockrell, but on joining him found the Federal forces had been repulsed. The assaulting column had struck Cockrell's works near the center, recoiled under the fire, swung around into a steep valley where – exposed to the fire of the Missourians in front and right flank and of Sear's men on the left – it seemed to melt away or sink into the earth to rise no more.

"From prisoners and from papers on their persons shown us, I learned my line had, from its position, been selected for assault by General McPherson, as that of Cheatham's had been by General Thomas."

Meanwhile, a mile and a half away to the south, the main Federal attack on Cheatham Hill was in terrible trouble.

Cheatham Hill

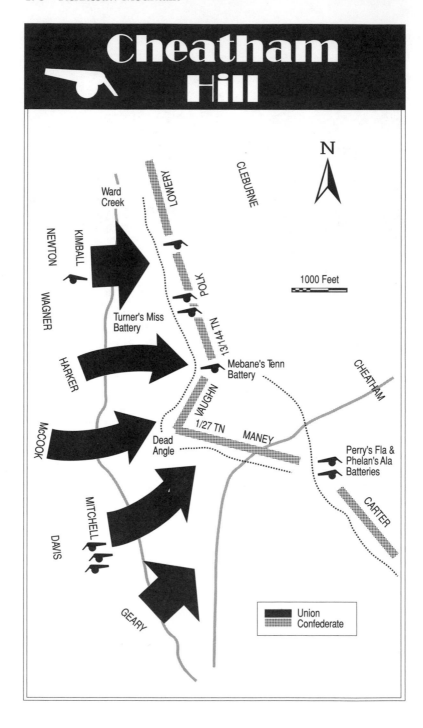

N

Ward Creek

LOWERY

CLEBURNE

NEWTON

KIMBALL

WAGNER

POLK

1000 Feet

Turner's Miss Battery

13/144 TN

HARKER

Mebane's Tenn Battery

CHEATHAM

VAUGHN

McCOOK

1/27 TN

MANEY

Dead Angle

Perry's Fla & Phelan's Ala Batteries

CARTER

MITCHELL

DAVIS

GEARY

Union
Confederate

The area Sherman has picked for his main thrust against the Confederate Line was not a good one. In Sherman's defense, however, it can be said that there really was no other choice; as strongly defended as the area was, all the others were even stronger. The mistake was in attacking Kennesaw at all.

The Confederate positions on Cheatham Hill were a maze of formidable earthworks, dirt embankments, and cleverly placed entanglements set out in front of the line of battle, giving little cover but making any advance extremely difficult. Defending these all-but-impregnable positions were the toughest and most battle-hardened Confederate troops in the entire Army of Tennessee, two full divisions under the command of General Patrick Cleburne – the general who had inflicted the devastating defeat upon Sherman at Pickett's Mill – and General Benjamin F. Cheatham.

To carry through his main thrust Sherman had chosen General Thomas's Army of The Cumberland. Thomas, in turn, had chosen two infantry divisions; the 2nd Division of the XIV Army Corps under the command of Brigadier General Jefferson C. Davis, and Brigadier General John Newton's 2nd Division of the IV Army Corps, about 8,000 men in all. The general idea was for the two divisions to make parallel advances, Davis on the right, Newton on the left, up the slopes toward the enemy position. As soon as the bombardment ceased, they would rush forward without stopping until they overran the enemy emplacements. At that point Thomas would send in the reserves.

At 8 o'clock that morning, Newton and Davis were in position but not yet ready to move out. The bombardment ended at 8:15 a.m. The Confederate defenders on the crest took heed of the warning and made preparations to receive the enemy attack, but the two Federal divisions were still not quite ready to make their move. At 9 o'clock, however, two Federal cannon boomed out the signal for the attack to begin, and Davis and Newton gave the order to advance.

As the Yankee divisions, line after line of massed infantry, burst from the trees into the valley in front of the lower slopes of Cheatham Hill, it became a Confederate turkey shoot. Thousands of muskets opened up all at once, but the Rebel cannon, more than 25 guns in five batteries, held their fire until, at a distance of less than 50 yards, they opened up a devastating barrage of double-loaded canister that decimated the advancing Federal ranks.

To the Federal left, Newton had begun his attack with two brigades of infantry under the command of Brigadier Generals Charles Garrison Harker and George Wagner, leaving his third brigade commanded by Brigadier General Nathan Kimball in reserve. General Harker moved forward on the right of the column with Wagner's brigade to his left. The two brigades managed to push forward almost to the line of Confederate trenches when, after a ferocious struggle, they broke and drifted back to the relative safety of the ravine through which they'd came. The two brigades regrouped, surged forward again, and once more reached a forward position only yards from General Cleburne's impregnable positions. General Harker himself managed to get within 20 yards of Cleburne's flaming trenches before being toppled from his horse mortally wounded, shot through the arm and chest.

As Harker's brigade retreated for the second time, the Confederate defenders in front of them turned their attention and a devastating flanking fire into the already badly distressed Wagner's brigade that had been advancing on Harker's left.

General Newton, seeing the state of the battle deteriorating in front of him, now committed his reserves under the command of Brigadier General Nathan Kimball. Unfortunately, Cleburne's division could see Kimball's brigade readying themselves for the attack. When it came, Kimball's men fared no better than had Harker's and Wagner's. Within a matter of minutes, they too had suffered the devastating fire of the massed Confederate infantry and artillery. Newton, realizing his position was hopeless, withdrew his forces and suspended all further action.

Meanwhile, further to the south, the battle still raged. As Newton's ill-fated brigades had moved out at around 9 o'clock, General Jefferson Davis too had committed two of his three brigades to rush the slopes of Cheatham Hill. His objective was the angle in the Confederate line commanded by Major General Benjamin F. Cheatham. His plan was for Colonel Daniel McCook's brigade to advance by regiment, one behind the other, each replacing the one in front should it become overwhelmed. McCook was a popular and well-loved leader known to his men as "Colonel Dan." Colonel John Mitchell's brigade was to advance on McCook's right and, simultaneously with McCook, attack the left flank of the angle.

The two brigades began their advance in fine order. Before long, however, they had entered the open space in front of the angle and

had come under heavy Confederate fire. The men of the 125th Illinois, McCook's leading regiment,
rushed forward and became involved in a deadly brawl with the
combined 1st and 27th Tennessee
Regiments. Meanwhile, to the
right, Mitchell's leading regiment,
the 113th Ohio, closely followed by
the 121st Ohio, had crested the hill
and had opened fire at close range
on the 19th Tennessee Regiment.
They, however, were undaunted
and waited their moment before
opening a devastating fusillade
into the advancing Ohio regiments. That single fusillade ended
the careers of six officers and scores
of other ranks. The leading Ohio
regiment panicked, turned, and

*Maj. General Benjamin F.
Cheatham.*

fell over those still advancing behind them until, not knowing
which way to turn next, and in desperation, they turned again and
rushed toward the well-entrenched Tennessee defenders. Those
who made it through the firestorm to the trenches wished they
hadn't; the Tennesseans took a deadly toll of the hapless enemy.
They shot them, bayoneted them, and took many of them prisoner.
The remainder of Mitchell's brigade fell back some 50 yards, took
cover, and from there maintained a steady fire upon the Confederate trenches in front.

On Mitchell's right, McCook's brigade was faring little better. The
initial hand-to-hand confrontation between the leading Federal
regiment and the 1st and 27th Tennessee had been short and
bloody. The dead and wounded of both sides lay piled one on top
of the other and, although the advancing Federals had the advantage of numbers, the climb up the steep slope had taken its toll. The
winded Union regiments were in poor condition for a fight when
they reached the top. The 125th Illinois was soon replaced by the
85th Illinois and then they, in turn, were replaced by the 22nd
Indiana, followed by the 52nd Ohio. McCook himself managed to
reach the parapet of the angle, where he stood slashing at the
enemy with his sword, shouting for his men to rally to him and
"Forward the flag." The story goes that, at this point, an Illinois
private grabbed at McCook's coattail and shouted to him *"Colonel*

Dan, for God's sake get down, they will shoot you." The gallant colonel shook him off and shouted angrily, "*God damn you, attend to your own business.*" Seconds later a Confederate minie ball hit him in the chest, throwing him backward from the parapet mortally wounded. As he was carried toward the rear he managed to gasp, "*Stick it to them, boys.*"

McCook's second in command took over the brigade for only moments before he too was hit by a minie ball through the heart, killing him instantly. Next in the chain of command were Colonels Caleb Dilworth and Allen Fahnstock. They quickly consulted and decided the Confederate line could not be broken, so they decided to pull back and dig in. The fight at the angle had lasted for less than an hour, during which time the Federal brigades had suffered more than 1,800 casualties; the Confederates under 700. From that moment on, Cheatham's heavily defended positions became known as the Dead Angle. For those who defended it, and for those who attacked it, the fighting had been the toughest of the entire war.

All along the six-mile line, from Kolb's Farm at the south to beyond the Western and Atlantic Railroad tracks at the north, the attack had failed. McPherson in the north was holding to a stalemate, Schofield to the south was faring no better, Morgan Smith's attack on Pigeon Hill had failed, and General Thomas's attack on Cheatham Hill also was in a position of stalemate. Sherman, unwilling to accept defeat, tried to persuade General Thomas to renew the attack. Thomas, ever blunt and to the point, told Sherman that, "*One or two more such assaults would use up this army.*"

All through the long afternoon the various units continued skirmishing to little or no effect until, by the time darkness had fallen, the battle had dwindled and ended. Sherman had lost more than 3,000 of his men, including two of his best brigade commanders. General Johnston had lost only a third that number. The battle of Kennesaw Mountain was Sherman's most devastating defeat of the Atlanta campaign.

For almost a week the two armies faced one another until, with little alternative, Sherman was forced to resume his flanking strategy. On July 2nd, under cover of darkness, the Confederate forces crept away from their Kennesaw positions. The battle for Atlanta proper was about to get under way.

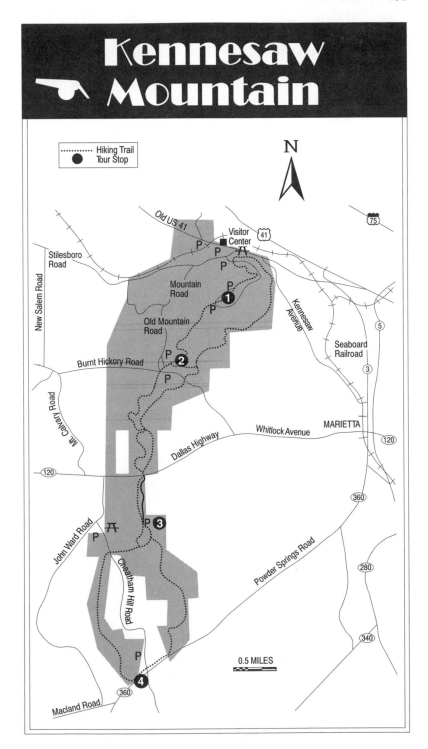

Touring the Battlefield

You should begin your tour of the Kennesaw Mountain Battlefield Park at the Visitor Center. The Center provides an audio visual account of the battle and the events leading up to it. The center also has a fine museum with authentic uniforms, maps and photographs, artifacts found on and around the battlefield, and a bookstore. The Visitor Center is also Stop 1 on your tour. When you leave the Center turn right and walk a few yards beyond the large tree in front of the building.

Stop 1: Northern End

As you look out across the field here, you are standing at the northern end of the battlefield in the general area of the Union diversionary attack against the Confederate positions on Kennesaw Mountain. If you turn around and face the Visitor Center, you'll see the mountain just behind and to the left of the building. Turn again, look out across the field toward the cannon, and try to imagine the scene as it must have been as the men of the 64th Illinois Regiment swept toward you and engaged the Confederate 25th Arkansas regiment in the woods at the foot of the mountain, drove them back, and then began to advance up the steep slopes of the mountain. From here you can either follow the trail and walk up the mountain or you can take your car and drive up the road for about a mile to Stop 2. If you decide to take the trail, your walk will lead past the rifle pits of the 1st Alabama Regiments and on to the main Confederate line of defense high on the mountain. The trenches there were built by soldiers from Tennessee and Alabama of Major General William Loring's Corps. If you decide to drive, you will pass the Georgia Memorial and eventually arrive at a parking lot on the crest of the mountain at Stop 2.

Stop 2: Observation Overlook

Leave your vehicle and go to the observation overlook just above. From here you will have a sweeping view over the North Georgia that Confederate General Joseph Johnston and his Army of Tennessee fought so hard to protect. Look to the south and you should be able to see the Atlanta skyline.

When you've taken time to enjoy the view, you should take the short walk along the trail that leads from the overlook to the peak of the mountain; you won't be disappointed. These positions were occupied by soldiers of General Walthall's brigade and the four Napoleon cannon represent those that exchanged fire with the Union batteries below. When you return to your vehicle, you will drive down the mountain the way you came up, past the visitor center. Follow the signs to Pigeon Hill, Stop 3.

Stop 3: Pigeon Hill

This was the scene of General Sherman's secondary thrust against Joe Johnston's army on the mountain. You will remember it was made by three Union brigades of Brigadier General Morgan Smith's 2nd Division of the XV Army Corps; a force of about 5,500 men. Leave your vehicle at the roadside parking area and walk the short trail to the Confederate positions held by the men of Confederate Brigadier General Frances Cockrell's Missouri brigade. As you walk up the steep trail, you will be following the line of attack used by the Federal soldiers of the 57th Ohio regiment of General Giles Smith's brigade. You will remember that the 57th Ohio managed to get within 40 yards or so of the Confederate positions, but encountered such a terrible firestorm of musket and canister they were forced to withdraw, leaving many of their men trapped among the boulders and rocky outcrops. As you will see, the Confederate fortifications are in an excellent state of preservation. If you continue on for a short distance beyond the open area to the boulders, you will reach the position where it is thought that General Cockrell had his command post. Return to your vehicle and then follow the park signs to Cheatham Hill, Stop 4.

Stop 4: The Dead Angle

Leave your vehicle in the parking lot and make your way along the short trail to the crest of Cheatham Hill, where you will find the magnificent Illinois Monument and an interpretive sign-board to the right. More than 8,000 Federals in two divisions under the command of Brigadier Generals Jefferson C. Davis and John Newton carried out the main thrust of General Sherman's attack on Kennesaw Mountain here against the Dead Angle on Cheatham Hill and two battle hardened Confederate divisions under the command of Major Generals Patrick Cleburne and Benjamin Cheatham. The position where you are now standing was that of General Cheatham and, in particular, that of the combined 1st and 27th Tennessee Regiment.

It is appropriate that you stand quietly for a moment at this spot. Look across the field that slopes away in front of the monument – it was much larger in 1864 – and reflect upon the momentous events that took place here. It's not difficult to see the now shadowy figures of the thousands of Union soldiers, one rank after another, charging up the hill across the field toward you, in one futile assault after another. Perhaps you can see the vast swarm of blue-clad soldiers of General Dan McCook's brigade, hear the incessant roar of musket fire from the Confederate defenders in the trenches behind you, and the constant booming of the Confederate batteries as they hurled load after deadly load of canister into the advancing Federal ranks. First came the 125th Illinois, closely followed by the 85th Illinois, then the 22nd Indiana, and finally the 52nd Ohio. The 125th Illinois was decimated by the combined musket and cannon fire, great holes blasted into their ranks; the three following Union regiments were dealt with in like manner. And perhaps you can see the brave Colonel Dan himself, swinging his sword and rallying his men, and then, the fatal shot to his chest and he was no more. The spot upon which you now stand saw some of the fiercest fighting of the war. Colonel McCook, as well as losing his own life, lost 397 his men here in only 30 minutes. Many were the deeds of bravery and heroism performed that day, the 27th of June 1864. The tunnel entrance at the foot of the monument is where Union soldiers, trapped and unable to retreat, dug in and huddled for six days under fire. Take all the time you need here, walk the trails and enjoy the quiet solitude of the countryside. Then return to your vehicle and follow the Park Service signs to Stop 5, Kolb's Farm.

Stop 5: Kolb's Farm

Kolb's Farm was the scene of an ill-fated attack on June 22nd by Confederate General John Bell Hood's Army Corps upon units of Sherman's army under the command of General's Schofield and Hooker. For several days, Sherman had been probing Joe Johnston's defenses on the way to Kennesaw Mountain. By the morning of the 22nd, Hood had deployed his corps on a ridge running north and south to the Powder Springs Road. General Thomas Hindman's division was on the right, Carter L. Stevenson in the center, with General A.P. Stewart on the left. To the west, Union Generals Hooker and Schofield were advancing toward Hood's position up the Powder Springs Road. Between the two armies, beside the road, stood a small four-room farm house – the one you see before you.

The Battle of Kennesaw Mountain

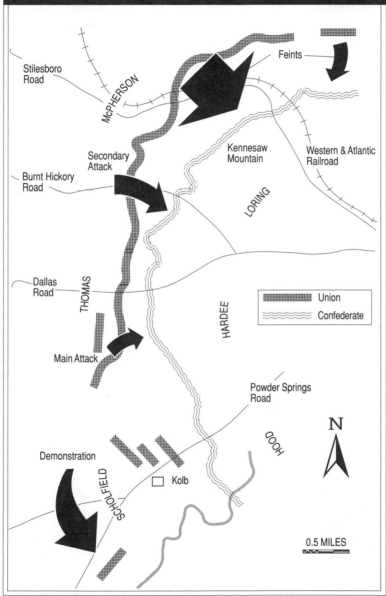

Stilesboro Road

McPHERSON

Feints

Secondary Attack

Kennesaw Mountain

Western & Atlantic Railroad

Burnt Hickory Road

LORING

Dallas Road

THOMAS

HARDEE

	Union
	Confederate

Main Attack

Powder Springs Road

Demonstration

SCHOLFIELD

Kolb

HOOD

N

0.5 MILES

The house was built in 1836 and, at the time of the battle, was owned by one Peter Valentine Kolb. By early afternoon on the 22nd, skirmishers of both armies had made contact and sporadic firing had broken out along the line of battle. Then, rather than waiting for Hooker to attack him, Hood decided to take the offensive. Hindman's and Stevenson's divisions swept forward, Stevenson leading with Stewart's division in reserve, smashing into the 123rd New York Regiment which was fanned out in open order formation some distance ahead of Hooker's main force. At that point, some 40 Federal cannon opened fire, causing great confusion in the Confederate ranks. For a moment or two the Confederate advance stumbled, then moved forward again, crossed the John Ward Creek, and ran into a devastating wall of cannon and musket fire that stopped them cold just 35 yards short of the Union line. The shattered Confederate divisions withdrew to the shelter of the creek, reformed, and charged again; the result was the same. The deadly crossfire of musketry and canister took a terrible toll on Hood's forces.

By late afternoon the Confederates had no option but to hold onto the ground close to the creek which afforded at least some protection from the enfilading Union cannon fire. The firing continued until well after dark, when Hood finally managed to withdraw his men. The action had been devastating for the Confederates. Carter Stevenson's division had been shattered. Of the 1,000 Confederate casualties, more than 870 were his. Hindman had lost about 200 men. Stewart, who hadn't really been engaged, suffered fewer than a dozen casualties. Union losses were estimated to be about 350.

No one knows why Hood decided to attack that afternoon. Certainly he had no such orders from General Johnston. It is thought that he might have been under the mistaken impression that his forces extended well beyond the Union right flank and that with a lightning attack, wheeling toward his own right, he could smash Hooker's right flank and roll it up. Had he pulled it off, he would have been something of a hero. Unfortunately for at least 1,000 of his men, he did not.

After the battle, Hooker set up his headquarters in the farmhouse you see before you. Today, Kolb's farm has been restored to its Civil War appearance. It's not open to the public, but it is worth a visit. The battlefield around it is now part of a modern subdivision.

What to See, Where to Stay

Nearby Attractions

Pickett's Mill State Historic Site and Battlefield Park is claimed to be "one of the best preserved Civil War battlefields in the nation" and may well be the best kept secret in Georgia. It was on this site that a full corps of General Sherman's Union army under the command of Major General Oliver O. Howard suffered a major defeat on its march toward Atlanta.

The Visitor Center at Pickett's Mill houses a fine museum, with authentic clothing and uniforms of the day, weapons, maps, photographs, and artifacts found on the battlefield. From time to time, the park service offers a variety of living history demonstrations in which authentically uniformed personnel act out the everyday lives of the soldiers of the Civil War era. Annual special events include the Battle of Pickett's Mill Commemoration.

For information contact Pickett's Mill State Historic Site, 2640 Mt. Tabor Road, Dallas, GA, 30132. Telephone 404-443-7850.

The site is located five miles northeast of Dallas just off Georgia Highway 381. From Interstate 75 take Exit 123 (the Red Top Mountain Exit), turn right and go about 500 yards to the junction of Highway 41 and turn left. From there go about eight miles to a red light at the junction of Highway 92 and turn right. Go four more miles to a four-way stop at the junction of Highway 92 and Highway 381. Drive straight through the stop light onto 381 and go two more miles until you see a Park Service sign on the right and Mt. Tabor Road on the left. Turn left onto Mt. Tabor road and drive about four fifths of a mile to the park entrance on your left.

For information on what to see, where to stay, and where to dine in the city of Marietta, see the previous chapter.

Chapter 11

Fort McAllister

December 13th, 1864

Fort McAllister is 10 miles east of I-95 on Georgia Spur 144; take Exit #15 off I-95 and follow the signs.

Located in a key position atop a bluff on the south bank of the Ogeechee River, the fort is probably the most complete and best preserved Confederate earthwork fortification in the country.

The Story of the Fort

The fort was the southernmost defensive position designed to protect the approaches to the Savannah River some 15 miles to the north, and defend Confederate blockade runners into Savannah and the approaches to the Ogeechee River. The fort was also expected to protect the vital Atlantic and Gulf Railroad trestle that lay only a short distance upstream from the fort, as well as the rice and cotton plantations that lay along the banks of the river.

The massive walls of the fort, still in much the same condition today as when they were built, were designed by Captain John McCrady of the Confederate States Engineers, and constructed by hand. Work was begun on the site in June, 1861. Once the site had been chosen, it was cleared of trees and the plan of the walls was laid out in the form of a wooden framework. Earth was piled against the wooden supports and allowed to settle. The framework was then removed and the entire structure was covered in sod to retain the loose earth.

Unlike its neighbors to the north, Forts Sumter and Pulaski, McAllister was not an imposing structure. The great brick forts to the north were thought to be impregnable at the beginning of the war. Time and the new large-caliber rifled guns, however, were to be the nemeses of the massive structures. Fort McAllister, however, would never fall to the great rifles that brought about the demise

Fort McAllister bomb-proofs.

of its northern neighbors. As the spinning projectiles hurtled across distances of more than a mile to shatter the great walls of Fort Pulaski, the earthen structure that was Fort McAllister was able to absorb the impact of the huge 11-inch guns ranged against it from the great ironclad, *U.S.S. Montauk,* on the 27th of January, 1863.

During the early days of the war, while on an inspection tour of the Confederate coastal defenses, Brigadier General Robert E. Lee came to Fort McAllister and suggested several improvements be made to the on-going construction of the works. These were mainly recommendations that would substantially increase the strength of the outer walls.

The fort, when completed, was equipped with 22 seacoast guns, including several massive eight-inch Columbiads and a 32-pounder rifled gun. There was also a 32-pounder hot-shot gun, a dozen or so smaller guns, and a 10-inch seacoast mortar.

In the early days, life at the fort was fairly easy and, if anything, quite boring. That changed when the famed Confederate blockade runner *Nashville* arrived in the mouth of the Ogeechee River seeking refuge from the U.S. Navy. The fast side-wheeler steamer had unsuccessfully tried to make it through the Union blockade into Charleston, South Carolina. After a long chase, during which she managed to elude her pursuers, the sleek ship had slipped unnoticed into the mouth of the river and the protection of the great guns of Fort McAllister. Things did not remain quiet for very long. After a thorough search of all the inlets south of the Savannah River, the Union navy found the *Nashville* nestled under the guns of the great Confederate fort at the mouth of the Ogeechee. To get to the ship, the Union navy first had to neutralize the fort. Four times during the fall and early winter of 1862 they attacked the fort to no avail; the great guns and solid earthen walls remained unscathed; the *Nashville* waited out the storm, up-river and out of sight.

48-pounder, eight-inch Columbiad, Fort McAllister.

On January 27th, 1862, however, the atmosphere at the fort changed with arrival of the great U.S. ironclad *Montauk* under the command of John L. Worden who had previously commanded the *U.S.S. Monitor* in her epic battle with the *C.S.S. Virginia* at Hampton Roads, Virginia on March 8th and 9th, 1862. The *Montauk* was a mighty ship, her sides were layered with sheets of four-inch armor plating, her great turret housed two guns: an 11-inch smoothbore Dahlgren and a 15-inch smoothbore Dahlgren. The 15-inch gun was the largest cannon ever mounted on a U.S. warship.

Early that morning the *Montauk* was anchored 150 yards below the barrier of river pilings, at which point she opened fire with her heavy guns on Fort McAllister. For almost five hours the great ship and the fort exchanged fire. During the battle, Fort McAllister was hit by the largest shells ever fired from a naval vessel against a shore-based enemy. The earthen construction of the fort, however, was more than a match for the great guns of the *Montauk*. She sustained little damage; nor was the ironclad damaged, attesting to the strength of her armored sides. Early in the afternoon, the *Montauk* withdrew from the river to refuel and to replenish her ammunition. She wasn't finished, however. On the 1st of February, she returned to finish the job. Again she sailed away without

success. The only casualty was
the fort's commander, Major
John B. Gallie. During the engagement the *Montauk* was hit
48 times by the eight-inch Columbiads and the 32-pounder
rifled gun, but suffered only
minor damage to her plating.
Meanwhile, the *Nashville*, unable to leave the protection of
the river, was converted into a
privateer and renamed the
Rattlesnake. On February 27th,
she headed toward the mouth
of the river under full steam,
trying to escape to the open sea.
Unfortunately, she didn't make
it and was forced to return up-

*Fort McAllister, December, 1864.
Union soldiers with Confederate
rifled gun.*

river under heavy fire from the Federal navy. As she rounded the
bend she ran aground and could not be re-floated. The following
morning, February 28th, the *Montauk* re-entered the mouth of the
river along with two Union gunboats and anchored some 1,200
yards from the *Rattlesnake*, then pounded her to bits with heavy
guns. The Union flotilla, the fort and the stranded *Rattlesnake*
engaged in a two-hour gun battle. The *Rattlesnake* wasn't built to
withstand such a mighty bombardment and eventually she exploded and burned to the waterline. Her remains lie in shallow
water just a couple of hundred yards from the Northwest Angle of
the fort. This time the *Montauk* did not leave the battle unscathed.
As she turned and made her way toward the mouth of the river
and the open sea she struck a Confederate mine, which exploded
just below the waterline, forcing the crew to beach her and make
repairs.

On March 3rd, 1863, Fort McAllister again came under fire from
the U.S. Navy. A fleet of three Union ironclads, the *Passaic*, the
Nahant, and the *Patapsco*, with several wooden gunboats in support, entered the mouth of the river and opened up a prolonged
engagement with the fort. This time the fort suffered some heavy
damage, but remained essentially intact after the Union fleet broke
off the engagement. That afternoon, the Union fleet sailed away; it
was the last time Fort McAllister would come under attack from
the sea.

After the Union fleet left, life at Fort McAllister resumed its quiet, easy-going atmosphere. All through the long summer of 1863, through the winter, Christmas and the New Year, and another long summer in 1864 the garrison of more than 200 men waited and watched. News from the fronts was not good. General Lee was being hard pressed in Virginia, and Atlanta had fallen to General Sherman. It was an uneasy period in the lives of the defenders. Everyone knew it was only a matter of time before Fort McAllister would have the full attention of the invading Federal forces; they were not wrong.

Soon word came that General Sherman was at Savannah, only 15 miles away to the north by sea. With McAllister guarding the southern approaches, Sherman's army, more than 60,000 strong, would be unable to receive supplies from the ships waiting off-shore. So, on December 10th, Sherman ordered General Oliver Howard, commander of the right wing of his army, to reduce the fort and open the way for his much needed food and supplies. Howard, in turn, ordered General William B. Hazen's veteran division of the XV Army Corps to march up the Ogeechee and take the fort.

Hazen arrived at the fort in the mid-morning of December 13th. For several hours he made preparations for his assault and finally, with dusk already falling, Hazen's men moved forward at about 4:15 p.m.

Meanwhile, the garrison had not been idle. Dozens of 13-inch shells had hastily been converted into land mines and placed at strategic positions on the landward approaches to the fort. The outer works were turned into a maze of formidable *abatis* and *chevaux-de-frise*, wooden structures bristling with wooden stakes sharpened to wicked points. Trees had been felled and left in confusion around the fort to slow the enemy down and provide slow-moving targets for the defenders. All the work, however, was for naught; 1,500 men of Hazen's crack division, watched by General Sherman on the top of Cheve's rice mill some two miles away, stormed over the outer defenses, up the earthen walls and into the fort. The fighting was, for a short time, desperate and hand-to-hand. The outcome, however, was inevitable; in only 15 minutes Major George Anderson's two hundred gallant defenders were overwhelmed. Confederate losses that day were 16 killed and 54 wounded; Union losses totaled 134, caused mostly by exploding mines in the outer defenses of the fort.

Chevaux-de-frise.

The fall of Fort McAllister marked the end of Sherman's "March to the Sea." With McAllister in Union hands, and supplies flowing into the Federal quartermasters' stores, it soon became obvious that further defense of the city of Savannah was useless and could only end in disaster. So, on December 20th, 1864, Confederate Lieutenant General William Hardee, a battle-hardened veteran of Shiloh, Stones River, Chickamauga, Chattanooga and a dozen other smaller, but no less important engagements, gathered together his 10,000 weary soldiers and left the city to General Sherman.

As for Fort McAllister? The tranquillity of southern Georgia returned to the banks of the Ogeechee. For many years only the raucous seabirds inhabited the once-bustling defenses. Then, in the late 1930s, Henry Ford, the owner of the site, undertook an extensive program of restoration. In 1958 the International Paper Company bought a large tract of the surrounding property, including the fort, from the Ford estate and deeded the site to the State of Georgia. It was then turned into a State Historic Site and placed under the protection of the Georgia Department of Natural Resources, Parks and Historic Sites Division. They, in turn, undertook extensive restoration of the property, returning it to much the same condition as it was during the years 1862 to 1864. A museum was built in 1963 to house the many mementos of the fort's turbulent history, including many artifacts recovered from the famous blockade runner, the *Rattlesnake*, now lying in shallow water within sight of the outer walls.

Visitors to the old fort will have no difficulty traveling back in time to the days when it was bustling with the soldiers of the Confederate garrison. The complex has been so well preserved that it could be re-garrisoned and defended again in very short order. Of course, modern technology would destroy it in a matter of seconds, but you get the idea.

Touring the Fort

Your self-guided tour of the fort begins, naturally, at Stop 1. But before you leave, you should keep in mind that the earthen walls of the fort are delicate, little more than sand with a thin protection of grass. They are very susceptible to weather erosion, and even more susceptible to erosion by foot traffic. Please DO NOT CLIMB ON THE WALLS OR THE BOMBPROOFS. Secondly, be careful. The terrain can, in places, be rugged; watch where you walk and avoid obstacles that can cause a fall.

Stop 1: The Construction of the Fort

Fort McAllister was constructed by hand. The land was cleared of trees and undergrowth, the site marked out, then a wooden framework was built and earth piled against the structure and allowed to settle. Later, the framework was removed and the earthen structure covered with sod, pegged in place and allowed to take root, to stabilize the loose sand against erosion. You will find Stop 2 just across the bridge.

Stop 2: The Parade Ground

The parade ground was the center of activities within the fort. As you can see, it's an open area and as such could also be a very dangerous place when under attack. During the naval actions of early 1863 when the *Montauk* and the accompanying fleets of

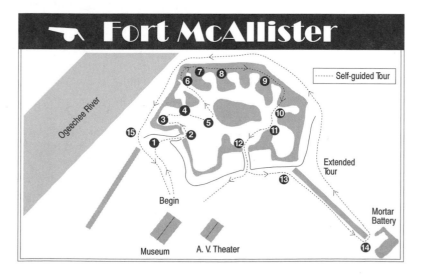

ironclads and gunboats attacked the fort, dozens of projectiles fell into the parade ground. Turn left and proceed to Stop 3.

Stop 3: The Hot Shot Gun

The 32-pounder, smoothbore gun you see here was used as a "Hot Shot Gun." Solid round-shot, cannon balls, would be heated in a furnace until they were red hot. They would then be brought to this gun and fired against wooden ships with the intention of setting them on fire. The gunners had to be pretty good; a ship was a small target, and the hot shot had to land fair and square in order for it to be effective. Go down the steps to Stop 4.

Stop 4: The Hot Shot Furnace

This is the furnace where the solid, 32-pounder cannon balls were heated to red hot. The gunners entered the furnace through a tunnel at the rear, removed the shot from the furnace and carried it, very carefully, to the waiting gun.

Stop 5: The Center Bombproof

Go on in and look around. This bombproof shelter had many uses. Not only was it designed as a shelter against falling shells during a bombardment, it was also used as a hospital and a supply area. During the naval attack on the fort of March 3rd, 1863, a 15-inch shell fired at the fort by one of the Federal Ironclads hit the top of the bombproof, bounced down over the door sill to the floor and exploded. Confederate officers in and around the shelter were burned by the explosion but no one was seriously injured. When you leave the interior of the shelter, turn left and proceed up the steps to the top of the wall and Stop 6.

Stop 6: The Left Angle

This gun position is one of the original four upon which the structure of the fort was founded. During the naval assaults of early 1863, the gun crews here saw a great deal of action. On February 1st, the *Montauk* fired a 15-inch gun that plowed right through the parapet. After the fort fell to Sherman's forces on December 13th, 1864, a signal station was established on the angle to communicate with the ships on the river.

Stop 7: Confederate Sharpshooters

It didn't take the Confederate defenders long to work it out that the Federal ships had found what they considered to be the position from which to bombard the fort. They always dropped anchor at the same place on the opposite side of the river. Noting this, Confederate volunteer sharpshooters were landed in the marshes opposite the fort. There, exposed to fire from the fort, they would harass the naval gun-crews inside the open turrets on the iron-clads. The response from the ironclads was to rake the marshes with load after load of grape-shot and canister, all to no avail. The Confederate sharpshooters came and went like ghosts in the night. From here, proceed to the right to Stop 8.

Stop 8: The Columbiad

It was this great gun that drew most of the attention during the Federal naval bombardments in the early months of 1863. On February 1st, 1863, most of the *Montauk's* fire was directed at this gun. The sustained, concentrated fire of the ship's 11-inch and 15-inch guns eventually reduced the wall in front of the gun, leaving it completely exposed. The gun crew, however, refused to leave the weapon, and fought on throughout the engagement, refusing to be relieved. During the engagement of March 3rd, the gun-carriage was hit by an 11-inch shell which exploded within the emplacement, causing great panic and confusion; incredibly, no one was injured, although the carriage itself was destroyed. Please feel free to go down into the gun emplacement and examine the weapon. When you've finished, climb the stairs again and continue along the front of the fort to Stop 9.

Stop 9: Support Position

This was one of two positions added on to the fort early in 1863. Its purpose was to support and reinforce the smaller battery. The eight-inch Columbiad gun that was mounted here was disabled during the naval bombardment of March 3rd, 1863, when a shell fragment struck and smashed one of the carriage's traverse wheels. According to the records, Private Carroll Hanson, under heavy fire from the ships in the mouth of the river, ran to the rear of the fort to get a new one. The wheel was too heavy for him to carry so he rolled it all the way, dodging shot and shell, arriving back here unscathed. The carriage was quickly repaired and the gun was soon back in action. From here proceed on down the steps and left to Stop 10.

Stop 10: The Reconstructed Service Magazine

What you see here is a reconstruction of the magazine that served the great 32-pounder rifled gun. It was here that the gun's ammunition (shells, powder, fuses, etc.) was kept. From here continue on to Stop 11.

Stop 11: The Rifled Gun Position

This position, along with that of the eight-inch Columbiad at Stop 9, was added to the fort early in 1863. The long-range 32-pounder gun was the only rifled gun mounted in the fort. Extremely accurate, and with a range more than twice that of the older smoothbore weapons, this gun was responsible for most of the fort's long-range defense. Please continue on to the right, past the center bombproof, to Stop 12.

Stop 12: The Sally Port

The Sally Port was added after the naval bombardment of March 3rd, 1863. At that time the rear of the fort was strengthened by the addition of light artillery emplacements whose job it was to defend the fort from attack by land-based troops. The Sally Port allowed easy access to the interior of the fort for supply wagons, etc. At this point you may either proceed out through the moat, turn right, and return to the museum, or continue your tour by turning left and following the boardwalk to Stop 13.

Stop 13: The Covered Way to the Mortar Battery

The earthen wall here provided shelter from heavy gunfire during the naval bombardments as the men made their way back and forth between the fort and the 10-inch seacoast mortar position. Proceed from here to Stop 14, where you will find the mortar battery position.

Stop 14: The Mortar Battery

The 10-inch mortar gun positioned here was commanded by Confederate Artillery Captain Robert Martin. The mortar was a short, heavy gun that was able to fire a huge shell high into the air in a long looping trajectory that brought the shell in on the intended target from an almost vertical angle. This gun saw heavy and continuous action during the naval bombardments of early 1863. On February 1st, after maintaining a continuous rate of fire for more than 90 minutes, the gun's wooden platform collapsed, dismounting the gun. Captain Martin had his men clear away the debris, remount the gun on the floor of the emplacement, and then resumed firing on the Federal ships. The battery was dismantled early in December, 1864, when it was realized that a land-based invasion of the fort was imminent. From here, walk up the steps and down to the exterior of the fort and follow the trail around to Stop 15.

Stop 15: The Northwest Angle

During the heavy fighting on December 13th, the defenders here put up a strong resistance and were able to repel the invading Federal forces. Their success, however, was to no avail, for the southwest angle fell to General Hazen's troops after less than 15 minutes of fighting. The first Federal flag to fly over Fort McAllister was raised here on the river wall.

This concludes your tour of one the nation's finest and best preserved Civil War fortifications. Before you leave, be sure to spend some time in the museum; it's packed with Civil War artifacts and bits and pieces recovered from the Confederate blockade runner, *Rattlesnake*.

If you'd like to stay for a while, or enjoy a quiet afternoon on the Ogeechee River, you will find the facilities at the park much to your liking; they include 1,700 acres of coastal parkland, 65 tent and trailer sites, hiking trails, boat ramps and a dock, two picnic shelters and one group shelter.

Popular activities include picnicking, boating on the river, bird watching, hiking, fishing, audio visual shows, and educational programs and tours.

Annual Special events at the park include a 4th of July Barbecue Picnic & Craft Show, year-round Tours of the Fort, and Labor Day and Winter Musters.

The park is open from 7 a.m. until 10 p.m., and the park office is open from 8 a.m. until 5 p.m. The fort itself is open all year round Tuesday through Saturday from 9 a.m. until 5 p.m. and on Sunday from 2 p.m. until 5:30 p.m. The fort is closed on Mondays except for legal holidays, and on Thanksgiving and Christmas Day.

For information and campsite reservations contact the Fort McAllister State Historic Park, Box 394-A, Fort McAllister Road, Richmond Hill, Georgia, 31324. Telephone 912-727-2339.

For local accommodations and visitor information on the surrounding area, contact either the Savannah Visitors Center at 301 Martin Luther King, Jr. Blvd., or the Savannah Area Convention and Visitors Bureau, PO Box 1628, Savannah, GA 31402-1628. Telephone 1-800-444-2427.

Chapter 12

The Petersburg Campaign

June 15th, 1864 to April 3rd, 1865

The main unit of the Petersburg National Battlefield is located just to the east of the city off VA Highway 36. From there you will be able to tour all six of the units that comprise the Petersburg complex. For more information, contact the Park Service, PO Box 549, Petersburg, VA 23804. Telephone 804-732-3531.

By June, 1864, the War Between the States had been raging back and forth for more than 36 months and no end seemed to be in sight anytime soon. True, Vicksburg, Gettysburg, and Chattanooga had all fallen to Union force of arms, and General Sherman was at the gates of Atlanta, but the Confederacy was far from beaten; General Lee's Army of Northern Virginia was intact, Richmond had not fallen to the Union, and the war in Virginia had reached a stalemate.

It was early in March, 1864, that President Lincoln decided he would, once more, make a change in command of the Armies of the United States. He had long thought that the North's superiority in numbers and resources must eventually turn the tide, and he was right. All that was needed, so it seemed, was a commander who, with a single-minded purpose, could marshal the mighty forces at hand and deliver a single tremendous blow against the southern armies to bring the Confederacy to its knees.

Lincoln decided that such a commander was the victor of Fort Donnelson, Vicksburg, and Chattanooga, Major General Ulysses S. Grant. And so, on March 9th, 1864, Grant was made Commander-in-Chief of all the Union armies.

Grant had long thought that the way to conquer the Confederacy was to initiate a massive offensive against the enemy on all fronts at the same time, and that General Lee's success was due, in part, to the fact that, up until now, he had only been required to fight one battle at a time, concentrating all his resourses on its successful conclusion. And he was right. General Lee's strategy had always

Lieutenant General U.S. Grant.

been that one must *"risk some points in order to have a sufficient force concentrated, with the hope of dealing a successful blow when the opportunity favors."* He further believed that, because the enemy could not attack all points at one time, his troops could be concentrated at a point where an assault should be made. Grant planned to change that by putting pressure on all Confederate armies at the same time.

Immediately after taking command, Grant began to organize his armies and put together a unified plan of operations. First General Sherman would march east from Chattanooga, smash General Joseph Johnston's Confederate Army of Tennessee, take Atlanta, and continue across Georgia to the sea, thus cutting the Confederacy in half. Second, General Benjamin F. Butler was to take his Army of the James and march up the south bank of the James River and attack Petersburg. General Franz Sigel was to take his army into the Shenandoah Valley and drive Confederate General John C. Breckinridge southward. General Nathaniel Banks, at present in New Orleans, was to attack the Confederate enemy at Mobile and finally he himself, at the head of General George Meade's Army of the Potomac, would move against General Lee's Army of Northern Virginia and Richmond. *"To get possession of Lee's army was the first great objective. With the capture of his army Richmond would necessarily follow."*

By early May Grant's plan was under way. He crossed the Rapidan River and the two great armies came together in the Battle of the Wilderness. Lee badly mauled Grant's army and expected the Federal army to run true to form and fall back and regroup, just as it always had done. Instead Grant moved south, trying to outflank Lee and put himself between the Army of Northern Virginia and Richmond. Lee, ever alert to such developments, moved quickly and a few days later the two armies clashed again at the Battle of Spotsylvania Court House. Again Lee inflicted devastating losses on the Federal army, and again Grant remained unperturbed, knowing that he could soon replace his casualties, whereas Lee could not.

Next, at Cold Harbor, Grant suffered a devastating defeat, but again he inflicted heavy losses upon Lee's ever-diminishing army. By the end of the first month of campaign Grant had lost more than 31% of his army. Lee had suffered even heavier losses, in the range of 32%. Slowly but surely, Grant was eating away at Lee's dwindling numbers, destroying his ability to conduct an offensive war.

Lee, by this time, had understood what Grant was about and he remained well entrenched behind the strong defensive line that had served him so well at Cold Harbor; Grant realized that any further attempt to dig him out would result in nothing less than the mass destruction of his troops. So he now had only two options open to him: he could either withdraw and return to Washington, or he could head south; he chose the latter. "*My idea from the start,*" he wrote to General Halleck, "*has been to beat Lee's army, if possible, north of Richmond; then after destroying his lines of communication north of the James River, to transfer the army to the south side and besiege Lee in Richmond, or follow him south if he should retreat.*" His plan was to isolate Richmond, and to do this he needed to cut the railroads into the city. With this strategy in mind, Grant now cast his eyes southward to the little town of Petersburg some 23 miles south of Richmond.

Petersburg, a small but thriving community of 18,000, nestled on the south bank of the Appomattox River, was the main source of supply, not only for Richmond, but for Lee's Army of Northern Virginia as well. Five railroads converged at Petersburg. Tracks ran into the city from every direction: the Richmond & Petersburg Railroad from the north, the South Side Railroad linked Petersburg with Lynchburg, the Weldon Railroad ran southeast into North Carolina and also joined with the Richmond & Danville Railroad, and the City Point Railroad joined Petersburg with City Point at the confluence of the James and Appomattox Rivers some eight miles away. If Grant could take Petersburg, Richmond must inevitably starve. Then it would only be a matter of time before it fell. Petersburg, then, was the gateway through which Grant must ride into the Confederate capital.

Unfortunately for Grant, he was not the only one to realize that Petersburg was the key to the Confederate capital and Lee's army.

Petersburg defenses.

For almost two years the Confederates had been working on the city's defenses and, by the time Grant had made the decision to attack, Captain Charles Dimmock had constructed a chain of massive breastworks and artillery emplacements that ran in a great semi-circle more than 10 miles long. It began and ended east and west of the city on the banks of the Rappahannock River. The 55 batteries on the defensive line, generally referred to as "The Dimmock Line," were numbered consecutively from east to west. As formidable as the Dimmock Line was, it had some glaring weaknesses. First, between batteries number seven and eight there was a deep ravine that could easily be penetrated by an attacking force. Second, the very length and size of the fortified line was in and of itself a disadvantage; it would take more men than were at that time available to man its defenses. General P.G.T. Beauregard, in charge of the defense of Petersburg, estimated it would take 10 times the 4,000 men he had available.

So in early June of 1864 Grant did not believe that Petersburg's defenses would offer him any great resistance, or that the city would be difficult to capture. His original plan called for General Butler's Army of the James to march northeast up the south bank of the James and attack the city from that direction. Unfortunately, Butler's army was soon neutralized by a much smaller Confederate army and bottled up in Bermuda Hundred; from there he was only able to send out small raiding parties that were more of a nuisance to the Confederates than they were a threat. General Beauregard, however, reading Grant's mind and realizing the greater threat, called upon General Lee for reinforcements.

The movement of Grant's (Meade's) army from Cold Harbor began on the evening of June 12th, 1864. By midnight on the 16th, the entire force of more than 90,000 men had safely crossed the James River at Wilcox's Landing. On June 14th Grant was at Bermuda Hundred in conference with General Butler and the order to attack Petersburg was given.

By first light on the morning of June 15th the first Union forces, the

Maj. General Winfield Scott Hancock.

XVIII Corps of the Army of the James under the command of General William F. Smith, began arriving in the approaches to the Petersburg defensive line. General Beauregard, with his tiny complement of fewer than 4,000 men, prepared to do battle with a vastly superior force of more than 15,000. In addition, General Smith was to be supported by General Winfield Scott Hancock's II Army Corps as soon as it could be brought onto the field, followed by General Burnside's IX Army Corps and General Warren's V Corps.

The Federal offensive began shortly after 7 o'clock that morning. Almost immediately, the line was breached when Battery Number Five, one of the strongest in the line, fell as Federal troops moved through the ravine between Batteries Seven and Eight and attacked it from the rear. Within hours, Beauregard had lost almost a mile of his first line of defense and had fallen back to hastily thrown up defenses along Harrison's Creek. To make matters worse, while Beauregard was falling back to Harrison's Creek, General Hancock arrived in support of Smith's advancing columns; things did not look good for Beauregard's tiny force. Had General Smith pressed on with his advance, there is no doubt that Petersburg would have fallen that day; General Smith however, was interested only in defending what he had already taken.

As the battle-hardened veterans of Hancock's leading division began arriving on the field in the late afternoon, it soon became obvious to them that General Lee's divisions had not arrived from Richmond, and that Petersburg was at their mercy. Consequently they wanted to attack the city before Lee's divisions could arrive. Smith, however, ordered them into bivouac; Hancock's men were enraged. *"The rage of the enlisted men was devilish,"* a Federal officer wrote later. *"The most bloodcurdling blasphemy I ever listened to I heard that night by men who knew they were to be sacrificed on the morrow."* General Grant himself did not seem to be too confident of success either, for later that evening Hancock received a message from him stating that, according to Hancock, *"the enemy were then throwing reinforcements into Petersburg, and instructed me that should Petersburg not fall on the night of the 15th it would be advisable for General Smith and myself to take up a defensive position and maintain it until all our forces had come up."*

Fortunately, for Beauregard at least, darkness ended the fighting on June 15th and Hoke's Confederate division arrived to give him a hand. In addition, realizing his situation to be desperate, he took it upon himself to order General Bushrod Johnson's division to abandon its duty of bottling up the Army of the James at Bermuda Hundred and move to the defense of the city, thus bringing his effective force up to about 10,000 men. Still, things looked hopeless. By the time all four Federal corps were present on the battlefield, Beauregard would face an army of more than 60,000 men; 40,000 were already there. Stiff as the odds were, they were better than those of the day before.

The fighting was renewed with vigor early in the afternoon of the next day, and lasted for more than three hours. More of Beauregard's line fell to the Federals, but the general fought like a rat caught in a trap and managed to hold on. Then at last as night began to fall on the second day of battle, and in response to Beauregard's urgent pleas, Lee's army was on the move and the first of his divisions began arriving to aid the beleaguered city.

During a council of war that evening, the 16th, General Meade outlined his plan for a general assault on the Confederate defenses the following morning. *"A vigorous assault on the enemy's works will be made tomorrow morning at 4 o'clock by the whole force of the Fifth, Ninth, and Second Corps."* General Smith's XVII Corps would be held back in reserve.

The following morning, General Warren's V Corps moved out along the Jerusalem road as planned, but soon ran into heavy Confederate resistance, Warren stopped to assess the situation, and there he stayed. To Warren's right, Hancock and Burnside were soon engaged in heavy fighting that lasted for most of the rest of the day. But their efforts were disconnected and uncoordinated, so very little was accomplished. Once again Beauregard's tiny force seemed to be blessed with a charmed life. By nightfall, when the fighting ended, Beauregard had fallen back to a line only a mile and a half from Petersburg itself. All night long, knowing that General Lee's entire army was on the move, the Confederates labored to fortify the new line of defense. By first light on the morning of the 18th, with more than 50,000 Confederate troops now manning Petersburg's new defensive line, Beauregard was ready to receive whatever force General Meade might care to throw at them; General Lee himself arrived a little after 11:30 that morning.

Meade ordered another general assault on the morning of the 18th, but it too was doomed to failure. With the entire Army of Northern Virginia strongly entrenched between them and Petersburg, the armies of the United States now knew that they were facing a situation similar to what they had just left at Cold Harbor; they did not want to face such a situation again.

The attacks were late starting; some units never got started at all and, by late afternoon, after a series of half-hearted assaults, the Federal field commanders had had enough. Earlier, at 2:30 that afternoon, General Meade, frustrated and angry at his commanders' timidity, sent the following telegram to Warren and Burnside, "*What additional orders to attack you require I cannot imagine. My orders have been explicit and are now repeated, that you each immediately assault the enemy with all your force, and if there is any further delay the responsibility and the consequences will rest with you.*" By then, however, whatever chance the Federal army might have had to take Petersburg had gone. During the four days of fighting, the Federal army had suffered more than 10,000 casualties for very little gain. On the evening of the 18th, after the hostilities had ended, Meade received the following telegram from General Grant, "*Now we will rest the men and use the spade for their protection until a new vein can be struck.*" The Battle for Petersburg moved into a siege operation, one that would last for almost 10 months.

At the close of the Battle for Petersburg, June 15th through 18th, the northern section of the Dimmock Line, Batteries 1 though 21 had fallen to the Federal army; Batteries 22, 23, and 24 were in a no-man's land between General Hancock's corps and the Confederate defenses; the rest of the line south and west was still intact, though weakly defended, because most of the Confederate army was deployed in the northern section of the line facing Burnside to the west on the banks of the Rappahannock, Warren to Burnside's left, then Hancock, with General Wright's corps on the extreme Union right. All along the lines, Federal and Confederate, the defenses bristled with forts and artillery batteries; in some places

Maj. General Ambrose Burnside.

the lines were less than a hundred yards apart. The area became one vast maze of breastworks and trenches; the mounds of earth thrown up by the furious digging on both sides served not only as defensive walls, but as burial grounds as well. For weeks, the two sides bombarded each other, sniped at each other with sharp-shooters and, when all else failed, yelled obscenities at each other. Thus the siege of Petersburg settled down to inevitable boredom and inaction. As the first month of the siege wore on, the mud and the filth in the trenches became a breeding ground for almost every deadly disease imaginable to man. Men died in their thousands and joined their fallen comrades within the walls of the defenses. Then, unable to withstand the boredom any longer, Lieutenant Colonel Henry Pleasants of the 48th Pennsylvania Volunteers of General Potter's division of the IX Corps, most of whom had been coal miners before enlisting, came up with an idea.

Pleasants' position was located just in front of a Confederate fortification beyond the crest of Cemetery Hill known as Elliott's Salient. It was a particularly strong emplacement of four heavy guns and two regiments of Confederate infantry at a point where the two opposing lines lay only 400 feet apart. Pleasants' idea was this: using his miners he would drive a mine shaft the 400 feet between the two lines to a point exactly beneath the Confederate work, load the end of the tunnel with black powder and then, in Pleasants' own words, *"blow that damned fort out of existence. That God-damned fort,"* he told his superiors, *"is the only thing between us and Petersburg, and I have an idea we can blow it up."* General Meade was skeptical, to say the least, but at this point in the siege anything was better than nothing, and so Pleasants was given the go ahead and the work on the shaft began.

The work on the mine began on June 25th. Pleasants' men, about 400 of them, without the help promised by the Federal high command, began to dig. At first, Pleasants was able to employ only a few of his men at any one time, and then, as the tunnel grew longer, he had to add more and more until at last every man in his regiment, including the officers, was employed. *"The great difficulty I had,"* Pleasants reported, *"was to dispose of the material got out of the mine. I found it impossible to get any assistance from anybody; I had to do all the work myself. I had to remove the earth in old cracker boxes; I got pieces of hickory and nailed them on the boxes in which we received our crackers, and then iron-clad them with hoops of iron taken from old pork and beef barrels. Whenever I made application I could not get anything,"* he complained. *"I could get no boards or lumber supplied to me for my operations. I had to get a pass and send two companies of my own regiment, with wagons, outside of our lines to rebel saw-mills, and get lumber in that way, after having previously got what lumber I could by tearing down an old bridge. I had no picks furnished me, but had to take common army picks and have them straightened into mine picks."*

Frustrated though he was, Pleasants made great progress and, by July 17th, the diggers had advanced their shaft more than 500 feet to a point 20 feet below the Confederate works.

On July 18th, the diggers branched out left and right, extending two branches paralleling the Confederate fortifications above. By July 23rd, a further 75 feet of tunnel had been dug beneath the Confederate line of fortifications for a grand total of more than 585 feet; it was a stupendous achievement. Now work changed from digging to carrying. Three hundred and twenty kegs of black powder, each weighing 25 pounds, were placed in the two branches off the main tunnel. The total charge when in place totaled exactly 8,000 pounds. Next, sand-bags were placed at the end of the main tunnel to direct the force of the explosion upward, and two fuses were linked together to form a line almost 90 feet long.

The Dictator at Petersburg, a 17,000-pound siege mortar.

On July 27th, everything was in place and General Burnside presented his plan for the attack to Generals Grant and Meade. He intended at first for a division of black troops under the command of General Edward Ferrero to lead the attack after the explosion. Meade, however, was concerned that leading with the black troops might have political repercussions. Grant agreed. So, with Grant's approval, Meade changed the plan and directed that the IX Corps would attack Elliott's Salient in a direct charge over the top of Cemetery Hill with the XVIII Corps ready to follow in support if necessary; the division commanders would draw straws to determine who would lead the charge. General James Ledlie of the First Division won.

Orders were then given for all Federal batteries located in the near vicinity of the action to prepare for a general bombardment of the Confederate works as soon as the explosion had occurred. Fifty-four heavy siege mortars and 110 heavy guns prepared to go into action. In addition, Grant gave orders for the II Corps to move across the James River at Deep Bottom and create a diversion; Lee responded and moved troops to meet what he perceived to be a new threat, leaving only 18,000 men in the defensive lines around Petersburg.

By 3 o'clock on the morning of July 30th, the entire Federal IX Corps was in position in the ravine to the rear of the mine entrance and at 3:15 Colonel Pleasants lit the fuse. Then they waited, and they waited, and they waited. By 4:15 it was obvious that something had gone wrong. Two men, Lieutenant Jacob Douty and Sergeant Henry Rees, volunteered to go into the mine and find out what had gone wrong. They discovered that the fuse had gone out just at the point where the first splice in the line had been made. They relighted the fuse and ran for cover. At 4:45 that morning the ground shook as the mighty explosion hurled the Confederate fortifications high into the air. Hundreds of tons of earth, along with guns, carriages, limbers, and men were flung skyward. At least 280 men were killed or wounded by the devastating explosion. The blast caused a crater more than 170 feet long by 80 feet wide and, in places, more than 30 feet deep.

The size of the blast itself caused a considerable delay in the Federal offensive. For several minutes the waiting soldiers stood and gaped at the spectacle. Removal of obstructions between the lines caused a further delay. Thus the disori-

The Crater, 1865.

ented Confederates were given valuable breathing space during which they were able gather themselves together and rally to their own defense. As the Federal forces began to move forward over the crest of Cemetery Hill and into the massive crater, the Confederates began to pour a deadly barrage of cannon and musket fire in upon them. Many Federal soldiers paused on the crest of the hill to view the devastation they had wreaked upon the enemy works, while many more dived headlong into the crater to take cover from the deadly Confederate fire. By quick reactions and decisive action, the Confederates were able to stop the Union attack. General Lee, at 6 o'clock in the morning and well aware of the dangerous situation at Elliott's Salient, sent General William Mahone with two brigades of infantry to the aid of the defenders at the threatened position.

In the meantime, more and more Federal troops were pouring into the massive crater. But the way out on the other side was blocked by the Confederate defenders. And still Federal reinforcements poured over the top of Cemetery Hill and down into the crater.

Mahone's brigades began arriving on the scene and were quickly deployed in a ravine about 200 yards to the west of the crater, between it and Petersburg. They hadn't been there many minutes when they saw hoards of blue-clad soldiers emerging from the crater. They realized that their comrades were in trouble and, though badly outnumbered, with a great yell Mahone's men leaped forward out of the ravine and charged across an open field right into the thick of the advancing Federal line, forcing them to flee back into the crater of horrors.

By 8:30 in the morning, almost an entire Federal division was trapped in the crater. And so the blood-bath began.

At 9 o'clock, three full batteries of Confederate artillery had trained their guns, 12 of them, on the unfortunate Federals in the crater and were hurling volley after volley of canister and shell into the now demoralized Federals. Then, as if the massed artillery bombardment were not enough, the Confederates brought forward a battery of mortars and that too began to rain shells in on the trapped Federal infantry in the crater.

Maj. General William Mahone. His men held the Crater.

By 10:30, the situation in the crater had turned into a circus of horrors. The hot sun beat down upon the thousands of men trapped there. There was no water to drink, no shade, and no leadership. The Confederate batteries continued to hammer the trapped Federal soldiers. As early as 9:30 that morning, General Meade had ordered General Burnside to withdraw his troops; the situation even then was obviously hopeless. Burnside, however, for some reason known only to himself, had decided to delay the withdrawal until noon. Many of his men tried to make it back to safety on their own, many of them died without ever leaving the gigantic grave they had dug for themselves; most stayed where they were, unable to move for fear of the devastating Confederate bombardment.

At 1 o'clock in the afternoon, General Mahone made his final charge on the Union lines. His men gained the slopes of the crater and beheld a terrible sight. Thousands of men clung hopelessly to the walls, while the dead and wounded lay in heaps all over the floor and walls. The Federals in the crater, however, were not yet ready to give up. As soon as the Confederates showed their heads over the rim of the crater they poured forth a deadly hail of fire that, for a moment, drove Mahone's men back. The Confederates put their hats on their bayonets and raised them over the rim of the crater. The hats were immediately torn to shreds by a volley of musket fire. Before the Federals had time to reload, Mahone's men charged over the rim, into the crater, and loosed off a deadly volley of their own, and then they set about them with bayonets and rifle butts. It was more than the devastated Federals could stand and they began surrendering en masse. The Battle for the Crater was over. Burnside's IX Corps had lost more than 4,000 men killed, wounded or captured; the Confederates lost under 1,500. And by now it had become painfully obvious that storming the Confederate fortifications was out of the question. The only option now left to Grant and Meade was a war of attrition against Lee; keep him busy and off-balance with a series of surprise attacks to the north, south and west, and thus gradually wear him down.

In the furtherance of this new Federal strategy, on August 18th, General Warren's V Corps left the lines, marched some three miles westward, and seized the Weldon Railroad at Globe Tavern. The next day Lee sent General A.P. Hill to recover the railroad. At first Hill was successful, inflicting heavy losses on Warren's corps, driving him back and taking more than 2,700 prisoners. But Warren held on; the railroad and a vital line of supply was lost to Lee. Lee now had only one direct line of supply between Richmond and the rest of the South, the Richmond and Danville Railroad.

By mid-September, the great Army of Northern Virginia was starving; Lee had to do something, and quickly. He sent General Wade Hampton and a force of 4,000 mounted troopers on a foraging expedition deep into enemy territory. Hampton returned on September 17th with more than 2,000 head of cattle and 300 prisoners, for a loss of only 60 of his men. Unfortunately, Hampton's success was merely a hiccup in the long months of the siege. Grant kept up the pressure, and slowly but surely the noose around Lee and Petersburg began to tighten.

Time and again Grant sent his corps and divisions this way and that, and time and again Lee was forced to take action to counter the ever more threatening Federal troop movements. And never for a moment did Grant give Lee and his beleaguered army time to rest.

On October 27th, Grant sent General Hancock's II Corps and two divisions of General Warren's V Corps west to the Boydton Plank Road. It seems by this time that the Federal commanders were growing ever more confident, because they became careless and

Confederate dead in a trench at Petersburg. Note the missing shoes.

allowed a gap to open up between the marching divisions. The Confederate commanders, however, were suffering no such problems of overconfidence and were alert to the situation. General Wade Hampton's cavalry and two Confederate divisions of infantry under the command of Generals William Mahone and Henry Heth struck Hancock a devastating blow at Burgess Mill, inflicting heavy casualties, driving the Federal force back from whence they came, and retaining the Boydton Plank Road. It was the last major action of 1864; the siege of Petersburg continued, and both sides settled down to a long winter. But even in the dead of winter, Grant continued to keep Lee off-balance.

On February 5th, 1865, Grant sent Hancock and Warren out again to take the Boydton Plank Road. This time they were successful. Lee's line was now more than 35 miles long and he had fewer than 36,000 men with which to defend it.

In the Shenandoah Valley on March 2nd General Sheridan defeated what remained of General Jubal Early's small army and marched east to join Grant. Lee was now in desperate trouble; he had no alternative but to abandon his positions around Petersburg and Richmond.

Lee, his back to the wall, pondered the question of what to do next. General Joseph Johnston was in the Carolinas. If Lee could retreat south and join him.... But how?

Ever the optimist, Lee decided the best way to open up a gap through which to move out was to attack Grant and take him by surprise. He gave orders to General John B. Gordon to choose a target where he might have the best chance for success. Gordon chose Fort Stedman, just 150 yards east of a strong Confederate position called Colquitt's Salient, and not far from one of Grant's main supply routes, the City Point Railroad.

Lee left the details of the attack to General Gordon, but gave him access to as many of his troops as might be needed to successfully carry it off. All through the night of March 24th, Gordon's men worked in silence, removing obstacles, overcoming Federal pickets without a shot being fired, and removing more Federal obstructions in front of Fort Stedman. When this was done a small force of 300 men wearing white strips of cloth tied around their heads so that Gordon's main body would be able to distinguish them from the Federals would rush the fort, take the defenders by surprise and capture it, and then move quickly onward to capture three more nearby Federal forts.

At 4 o'clock in the morning of March 25th, General Gordon gave the order to attack. At first it was successful. The 300 had little trouble taking the surprised garrison of Fort Stedman. Thereafter, things began to go badly wrong. Moving onward, as Gordon's plan had called for, the 300 rushed what was supposed to be the second Federal fort. It wasn't. It didn't exist. Neither did the other two. The 300 floundered around in the dark until eventually they were forced to return to Fort Stedman. Unfortunately, by this time, the Federals had been alerted and were pouring a deadly storm of rifle fire and canister into the massed Confederate ranks. At 7:30 that morning General Lee gave the order to withdraw. The movement to the rear began, but the heavy Federal fire made it almost impossible. Many of Gordon's men preferred surrender rather than certain death. General Lee lost more than 4,000 of his already depleted army in the Battle for Fort Stedman; the end of the Battle for Petersburg was in sight.

On March 31st, General Sheridan's army pushed northwest to Five Forks, just 18 miles southwest of Petersburg, where they were stopped by a strong Confederate force under the command of Generals George Pickett and Fitzhugh Lee and were forced back to Dinwiddie Courthouse. Lee sent urgent orders to his generals that they must "Hold Five Forks at all hazards." And that's just what they meant to do. In a feverish haste the Confederates constructed a network of defenses and prepared to defend them to the last man. But April 1st was a glorious day. The sun shone brightly and, as far as anyone could tell, there was no indication that a Federal attack was imminent. It had been a very long winter with little cheer or enjoyment and so, when Pickett and Fitzhugh Lee received an invitation from General Rosser to join him for an afternoon shadbake, they had no hesitation. It was a fatal mistake.

Late that afternoon, with a force of 3,000 cavalry and infantry, General Sheridan attacked the leaderless Confederates and soundly defeated them. By nightfall that evening Five Forks was in Federal hands, along with more than 3,000 Confederate prisoners; the western side of General Lee's line had collapsed.

After the Confederate defeat at Five Forks, Grant knew that the end was in sight. The next day, April 25th, he ordered a general assault all along the Confederate line. One by one the Confederate forts along Lee's line began to go. By mid-day almost all of the Confederate line to the west was in Federal hands. Only Forts Gregg and Whitworth, just in front of the city, remained intact. Petersburg was now completely surrounded except to the north across the river. That was the only way left open for Lee to make his escape and he took it.

But Lee needed time. Forts Gregg and Whitworth must buy that time. Lee sent word to the garrisons that General Longstreet was on his way to their aid, but they must hold for at least two hours until he could get there. There were only 274 men in the garrisons of the two forts to hold back an entire Federal army corps. General John Gibbon, in command of the XXIV Army Corps, gave orders for General Foster's division to open the attack on the Confederate forts. Confidently, Foster's men sallied forth, flushed with the Federal victories earlier in the day and expecting little resistance from the defenders in the two forts. They were entirely surprised, however, when they came under a veritable firestorm of canister and shell from Fort Gregg and were forced to withdraw in disarray.

The action stepped up. Time and again the defenders in Fort Gregg threw back concentrated Federal attacks. Gradually the separate attacks turned into one long sustained assault as the Federal troops tried desperately to overwhelm the fort.

Inside Fort Gregg, the men of Lee's finest artillery corps were doing stalwart work. For an hour and a half the tiny garrison held back the might of Gibbon's corps, more than 14,000 men. The wounded in the fort lay on their backs and reloaded rifles with bloody hands and then handed them to their comrades on the breastworks. Then Gibbon received two more brigades of infantry and together they hit the beleaguered fort on all sides. Soon they had forced an entry and were inside, but still the fort's defenders refused to give up. For more than 25 minutes they engaged in fierce hand-to-hand combat; even the Confederate wounded joined it. They went crazy, fighting like demons with bayonets, knives, chunks of wood, and even fists. At one time six Federal battle flags were seen on the parapet. When the battle was over one Confederate survivor described the action as follows: *"Those twenty-five minutes were the most desperate and infernal we ever experienced. We lost all sense of reason, and were driven by a blinding urge to kill. I have never seen men struggling more frantically to clamber up the high parapet, and only after twenty-five or thirty minutes of awful slaughter was that heroic garrison conquered."*

By 3 o'clock that afternoon, the battle for Fort Gregg was over, and Gibbon turned his attention to Fort Whitworth. In Fort Whitworth Colonel Joseph M. Jayne and his 60 men prepared to do battle in the same grand tradition as had just been set by the heroic garrison in Fort Gregg. The Federals, however, had no intention of going through it all again, and they turned the captured Confederate cannon in Fort Gregg on Fort Whitworth, leaving Jayne no alternative but to surrender his tiny garrison. The two forts were at last in Federal hands, but at what a cost. Of the 14,000 Union soldiers involved, 122 were killed and almost 600 were wounded. Of the 214-member garrison that had so well defended Fort Gregg, 55 lay dead and 129 were wounded, for a staggering 86% casualties. Only 30 men of the Confederate garrison survived the battle uninjured.

Confederate dead in the trenches around Petersburg.

Petersburg Courthouse, 12 hours after the fall of the city to U.S. Grant, April 3rd, 1865.

Heavy as the cost had been to the defenders of the two Confederate forts, they had achieved their objective, having bought General Lee the time he needed. That evening the Confederate army was able to make an orderly retreat westward toward Appomattox. The next morning, the Federal army entered Richmond and Grant was in Petersburg. During the 10 months of fighting around the city Grant had suffered some 42,000 casualties; Lee more than 28,000, including one of his greatest commanders, Lieutenant General A.P. Hill. The once great Army of Northern Virginia was at last slowly dying. The end was less than 10 days away.

Touring the Battlefield

The four-mile driving tour of Petersburg National Battlefield, and the extended 16-mile driving tour of the Siege Line, will take you around most of the important sights of the Campaign of 1864-65. Along the way you will find many wayside exhibits and audio stations designed to interpret the battle for you. There are also several short walking trails that will give you fine views of some of the most important sites; it is recommended that you take them. Take plenty of time. Your visit to Petersburg should not be rushed. After all, General Lee and Grant were here for almost 10 months. As always, you will begin your visit at the Visitor Center.

The Petersburg Battlefield

Stop 1: The Visitor Center & Battery Number 5

You will find many interesting interpretive exhibits in the Visitor Center designed, to give you an insight into the complex operations of the 10-month siege. When you've finished there, take the short walk along the path to Battery Number 5.

By June, 1864, the Confederates had been working on the city's defenses for almost two years and, by the time Grant had made the decision to attack the city, the Confederate engineer in charge of the works, Captain Charles Dimmock, had constructed a chain of massive breastwork artillery emplacements that ran in a great semi-circle more than 10 miles long. The line began and ended east and west of the city on the banks of the Rappahannock River. The 55 batteries on the defensive line, generally referred to as "The Dimmock Line," were numbered consecutively from east to west. This Confederate battery, Number 5, was a part of that Dimmock Line which fell to the Federal forces of General William F. Smith's division of the XVIII Corps of the Army of the James on the evening of June 15th, 1864. You will recall that Smith's men pierced the Dimmock Line by way of a ravine between Batteries 7 and 8 and attacked this battery from the rear. By the morning of the 16th, General Beauregard, commanding the Confederate garrison, had lost not only this battery, but all the defensive line for more than a mile to the south.

After the first Battle for Petersburg ended on June 18th, Battery Number 5 was manned by Federal artillerists who placed a massive, 17,000-pound siege mortar they affectionately called The Dictator, or sometimes The Petersburg Express, here at Battery Number 5. The great mortar hurled huge 13-inch shells into the Confederate defenses. When you have finished here, walk back along the path to the Visitor Center, get into your vehicle and follow the tour signs to Stop 2.

Stop 2: Battery Number 8

This position, along with Battery Number 9, the next stop on your tour, also fell to General Smith's forces on the evening of June 15th. It was turned into a Union artillery post and renamed Fort Friend. Ironically the captured Confederate guns in place here were used to repel the Confederates who had broken the Union line at Fort Stedman on March 25th, 1865. From here return to your vehicle and continue on along the park road to Stop 3.

Stop 3: Battery Number 9

This Confederate artillery position was also a part of the Dimmock Line and, like Batteries 8 and 5, fell to black troops of General Hink's Federal division on June 15th, 1865. From here you can take the 10-minute walk to Meade Station, an important Union supply

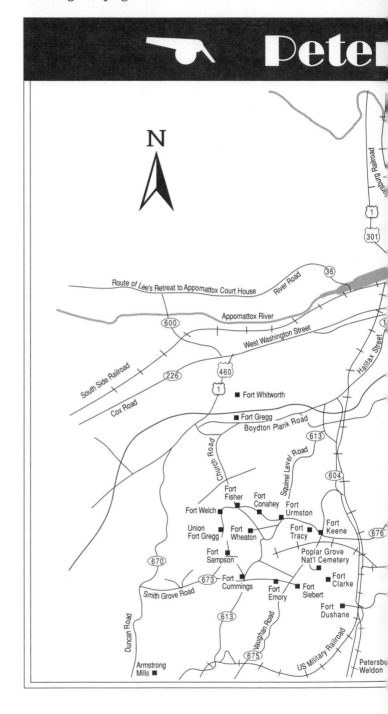

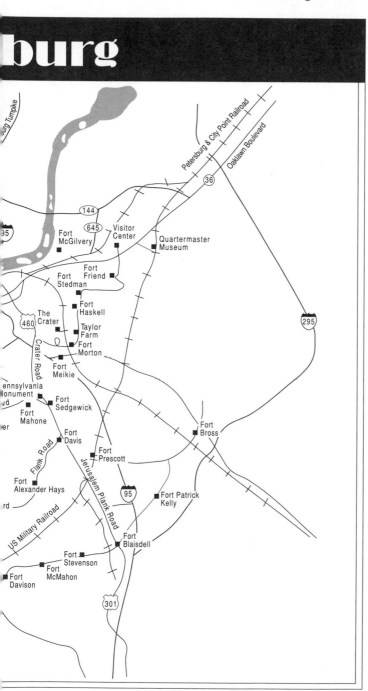

burg

Petersburg & City Point Railroad

Oaklawn Boulevard

rg Turnpike

36

144

95

645

Fort
McGilvery

Visitor
Center

Quartermaster
Museum

Fort
Fort   Friend
Stedman

Fort
Haskell

The
Crater

Taylor
Farm

Fort
Morton

Fort
Meikie

295

Crater Road

460

ennsylvania
onument
d

Fort
Sedgewick

Fort
Mahone

er

Fort
Davis

Flank Road

Fort
Bross

Fort
Prescott

Jerusalem Plank Road

Fort
Alexander Hays

rd

95

Fort Patrick
Kelly

US Military Railroad

Fort
Blaisdell

Fort
Stevenson

Fort
Davison

Fort
McMahon

301

depot and hospital site on the Army Line of the City Point Railroad. When you have finished at Meade Station, return to your vehicle and continue on along the park road to Stop 4.

Stop 4: Harrison's Creek

Harrison's Creek is a major point of historic interest on the park road. It was here on the banks of this creek that the Confederate drive to break out of Petersburg on March 15th, 1865, was checked by an artillery barrage from a low ridge just to the east. Stop 5 is just a short distance on along the road.

Stop 5: Fort Steadman

Fort Stedman was the place chosen by Confederate General John B. Gordon for his attempt to break the Union line and open up an escape route for Lee's Army of Northern Virginia on March 25th, 1865.

You will recall that by mid-March General Lee, his defensive line now stretched to more than 35 miles long and his back to the wall, had decided that he would not be able to hold the city much longer and that his best course of action was to join General Joseph Johnston in the Carolinas.

Lee decided the best way to open up a gap through which he could escape was to attack Grant and take him by surprise. He gave orders to General Gordon to choose a target. Gordon chose Fort Stedman just 150 yards east of a strong Confederate position called Colquitt's Salient, and not far from one of Grant's main supply routes, the City Point Railroad.

All through the night of March 24th, Gordon's men worked in silence, cleaning away the obstacles in front of the fort and removing the Federal pickets. When this was done a small Confederate force of 300 men would rush the fort, take the defenders by surprise, capture it, and then move quickly onward to capture three more nearby Federal forts.

At 4 o'clock in the morning of March 25th General Gordon gave the order to attack. The 300 had little trouble overwhelming the surprised garrison. Thereafter, however, things began to go badly wrong. The second Federal fort didn't exist, neither did the other two. The 300 were forced to return to Fort Stedman and back to the

Confederate line. Unfortunately, by this time, the Federals stood solidly between them and safety.

At 7:30 that morning General Lee gave the order to withdraw. The movement to the rear began, but the heavy Federal fire made it almost impossible. General Lee lost more than 4,000 men in the Battle for Fort Stedman.

Inside the fort you will find a monument erected by the State of Pennsylvania to the memory of the Third Division of the IX Corps of the Army of the Potomac, which participated in the Battle of Fort Stedman on June 18th, 1864. When you have finished your tour of Fort Stedman, you might like to walk the Loop Trail that leads from the fort to Colquitt's Salient where General Gordon's Confederate attack originated. As you walk the trail, you will pass the monument erected to the memory of the 1st Maine Infantry Regiment, who suffered the greatest regimental loss in a single action during the Civil War. On June 18th the 1st Maine, during the general Union offensive involving elements of all four Federal corps, charged from the concealment of Prince George Court House Road just to the north of where Fort Stedman is today, and was hit by a withering Confederate crossfire. In a matter of minutes the regiment had lost more than three-fourths of its number. Of the 850 men who made the charge, 632 fell dead and wounded on the field where you now stand. When you have finished your visit to Colquitt's Salient, return to your vehicle and continue on along the park road to Stop 6.

Stop 6: Fort Haskell

Fort Haskell is one of the best preserved sections of the Union earthworks. Federal artillery and heavy infantry fire from this position helped to turn the tide against General Gordon's Confederate troops in the Battle for Fort Stedman on March 25th, 1865. The ditch around the embankments was turned into a formidable obstacle by the deployment of chevaux-de-frise, large timbers with sharpened stakes driven through at right angles. Sandbags and gabions, cylindrical wicker baskets, were placed on the fortifications to protect them from artillery fire. The Federal defenders of Fort Stedman were driven down the line of works until they ended up here in Fort Haskell. So many of them, in fact, were jammed inside that it became almost impossible to fight. From Fort Haskell, continue on along the park road to Stop 7.

Stop 7: Taylor Farm

Today nothing is left of the Taylor Farm. All the buildings were destroyed during the siege of the city. During the Battle of the Crater, Federal batteries located along this ridge employed 54 heavy siege mortars and 110 heavy guns in a general bombardment of the Confederate positions as soon as the explosion had occurred. This was to prepare the way for General James Ledlie's First Division of the XVIII Corps in their attack. Stop 8 is just a little further on along the park road.

Stop 8: The Crater

You are now at the scene of the Battle of the Crater that took place on the morning of July 30th, 1864. Unable to withstand the boredom of the long siege, Federal troops drove a mine shaft the 400 feet between the two lines to a point exactly beneath the Confederate work. Once this was done, 320 kegs of black powder, each weighing 25 pounds, were placed in the tunnel.

At 4:45 in the morning on June 30th, 1864, the ground around here shook as a mighty explosion hurled the Confederate fortifications high into the air. The crater caused by the blast was more than 170 feet long and 80 feet wide. Today, time and the elements have smoothed the edges of the mighty hole. Even so, it's still possible to get an idea of the magnitude of the blast that so devastated the Confederate line.

Shortly after the explosion, the Federal forces began to move forward over the crest of Cemetery Hill and into the crater. The Confederates, however, had had time to recover and hammered the advancing Federal brigades with cannon and musket fire. The blue-clad soldiers dived for cover into the crater; many of them would never leave it alive.

General Lee, well aware of the dangerous situation at Elliott's Salient, sent General William Mahone and two brigades of infantry to the aid of the defenders at the threatened position.

By 8:30 in the morning, almost an entire Federal division was trapped in the crater. By 9:30, three Confederate batteries of artillery and mortar battery had trained their guns on the trapped Federals and were systematically cutting them to pieces.

By 10:30, the situation in the crater was desperate. The hot sun beat down upon the thousands of men trapped there. There was no water to drink, no shade, and no leadership, and the Confederate batteries relentlessly continued to smash the trapped Federal brigades.

At about 1 o'clock in the afternoon, General Mahone's brigades charged forward again. When they gained the slopes of the crater they beheld hundreds of dead and wounded Federal soldiers lying in heaps where they had fallen.

Eventually, the devastated Federals dropped their weapons and surrendered; the Battle for the Crater was over. Burnside's IX Corps had lost more than 4,000 men killed, wounded or captured, the Confederates fewer than 1,500.

The Siege Line Tour

The Siege Line Tour will take you on an extended drive for several miles to the south and west of the town. Return to the Visitor Center and leave the main unit of the park by turning left onto Crater Road (U.S. Highway 301) and follow the Park Service signs to Stop 9.

Stop 9: Fort Sedgewick

Today, nothing remains of the fort built by Union troops during July and August, 1864. Sedgewick was a key Federal position on the eastern section of the siege line. It was nicknamed Fort Hell by the men who garrisoned it due to the almost continuous Confederate artillery and sniper fire that rained in upon it. Fort Sedgewick was also the scene of a major assault on the last day of the Battle for Petersburg, April 2nd, 1865 against two Confederate works – Rive's Salient and Fort Mahone – during which Federal Colonel George Gowan of the 48th Pennsylvania Volunteers was killed. The nearby Gowan monument honors his memory. From here, continue on along Crater Road until you reach the junction with Flank Road, the site of Fort Davis. Turn right onto Flank Road which follows the Union siege line south and west of Petersburg. Along the way to Stop 10 you should be able to spot many of the low sections of breastworks that still remain, including Fort Alexander Hayes to your right, Union Batteries 24 and 25 on the left, the site of Fort Howard to the right of the road (not visible), Battery 26 on the left, and finally Fort Wadsworth, just a short distance past the junction with Route 604 on the left.

Stop 10: Fort Wadsworth

Fort Wadsworth was located at one of the major strategic sites along the siege line. The fort stands on the site of the Battle of the Weldon Railroad that took place on August 18-21, 1864. The Railroad fell to the Federal forces of General Gouverneur K. Warren's V Army Corps and the fort was built to strengthen the Federal hold on the important railroad line of supply into the city of Petersburg. Inside the fort you will find a monument to the memory of the soldiers from South Carolina of Confederate Lieutenant General A.P. Hill's Corps, who broke through the Union line near here on August 21st. Continue on along the Flank Road for a short distance until you come to the junction with Vaughan Road, turn left and drive a short distance more to Stop 11.

Stop 11: Poplar Grove Cemetery

This cemetery was established on ground captured by the Union Army in the Battle for the Weldon Railroad, August 18 through 21, 1864. During the winter of 1864-65, the 50th New York engineers were encamped in this area and constructed a log church. Of the 6,178 Union soldiers buried in the cemetery, 4,110 are unknown. Most of the Confederate soldiers who died here are buried in the Blandford Cemetery in Petersburg. Return to your vehicle and follow the park road back to Vaughan Road, turn right and follow it to the junction with Flank Road, turn left onto it, and continue your tour along the Siege Line to Stop 12.

Stop 12: Forts Urmston and Conahey

These two forts were constructed in the fall and early winter of 1864 on ground captured by the Union Army during the Battle of Peeble's Farm, September 30th through October 2nd. There is an interpretive sign which explains the significance of this position on the siege lines. When you have finished here, continue to follow the Flank Road to Stop 13 on your tour.

Stop 13: Fort Fisher

Fort Fisher is located on the right side of the road and was the largest earthen fortification of the siege line. As you will see, it is still in an excellent state of preservation. Although there was little fighting on this section of the line, Fort Fisher was important for several reasons. On April 2nd, 1865, after the battle of Five Forks, Union forces of the VI Corps came through the Confederate defenses between Forts Fisher and Welch. Also nearby was a Union watchtower, almost 150 feet high, which was used to observe Confederate troop movements, and to spot artillery fire. Behind the fort, a short distance away to the south, was a field of execution where almost every week military offenders, deserters, and spies paid with their lives for their transgressions. When you've finished your tour of Fort Fisher, return to your vehicle and continue on along the Flank Road for a short distance to the junction of Church Road. Turn left onto Church Road and drive on to Stop 14.

Stop 14: Confederate Fort Gregg

You will recall that on April 2nd, 1865, Fort Gregg, along with Fort Whitworth, was all that stood between the retreating Army of Northern Virginia and Grant's victorious forces.

After the Confederate defeat at Five Forks on April 1st, General Grant knew that Petersburg was almost within his grasp. The next day, April 2nd, he ordered a general assault all along the Confederate line.

By mid-day almost all of the Confederate line to the west was in Federal hands. Only Forts Gregg and Whitworth remained. Grant had Petersburg almost completely surrounded. Only a small section to the north across the river remained open. If Lee was to make his escape, he would have go out that way, but to do so he needed time. Forts Gregg and Whitworth would have to buy him that time.

There were only 274 men in the garrisons of the two forts to hold back an entire Federal army corps, and the Federals expected to encounter little resistance. General Foster's division of General John Gibbon's XXIV Army Corps opened the attack on Fort Gregg and were surprised when they were hit by a firestorm of canister and shell from the fort. It was something they hadn't been prepared for and they were quickly driven back in disarray.

For more than 90 minutes, the tiny Confederate garrison held the might of an entire Federal corps at bay, more than 14,000 men, until at last Gibbon received two more brigades of infantry and they were hit on all sides at once. It was only a matter of minutes before the Federal troops had forced an entry and were inside the fort, but still its defenders refused give up. For more than 25 minutes they fought a fierce hand-to-hand contest. The end, however, was inevitable. After almost two hours of the fiercest fighting of the 10-month siege Fort Gregg fell to Gibbon's forces. The cost, however, had been very high. Of the 14,000 Union soldiers involved in the assault, 122 lay dead, and almost 600 more were wounded. Of the 214 members of the Confederate garrison, 55 were dead and 129 wounded. Only 30 Confederate soldiers survived the battle uninjured.

Heavy though the cost had been, the defenders of Fort Gregg had achieved their objective: they had bought General Lee the time he needed. That evening the Confederate army was able to make an orderly retreat westward along the long road to Appomattox Court House.

This concludes your tour of the Petersburg National Battlefield. From here you can either turn right and return to the Visitor Center or you can follow the Park Service signs to the site of the Battle of Five Forks, about 10 miles away to the west.

What to See, Where to Stay

What to See

The Siege Museum. 15 W. Bank Street. A Greek-revival building housing exhibits that describe the Siege of Petersburg, including a film, *"The Echoes Still Remain."* Open daily, but closed Thanksgiving and December 24th-25th. Telephone 804-733-2404.

The Center Hill Mansion. Center Hill Court. A circa 1823, Federal style mansion visited by Presidents Tyler, Lincoln and Taft. Fine carvings and antique furniture. Open daily, but closed Thanksgiving, December 24th, 25th, and January 1st. Telephone 804-733-2401.

Lee Memorial Park. South part of town, off Johnston Road. 864-acre park with a fishing lake, ball fields, courts, and picnic areas. Open daily, but closed from mid-October through mid-April. Telephone 804-733-2394.

Hotels

Best Western. 405 E. Washington Street, Petersburg, VA 23804. Telephone 804-733-1776. Crib free, cable TV, pool, cafe, bar, meeting room, valet service, airport transportation, accepts credit cards.

Comfort Inn. 12001 S. Crater Road, Petersburg, VA 23805. Telephone 804-732-2000. Children under 18 stay free, crib free, cable TV, in-room movies, free continental breakfast, pool, cafe, bar, meeting room, accepts credit cards.

Days Inn. 12208 S. Crater Road, Petersburg, VA 23805. Telephone 804-733-4400. Crib free, cable TV, pool, playground, cafe, meeting room, accepts credit cards.

Quality Inn-Steven Kent. I-95, Exit 45. Telephone 804-733-0600. Children under 16 stay free, crib free, cable TV, pool, cafe, bar, accepts credit cards.

The High Street Inn. 405 High Street, Petersburg, VA 23803. Telephone 804-733-0505. An 1890s Queen Ann mansion in the historic district. Five rooms, antiques, free continental breakfast, complimentary afternoon tea, movies, accepts credit cards.

Where to Eat

Alexander's. 101 W. Bank Street, Petersburg, VA. Telephone 804-733-7134. Hours: 9 a.m. to 8:30 p.m. Closed Sundays, Thanksgiving, December 25th, and January 1st. Italian, Greek, and American menu. Wine & beer. Semi-à la carte. Specialties are veal à la Greca, souvlaki, and Athenian chicken. Parking available. NO CREDIT CARDS ACCEPTED.

Chapter 13

Lee's Retreat

From Petersburg to Appomattox Court House

April 3rd-12th, 1865

The Appomattox Court House National Historic Park is in south central Virginia 92 miles west of Richmond and 18 miles east of Lynchburg on VA Highway 24. The park is three miles northeast of the town of Appomattox, which is located on U.S. Highway 460.

After the fall of Petersburg and Richmond on April 2nd, 1865, General Robert E. Lee headed west toward Amelia Court House along the long road that would lead eventually to Appomattox Court House.

The divisions under the commands of Generals Pickett and Heth, along with Lieutenant General Anderson's Corps (of which only Bushrod Johnson's division remained), and most of Lee's cavalry corps were cut off from Lee after the Battle of Five Forks. They would have to cross the Appomattox River at Bevill's Bridge several miles to the west in order to eventually join with General Lee at Amelia Court House.

General A.P. Hill's men joined with General Longstreet's Corps, crossed the Appomattox, and then they too headed west. Major General John Gordon's Second Corps followed on behind, acting as the Confederate rear guard. General Mahone abandoned his position in front of the Army of the James at Bermuda Hundred and followed Lee. General Ewell's two Confederate divisions left Richmond later that evening, the 2nd of April, and they too headed west toward Amelia Court House, leaving the Confederate capital to its Federal conquerors. As Lee said, it was a sad business.

By the evening of April 3rd, things must have seemed a little brighter for Lee and his officers. Amelia Court House and fresh

General Robert E. Lee.

supplies were not far away. Henry Heth with his division had managed to cross the river and join up with the main body of the retreating Confederate army. General Anderson was close to Bevill's Bridge and had been joined by General Pickett. By nightfall General Longstreet and his corps, after a march of more than 25 miles, had reached Goode's Bridge on the Appomattox and had already transferred two divisions under the command of Generals Field and Wilcox across the river. Longstreet held Goode's Bridge until General Gordon was able to make the crossing, and then Gordon, in turn, held it until General Mahone arrived. Mahone, taking his turn, would hold the bridge for General Ewell. Lee's retreat from Petersburg and Richmond was turning into a successful and coordinated withdrawal.

On the morning of April 3rd, General Grant gave orders to General Weitzel to invest Richmond, and then waited to confer with President Lincoln later that day. In the meantime he sent General Meade with three army corps, the II, V, and VI, westward after General Sheridan in pursuit of General Lee.

By 8 o'clock on the morning of April 4th, General Lee had joined with Longstreet and the two generals arrived at Amelia Court House with their advance guard by 8:30. Soon, with units of his army arriving from all directions, Lee's force numbered more than 30,000 men, and they were all hungry. Unfortunately, by some quirk of communications, the 350,000 rations Lee had ordered and was expecting to find waiting for him at Amelia Court House had gone astray. Once again his army was in trouble.

Lee sent an urgent message to Danville requesting that 200,000 rations be shipped to him immediately. In the meantime, he sent his men off into the countryside to forage for whatever food they could find. It was a sad day for the Army of Northern Virginia. Most of the men had given their all, and this final blow was too

General-in-Chief of Armies of the United States, U.S. Grant.

much for many of them to handle; soon they were deserting in ever-increasing numbers. Most of Lee's men, however, had grown used to the constant setbacks that had beset them for more than a year and accepted the new situation with good grace. As always, a loud hurrah went up whenever the gentle commander of the once-great Confederate army rode by.

All through the night of April 4th, Lee and his men waited for the foraging wagons to return. It was a miserable time, desperately cold as the rain and the wind blew through the Confederate camp. The lights in Lee's tent burned into the early hours of the morning of April 5th as he and his generals examined the situation and tried to decide what to do next.

The wagons returned, bringing little with them. The land that had been so good to the Confederate cause had, at last, nothing left to give. Lee's last hope now was that supplies would arrive soon from Danville. And it was still raining when General Mahone and his men marched into Amelia Court House later that morning.

As soon as Mahone arrived, he made his way straight to General Lee to report and was amazed to find Lee in full dress uniform, including his golden spurs and famous "Maryland Sword." It seemed to Mahone that Lee had perhaps had some sort of premonition of death or disaster and that he wanted to be found at his very best: *"He was wearing all his best clothes. It impressed me that he anticipated some accident to himself and desired to be found in that dress."* Could it really have been that Lee already knew the end was at hand? Maybe, but if so he never admitted it.

There was nothing for Lee to do now but to head southwest along the Richmond & Danville Railroad tracks. So, everything that could be was loaded onto the wagons, what little was left was burned, and then the long column moved out from Amelia Court

House. General Longstreet's Corps led the way, followed by General Mahone, then General Anderson, General Ewell, General Custis Lee, and General Kershaw. General Gordon, once again, brought up the rear. In order that the army might make the best possible time, the wagons were ordered to move south toward Danville by a separate, parallel road.

While the men marched, Lee and Longstreet stayed behind at Amelia Court House gathering intelligence. It wasn't long before they received news that the wagons had been attacked by Federal cavalry, and already the sounds of fighting could be heard in the distance. So, shortly after 1 o'clock that afternoon, Lee and Longstreet rode south to assess the situation for themselves. Eight miles south of Amelia Court House at Jetersville, they found General Sheridan's dismounted cavalry in line of battle blocking the route south, and they also knew that the main body of the Federal army was fast approaching from the rear.

Lee now knew that, unless he could force his way through the enemy lines, his army would be unable to reach either Danville and his supplies or General Johnston. He was left with only two possible options: he could either fight here, further taxing his tired and starving army, or he could take the only other route open to him and march 15 miles west to Farmville, rejoin the South Side Railroad there, march south along the tracks, and join Johnston south of the Roanoke River. After a long consultation with General Mahone – his troops were relatively fresh and would lead the fight if that was the decision – Lee decided to spare his army and march to Farmville. The decision made, he sent couriers to request that supplies for his army be sent from Lynchburg to Farmville with all speed.

The situation for the retreating Confederate army was rapidly deteriorating. With his lead on General Grant's pursuing army now reduced to only a matter of hours, Lee knew he had to make use of every minute of the waning daylight; he would have to march his army onward through the dusk and well into the night. General Mahone took the lead followed by General Field, then the remnants of Wilcox's and Heth's divisions, then Anderson and Ewell, and finally General Gordon. Forced to march on the same road as the wagons, the distressed Confederates stumbled along in the dark. Many lost their heads and retreated into the relative safety of insanity. Men panicked and fired at shadows – even at each other. The march to Farmville was a nightmare.

Maj. Richard S. Ewell.

When General Mahone reached the bridge over Flat Creek he found it had collapsed and further time was lost while the army had to wait until Mahone's engineers repaired it. Mahone waited alone in a nearby farm house. When the work was complete, Colonel Charles Marshall of General Lee's staff, more than a little under the weather from drinking pine top whiskey, and without consulting Mahone, gave orders for Mahone's lead brigade under the command of Brigadier General Nathaniel Harris to resume the march. Mahone, under terrible stress and suffering from the horrors of the night march, lost his temper and informed Lee that if ever again Marshall interfered with his command, Lee would be short one staff officer.

The night march to Farmville, now turned into a race for life or death, took its toll, and there's no doubt it hastened the end for the Army of Northern Virginia. Mahone gathered together his disorganized brigades and resumed the march; General Gordon at the rear also maintained good order. Unfortunately, Anderson and Ewell at the center of the column were not doing quite so well. They struggled onward, straggling along in the dark, trying to keep up. The next day, the 6th of April, they would have to cross Sayler's Creek.

On the Federal side, things were going much better. By the afternoon of April 4th, General Sheridan's cavalry, along with elements of the V Army Corps, had cut the road to Burkville and Lee's route to the south. The following afternoon, the 5th, General Meade arrived in the field with the II and VI Corps. Later that evening, Grant, several miles away to the rear, and after hearing that Meade was unwell, set out to join the main body of the army. Meade, with Grant's approval, had planned to attack the Confederate army at Amelia Court House on the morning of the 6th, while General

Maj. General Philip Sheridan.

Sherman would take his cavalry and move to Farmville, should Lee decide to go in that direction. On the morning of the 6th of April, however, when Meade arrived at Amelia Court House, he found that Lee had already gone.

In the meantime, after the last elements of his army had crossed Flat Creek, Lee ordered the bridge destroyed and his army moved slowly onward through Deatonville and along the road toward Rice's Station some 12 miles away. Once at Rice's Station, Lee knew they would be within two hours of Farmville and the 80,000 rations already waiting for them there. But they had to get there. Sheridan's Federal cavalry was harassing his army left and right and, time and again, they had to deal with lightning attacks against the rear and center of the column; it was heavy going for the exhausted Confederate troops.

Shortly after mid-day, General Longstreet, now in the lead, crossed Sayler's Creek and moved on toward Rice's Station. General Mahone followed soon after Longstreet. Then came word that Federal cavalry was ahead of them and moving on Farmville. Longstreet sent Fitzhugh Lee with a section of the Confederate cavalry to stop them and then turned his own corps to face an enemy force reported to be approaching from the south.

By this time, however, Lee had other and more pressing problems. A gap had opened in the Confederate column between Mahone and Anderson. General Ewell had ordered his own and Anderson's corps to halt while the wagons moved past, and he did it without informing Lee. Thus Mahone moved on ahead without being aware of the gap opening up behind him. General Sheridan, as always, was ready and waiting to take advantage of just such an opportunity.

Maj. General John. B. Gordon, commanding the Confederate rearguard from Petersburg, became separated from the main body of the army at Holt's Corner.

Sheridan, tired of harrying the Confederate rear guard under General Gordon without success, had moved the main body of his cavalry northward and had already crossed Sayler's Creek when he saw the unprotected Confederate wagons moving ahead of Ewell and Anderson toward Rice's Station. Ewell's order to halt the column was about to have disastrous results for the Confederate army.

Like a tiger, Sheridan pounced on the unprotected wagon train. Two divisions under the command of Generals George Crook and Wesley Merritt were sent in to attack the wagons; it was over in a matter of minutes. Hundreds of wagons were destroyed or captured. Sixteen guns fell into Federal hands and dozens of prisoners were taken. Best of all, Sheridan now had two divisions in line of battle astride the Confederate route northward, isolating Lee, Mahone and Longstreet from the rest of the army. What happened next can only be described as a fiasco.

General Anderson, finding Federal General Crook blocking the route, halted his column and waited for orders. Almost at the same moment he received an urgent message from General Gordon at the rear of the column saying that he was being attacked and that the advance must continue. So, without further orders, one of Anderson's brigades attacked General Crook's positions and, at first, had some success. Unfortunately, there was no one there to back them up and they were forced to fall back. In the meantime, in an effort to save what few wagons remained, General Ewell ordered them to take a side road to avoid the Federal cavalry ahead. It was an astute move, but unfortunately, just as he forgot to tell Mahone that he was halting the column, Ewell forgot to inform General Gordon that he was redirecting the wagons. General Gordon, who had been following the wagons ever since the march to Farmville had begun, continued to do so. Ewell and Anderson were completely isolated.

Realizing what had happened, and now fully aware of their potentially deadly predicament, Ewell and Anderson couldn't immediately decide upon what to do next. They could either attack the Federal positions held by Crook and Merritt, already being reinforced by more cavalry divisions, or they could move off to their right and north in the hopes that they might hit the same road that General Gordon was traveling, still unaware of the desperate situation building behind him. Ewell preferred to move out across country. Had they done so, that would probably have saved them. Anderson, however, confused and close to panic, could think only of attack. The Battle of Sayler's Creek was about to begin.

Sayler's Creek was not the best place to engage in an offensive action. The two Confederate generals were trapped on the south side of Little Sayler's Creek with several hundred yards of heavy timber in front of them. Beyond that was Sayler's Creek itself. The ground all around was covered in dense woodlands with odd clearings only two or three hundred yards wide dotted here and there. To the north of Sayler's Creek there was a low ridge that ran past the Hillsman House and back to the road where Gordon had followed the wagons. Ewell and Anderson had only 7,000 men and no artillery with which to face Sheridan and his divisions now in position between the two creeks.

General Anderson ordered his men to attack Sheridan's positions and Ewell gave orders for his men to come up in support. As he did so he received an urgent message from the rear that General Wright and the Federal VI Corps was at his rear, where General Gordon should have been, and was preparing to attack. While General Ewell made preparations to face Wright, Anderson's brigades moved forward toward Sheridan. The men, however, had all but reached the end of their endurance. Disheartened, dejected, totally exhausted, and knowing that they had just been ordered to almost certain death, they were able only to make what Anderson called "*a feeble effort.*" Soon they were falling back, surrendering, or simply sitting down where they were, waiting for the inevitable. But one brigade, that of Brigadier General Henry Wise, fought like tigers, managed to break out, then reached the road beyond the Federal cavalry and the relative safety of the main body of Lee's army at Rice's Station. The rest of what was left of Anderson's force took cover behind hastily erected breastworks and prepared to face Sheridan's counter attack.

Meanwhile, General Ewell was preparing to do battle with General Wright. He had taken up a strong position on the crest of the ridge some 300 yards back from Little Sayler's Creek. He placed Custis Lee on his left and General Kershaw with three brigades on his right. Across the creek, near the Hillsman House, General Wright was in position with two full divisions of infantry. Wright, knowing he had all the time in the world, brought forward his artillery, put them into battery around the Hillsman House, and ordered them to open fire on Ewell's position. Ewell, without artillery of his own, could do little else but endure the bombardment. Then, thinking that Wright had committed to driving him off the crest of the ridge with his artillery, and that nothing was likely to happen at his front anytime soon, Ewell rode to the rear to find out what was happening to Anderson. No sooner had he done so than Wright launched his attack against the Confederate positions on the ridge. The Confederates, though confused and disheartened, stood firm. On the Federal infantry rushed, up the hill toward the Confederate line of battle. Everyone knew it was the end. The Confederate units, torn apart by barrage after barrage of case-shot and shell, returned fire as best they could, and still the Federal infantry rushed on. As the Federal line came to within a hundred yards of Custis Lee's position the Union officers waved white handkerchiefs and called for surrender. The answer was a devastating volley of musket fire right into their faces. They staggered and fell back a yard or two. The Confederates, thinking they had broken the Federal attack, abandoned their positions and, with a great yell, rushed the Federal line. From there, the battle deteriorated into a blood bath.

As soon as the Confederate ranks came out into the open the Federal artillery began to cut them to pieces. Confederate Major Robert Stiles described it later as follows: "*Quicker than I can tell it, the battle degenerated into a butchery and a confused melee of brutal personal conflicts.*" The fighting reached almost insane proportions. Bayonets flashed silver and then red; rifle butts smashed faces and then were either dropped or thrown down as the demented Confederate soldiers resorted to fists, feet and teeth, biting, kicking and scratching like demons until, at last, surrounded and outnumbered, they surrendered.

Confederate General Kershaw's three brigades fought on until, at last, he too was forced to surrender. The Battle of Sayler's Creek, the last great battle the Army of Northern Virginia would ever fight, were over. Lieutenant General Richard Ewell, along with seven other Confederate generals and more than 6,000 Confederate soldiers, were captured. Generals Anderson, Pickett, and Bushrod Johnson all managed to escape and ride to Rice's Station. General Gordon also was attacked as he tried to cross Sayler's Creek near the Lockett House. He lost another 1,700 men.

Maj. General George Pickett.

As all this was happening, General Lee at Rice's Station had little idea of what was going on. On hearing that his wagon train had been captured, and realizing that something had gone badly wrong, however, he and General Mahone and a full division of infantry rode back toward Sayler's Creek. As the two commanders crested a ridge overlooking the battlefield, Lee and Mahone were able to see the full extent of the disaster that had befallen Generals Ewell and Anderson. Some time later Mahone wrote that, "*Here the scene beggars description.*" Lee himself said as he looked down upon the chaos at Sayler's Creek, "*My god has this army dissolved?*" to which Mahone replied, "*No, General, here is a division ready to do its duty.*"

Lee nodded and said, "*Yes, General, there are some true men left.*" And then he said wearily, "*Keep those people back.*" He was referring to the Federals already making movement in the direction of Rice's Station. Mahone deployed his division in line of battle ready to do as his general had asked, but night was almost upon them and it was already too late in the day for further fighting.

As night began to fall, the remains of Ewell's and Anderson's fleeing divisions came streaming past the two watching generals. Then Anderson himself arrived. Lee refused even to look at him. He simply jerked his thumb toward the rear, told him to take charge of the stragglers, and get them out of there. Later, at Rice's Station, thoroughly disgusted by the whole shabby affair, Lee relieved him, along with Generals Pickett and Bushrod Johnson of their commands and told them to go home. Three fine careers, especially those of Pickett and Johnson, had gone down the drain in a matter of hours.

Lee, of course, now had serious problems. He still had to reach Farmville and his precious supplies of food, and that meant crossing the Appomattox. He ordered General Longstreet to take his corps and cross at Farmville, General Mahone was to go to High Bridge, follow General Gordon across the river there, and then burn the structure once he and his men were safely across. Longstreet made it across the river early the next morning, April 7th, and marched into Farmville where food was waiting; it was the first his men had seen in more than five days. General Gordon arrived soon after, followed by General Mahone.

And still things continued to go wrong. As Lee's men were receiving their rations, word came in that the Federals were crossing the river at High Bridge. Obviously Mahone had not done a proper job of destroying it. Lee, wondering what in the world he had done to deserve this long string of disasters, was furious. With the wolves once again at his heels, it was already time to move on again. And, even before all of his men could be fed, he had to send the rail cars back to Lynchburg. It was devastating. All he could hope for was that he might meet them again further on down the line. The next stop on the journey west was Cumberland Church.

At Cumberland Church Lee's men clashed with elements of General Humphrey's II Corps, and then moved on again to New Store, still heading west. Meanwhile Grant and General Wright's corps had arrived in Farmville. Without waiting for a moment, he ordered Meade and Wright to set of after Lee. Generals Ord, Gibbon and Sheridan were to move in a more southerly direction in the hopes that they might head Lee off. The next day, however, Sheridan learned that a trainload of rations was waiting for Lee at Appomattox Station some 22 miles to the west; Sheridan decided he would get there first.

Later that afternoon Grant received news from General Sheridan that Lee's provisions had arrived at Appomattox by rail and that he expected to capture them before Lee could reach them. Grant was, by now, firmly convinced that the end was only a matter of days away and was determined to do what he could to avoid a continued and needless loss of life. So, in the early evening of April 7th, 1865, he sent the following communication to General Lee.

Headquarters, Armies of the U.S.
5 p.m., April 7th, 1865
General R.E. Lee, Commanding C.S.A.:
The results of last week must convince you of the hopelessness of further resistance on the part of the Army of Northern Virginia in this struggle. I feel that it is so, and regard it as my duty to shift from myself the responsibility of any further effusion of blood by asking of you the surrender of that portion of the Confederate States army known as the Army of Northern Virginia.
U.S. Grant, Lieutenant-General

Lee received Grant's communication late that evening, just as he was about to retire. It may have been that Grant's letter brought some relief; if so he didn't show it. Instead he showed the letter to General Longstreet, who shook his head and said, "*Not yet!*" Lee agreed but, still wanting to keep the lines of communication open, he replied to Grant's letter as follows:

April 7th, 1865
General: I have received your note of this date. Though not entertaining the opinion you express of the hopelessness of further resistance on the part of the Army of Northern Virginia, I reciprocate your desire to avoid useless effusion of blood, and therefore, before considering your proposition, ask the terms you will offer on the condition of its surrender.
R.E. Lee, General
Lieutenant-General U.S. Grant, Commanding Armies of the U.S.

Meanwhile, the Confederate army marched westward, on through the night, with Longstreet's Corps leading. As dawn broke the next morning, the 8th, the sun came up and warmed the weary soldiers; and, even as most men in the ranks were well aware of what was developing between Lee and Grant, spirits began to rise again. During the morning General William Pendleton, a man who was often mistaken for Lee, representing corps commanders Mahone, Gordon, and Anderson, as well as several other generals, approached Lee and suggested that perhaps it was time to capitulate. Lee, however, told Pendleton in no uncertain terms that it was not. By nightfall, however, he had received the following note from General Grant:

Sheridan and his staff, 1865. Left to right: Wesley Merritt, David McM. Gress, Sheridan, Henry Davis (standing), James H. Wilson, Alfred Torbert.

April 8th, 1865
General R.E. Lee, Commanding C.S.A.:
Your note of last evening in reply to mine of the same date, asking the conditions on which I will accept the surrender of the Army of Northern Virginia, is just received. In reply I would say that, peace being my great desire, there is but one condition I would insist upon – namely, that the men and officers surrendered shall be disqualified for taking up arms against the Government of the United States until properly exchanged. I will meet you, or designate officers to meet any officers you may name for the same purpose, at any point agreeable to you, for the purpose of arranging definitely the terms upon which the surrender of the Army of Northern Virginia will be received.
U.S. Grant, Lieutenant-General

To which Lee immediately replied:

April 8th, 1865
General: I received at a late hour your note of to-day. In mine of yesterday I did not intend to propose the surrender of the Army of Northern Virginia, but to ask the terms of your proposal. To be frank, I do not think the emergency has arisen to call for the surrender of this army, but, as the restoration of peace should be the sole object of all, I desired to know if your

proposals would lead to that end. I cannot, therefore, meet you with a view to surrender the Army of Northern Virginia; but as far as your proposal may effect the Confederate States forces under my command, and tend to the restoration of peace, I should be pleased to meet you at 10 A.M. to-morrow on the old stage road to Richmond, between the picket lines of the two armies.
R.E. Lee, General
Lieutenant-General U.S. Grant

It was not what Grant wanted to hear and, because of the terms of the note, he decided not to meet with Lee that morning and sent Lee a note saying as much.

Lee did not, however, receive Grant's note until early the following morning, almost at the same time as he received the news that he had lost the race. General Sheridan was at Appomattox Station, had captured Lee's supplies and rations, and was now blocking the Confederate route south to North Carolina and General Johnston; and with two Federal corps snapping at his heels, Lee and the Army of Northern Virginia was trapped. In a desperate, last ditch attempt to break out, Lee sent his son, Fitzhugh Lee, with his cavalry and General Gordon's infantry to try and drive Sheridan out of the way. It was no good. Sheridan held and the last hopes for escape were gone. Lee, now knowing that surrender was inevitable, put on his dress uniform and made ready, saying, *"I have probably to be General Grant's prisoner, I must make my best appearance."* Lee decided then to talk once more with Generals Longstreet and Mahone; both urged him to surrender. Lee shook his head in sorrow and said, *"Then there is nothing left for me to do but to go and see General Grant, and I would rather die a thousand deaths."* It was a sad time for all concerned.

At 8:30 that morning, Lee mounted his horse, Traveller, and with Colonel Marshall and Sergeant G.W. Tucker rode to the rear toward the appointed place. Lee, however, had forgotten to send out orders to fly flags of truce, thus establishing a cease-fire. The sounds of General Gordon's guns in the vicinity of the Station, however, reminded him and orders were given at once. Minutes later, Federal Colonel Charles Whittier arrived under flag of truce with Grant's note refusing the meeting. Lee sent him back to Grant with a note telling him that he was now prepared to discuss the surrender of the Army of Northern Virginia, and requesting that they meet as soon as possible.

As Lee waited for Grant's reply, Colonel Whittier returned again with news for General Longstreet that his General, Humphrey, was under orders to attack him, that he could not find General Grant to authorize a change in the orders, and that he therefore had no alternative but to attack Longstreet. Humphrey, however, also wanted to avoid further bloodshed and offered Longstreet an astounding proposal. It was suggested that as Humphrey's brigades slowly advanced, so those of Longstreet would fall slowly back before him. And so the final dance began. Colonel Whittier arrived back in front of Lee at noon with a letter from Grant agreeing to meet. Thus it was that Lee finally rode out to meet his destiny at the tiny village of Appomattox Court House.

The place chosen for the meeting provided one of the last, and perhaps one of the most amazing coincidences of the war: the house chosen for the historic meeting between the two generals belonged to one Wilmer McLean. In June of 1861, before the war had begun, McLean was living on a small plantation near Manassas Junction. At that time he was a staunch Confederate and, before the Battle of 1st Manassas, had helped General Beauregard survey the area in anticipation of the hostilities that

The McLean House, where Lee and Grant met.

were sure to come. McClean's house at Manassas became Beauregard's field headquarters and, on July 17th, three shots from a Federal battery were fired at the house. only one of which did any real damage; those three shots were the first fired between the two major armies. And now the wheel had turned full circle. Once again McClean's home, now at Appomattox, would play an important role in American history. This time the war in the East would end within its walls.

When the two generals met in the parlor of the McLean House, the atmosphere was at first somewhat stiff. Neither man knew what to say to the other. Grant opened the conversation with some small talk, to which Lee replied and then, obviously uncomfortable, asked Grant what terms he would offer for the surrender of his army. Grant replied that all he asked was that Lee lay down his arms and not pick them up again until and unless properly exchanged, and that all arms and supplies were to be surrendered along with the army.

Lee nodded and, relieved at Grant's obvious generosity, accepted the terms as laid out and suggested that Grant write out a formal letter of proposal. Grant called for his order book and, with a great deal of thought, began to write. He had all but finished the letter when he glanced up at Lee, observed that he was wearing his famed Maryland sword, and then added another sentence: *"This will not embrace the side arms of the officers, nor their private horses or baggage."* He added a further sentence promising that Lee's men would not be molested by the Federal Government so long as they held to the terms of their paroles, and then he signed it, *"Very respectfully."*

When the letter was finished he handed it to Lee, who read it and, with Grant's permission, corrected an error, and then said, *"This will have a very happy effect on my army."* Even so, and as generous as the terms were, Lee still felt he had one more request to make. He informed Grant that, in his army, his men owned their own horses, and that they would need them to work their farms when they returned home. And then he asked Grant if they might take them home with them. Grant observed that the terms of his letter did not allow for such a request, but that he saw no reason why Lee's men should not keep their horses. Lee nodded gratefully, and than told Grant that he had not enough food to feed his men. Grant asked if 25,000 rations would be enough. Lee said that they would, and orders were given for food to be sent immediately to Lee's men. The alterations were made to the letter of surrender, Lee signed it, and with his signature the Army of Northern Virginia was officially surrendered.

Lee, accompanied by Colonel Marshall and Sergeant G.W. Tucker, rode back to his men in deep depression. As he reached his lines his men ran forward, some with tears in their eyes, and reached up to touch his hand. By the morning of April 12th the terms of surrender had almost all been carried out, the paroling was complete. Only the formal surrender of the army remained. Grant, also depressed, was unwilling to watch the final hours of this once-great army and he returned to Washington, leaving General Joshua Chamberlain to receive the formal surrender. That morning Chamberlain formed his command on either side of the road, and the rag-tag Confederate Army of Northern Virginia, battle flags flying, marched forward. Chamberlain ordered his men to attention, and then, as the defeated army marched past, to the salute. Confederate General Gordon, leading the parade on horseback, turned in the saddle to face Chamberlain, dropped the tip of his sword to touch the toe of his boot in return salute and called for his marching men to do the same. It was a poignant moment – two great armies honoring each other, and then it was over. The Confederate arms were stacked, the battle flags torn to shreds by their bearers, unable to part with them, and divided among the men as mementos. Then, sadly, the defeated army went home.

The war continued on for only a short time longer. General Joseph Johnston surrendered his army to General Sherman on April 26th. Lieutenant General Richard Taylor surrendered the Department of Alabama, Mississippi, and East Louisiana to Major General E.R.S. Canby on May 4th. Simon Bolivar Buckner surrendered Lieutenant General E. Kirby Smith's Trans-Mississippi Department in New Orleans on May 26th, and, finally, Cherokee Brigadier General Stand Watie surrendered his regiments of Indians to Lieutenant Colonel Asa C. Matthews on June 23rd. The American Civil War was at an end. More than 620,000 Americans had given their lives for one cause or the other, and the face of the nation had changed forever.

The Road to Appomattox

If you decide to take the driving tour along the route of General Lee's retreat from Petersburg to Appomattox Court House you should make plans to start early in the morning and expect to spend most of the day on the road. The tour is well marked and features many interesting and informative stops along the way, culminating with a visit to the Appomattox Court House National Historic Park. Tune your radio to AM 1610 and turn it on as you reach each stop along the way for a broadcast of an interpretive message that describes the action that took place there.

Leave Petersburg on Route 460 and drive to Stop 1 at Sutherland.

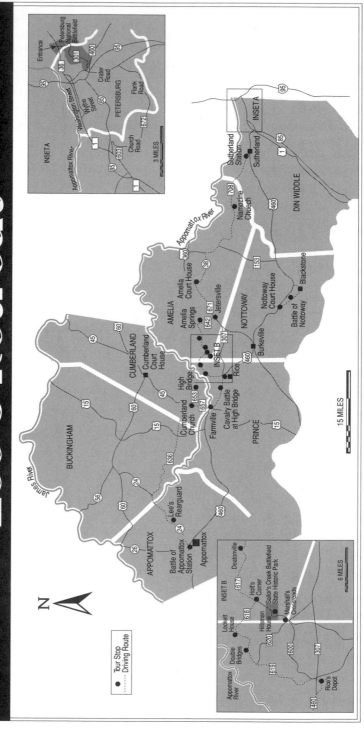

Lee's Retreat

N

● Tour Stop
⋯⋯⋯ Driving Route

INSET A

Petersburg National Battlefield
Entrance
301
460
95
Crater Road
PETERSBURG
Flank Road
Appomattox River
Washington Street
Wythe Street
85
672
603
Church Road
85
1
1
3 MILES

95
85
DINWIDDLE
Sutherland Station
Sutherland
1
708
460
Namozine Church
Blackstone
153
Nottoway Court House
Battle of Nottoway
NOTTOWAY
Burkeville
460
Appomattox River
360
38
AMELIA
Amelia Court House
Jetersville
Amelia Springs
671
642
307
INSET B
Rice
CUMBERLAND
Cumberland Court House
45
60
High Bridge
45
653
657
Cumberland Church
Farmville
Cavalry Battle at High Bridge
15
PRINCE
636
BUCKINGHAM
15
James River
24
60
56
Lee's Rearguard
26
24
APPOMATTOX
Battle of Appomattox Station
Appomattox
460
15

15 MILES

INSET B

Deatonville
617
Holt's Corner
618
Hillsman House
Sailor's Creek Battlefield State Historic Park
620
Marshall's Crossroads
600
307
Lockett House
Double Bridges
619
460
Rice's Depot
Appomattox River
6 MILES

Stop 1: Sutherland Station

The engagement here on April 2nd, 1865, enabled General Grant's forces to sever the South Side Railroad, thus depriving Lee of his last line of supply into Petersburg.

Stop 2: Namozine Church

From Sutherland Station take Route 708 and drive about 10 miles to Namozine Church where, on April 3rd, a rearguard cavalry skirmish took place as Lee's army marched toward Amelia Court House.

Stop 3: Amelia Court House

From Namozine Church continue on along Route 708 for about eight miles to the junction of Highway 153, turn right and go about three miles to the junction of Highway 30, turn left and continue on to Stop 3 at Amelia Court House.

It was here, as you will remember, that General Lee camped on the evening of April 4th with his entire army. His plan was to skirt the Federal army, turn southward, and eventually join his Army of Northern Virginia with that of General Joseph Johnston somewhere in the Carolinas. From Amelia Court House, on the evening of April 5th, Lee turned and marched southwest along the railroad tracks toward Danville on the Virginia/North Carolina border, where he hoped supplies would be waiting for him.

Maj. General Bushrod R. Johnson.

Stop 4: Jetersville

From Amelia Court House, take Route 360 southwest and drive about eight miles.

Lee's intention was to march his army along what is now modern Route 360 to Danville. Eight miles south of Amelia Court House at Jetersville, however, they found General Sheridan's dismounted cavalry in line of battle blocking the route. Lee also knew that the Federal infantry was in hot pursuit and approaching fast. He now had only two alternatives: he could force his way through Sheridan's cavalry, or he could take the only other route open to him and march some 15 miles west to Farmville, rejoin the South Side Railroad there, march south along the tracks, and join Johnston south of the Roanoke River. He chose Farmville and sent a message to Lynchburg urgently requesting that supplies be sent to him there.

Stop 5: Amelia Springs

From Jetersville take Route 642 and drive for about two and a half miles to Stop 5.

The Union army made contact with the Confederate rearguard here at Amelia Springs on the morning of April 6th.

Stop 6: Deatonville

From Amelia Springs turn right onto Route 617 and drive for about three miles to Stop 6.

During the morning of April 6th, the Confederate army moved slowly from Amelia Springs, across Flat Creek, and on toward Rice's Station some 12 miles away. After crossing the creek the army moved slowly on through Deatonville, where you are now and where they clashed briefly with elements of General Sheridan's cavalry.

Stop 7: Holt's Corner

From Deatonville, continue on along Route 617 to Stop 7 at Holt's Corner.

You will recall that General Ewell ordered the Confederate wagons to take a side road to avoid the Federal cavalry ahead, and that he neglected to inform General Gordon. General Gordon, who had been following the wagons, continued doing so, leaving Ewell and Anderson isolated and at the mercy of the Union Army. Holt's Corner is the point at which the Confederate wagons, followed by

General Gordon, turned west, leaving Anderson and Ewell to continue on along the route to Sayler's Creek.

Stop 8: Sailor's Creek Battlefield; The Hillsman House

From Holt's Corner continue on along the road for about a mile to Stop 8 at the Hillsman House on Sailor's Creek Battlefield.

Finding himself forced to deploy for battle, General Ewell took up a strong position on the crest of the ridge some three hundred yards back from Little Sayler's Creek. He placed General Custis Lee on his left and General Kershaw with three brigades on his right. Across the creek, near the Hillsman House, General Wright, with two full divisions, deployed his men and, in preparation for an attack on Ewell's positions, brought forward his artillery, put them into battery here around the Hillsman House and, at about 5:15 in the afternoon, ordered them to open fire. The battle ended in the defeat of Ewell's Corps and his capture, along with seven other Confederate generals. The Hillsman House was used as a hospital after the battle.

Stop Number 9: Marshall's Cross Roads

From the Hillsman House continue on along the road for about a mile to Stop 9 at Marshall's Cross Roads.

It was here, about a mile south of General Ewell's position on the ridge, that General Richard Anderson set up his defensive line and waited for the Federal Cavalry under the command of General Philip "Little Phil" Sheridan's assault. Anderson deployed two divisions under the commands of Generals Bushrod Johnson and George Pickett to the left and right facing south and west, just in front of the main road, and behind a hastily thrown up line of log breastworks. Sheridan's forces, under the overall command of General Wesley Merritt, formed a line of battle some 800 yards away to the south. Federal General George Crook's division was facing Bushrod Johnson, General Thomas Devin was at the center and to the rear of the Federal line, while General George A. Custer took the Federal right in front of Pickett. The ensuing battle was a decisive victory for the Federals and for Custer in particular, whose men captured no fewer than 31 Confederate battle banners. Confederate Generals Anderson, Pickett and Johnson managed to escape after the battle and reach the relative safety of the main body of the army at Rice's Station, where General Lee removed them from field command. The Battle of Sayler's Creek was a devastating defeat for General Lee and, no doubt, had a great deal to do with his decision to surrender the army only a few days later at Appomattox Court House.

Stop 10: The Lockett House

From Marshall's Crossroads, return along the road to the junction with Route 618 at Holt's Corner. Turn left onto 618 and drive for about three miles to Stop 10 at the Lockett House.

The fighting on the afternoon of April 6th spread to this position when General Gordon, following the redirected wagons, was attacked by units of General Andrew Humphrey's II Corps. The engagement was disastrous for Gordon. He lost 1,700 men, including his artillery commander, Lieutenant Wilfred E. Cutshaw, and a regimental brass band, 200 wagons, 70 ambulances, and 13 regimental battle flags. The Federals lost 550 of their number. After the battle, the Lockett House was used as a hospital.

Stop 11: The Double Bridges

From the Lockett House turn left onto Route 619 and proceed for about a mile and a half to Stop 11.

For the last few miles you have been following the route taken by the Confederate wagon train redirected from the main road to Rice's Station. General Gordon, you will recall, tailing along after the wagons, also turned off the main road at Holt's Corner. The Federals caught his column at the Lockett House and a desperate battle ensued with heavy losses for the Confederate column. After the fighting ended at the Lockett House, Gordon's column continued on along the road, crossed the creek here, and once again came under attack from the pursuing Federals.

Stop 12: Rice's Station

From Double Bridges continue on along Route 619 to the junction with Route 307. Turn right onto 307 and proceed a short distance to Stop 12.

Once at Rice's Station Lee's army was less than two hours march from Farmville and the supplies already waiting for them.

High Bridge, after repairs had been made to the first three spans, 1865.

Stop 13: High Bridge

From Rice's Station continue on along Route 307 for about three and a half miles to Stop 13.

Early on the morning of April 6th, Federal General Edward O.C. Ord of the Army of the James ordered a task force under the command of Lieutenant Colonel Horace Kellogg, along with two companies of cavalry under Colonel Frances Washburn, about 800 men in all, to burn the bridges across the Appomattox River near Farmville, thus cutting off General Lee's retreat in that direction.

General Longstreet, you will recall, was leading the long Confederate column toward Farmville. Sometime around mid-morning, Longstreet received word that Kellogg and Washburn were closing in on the great trestle bridge and immediately ordered his cavalry under Generals Thomas Rosser and Fitzhugh Lee to find and destroy them.

General Ord soon learned of Longstreet's move and sent General Theodore Read at full speed to warn the raiding party. Read arrived, took command of the small Federal force, and decided to continue on and complete the mission. Longstreet's cavalry, true to tradition, arrived on the scene in the nick of time, just before the destruction of the bridge could be completed. Heavy fighting broke out immediately and ended in defeat for the Federal raiders; all 800 men were captured, including six regimental flags and a brass band. Confederate losses were estimated at around 100 men killed and wounded.

Unfortunately, the main body of General Ord's Army of the James was rapidly approaching Rice's Station from Burkville with the express intention of cutting Lee's route to the south. General Longstreet deployed his corps in line of battle covering the roads to Rice's Station, and at right angles to the South Side Railroad. General Robert Foster with the 1st division of the Federal XXIV Corps discovered Longstreet's positions and he too went into line of battle. Sporadic fighting broke out in some places, but the main Federal assault on Longstreet's positions never came. Darkness fell over the battlefield and when Lee arrived at Rice's Station he ordered Longstreet to retreat toward Farmville.

During the night of April 6th the rest of the Federal Army of the James arrived and joined with General Foster's division; the Confederate army, however, was already on the move. General Longstreet ordered General Mahone and Gordon northward to High Bridge with orders to burn it, thus cutting off the pursuing Federals approaching in that direction. Mahone and Gordon crossed High Bridge in the early hours of the morning of the 7th and, just as the Federal forces began arriving, set fire to it. The tarred timbers of the trestle burned brightly in the darkness as the Confederate rearguard fought hard to prevent the Federals from saving the structure and did, in fact, manage to hold them off long enough for three spans to be completely destroyed and two more heavily damaged.

Stop 14: Farmville

From High Bridge, continue on along Route 307 for about four miles to Stop 14, the small tobacco town of Farmville.

Lee's army marched into Farmville on April 7th; the food waiting for them was still in the railroad cars in which it had arrived. It was the first his men had seen in more than five days. Unfortunately, many of them never received their rations. As Lee's men were lining up, word came in that the Federals were crossing the river at High Bridge. Lee had no alternative but to send the still loaded rail cars back to Lynchburg. The next stop on the journey west was Cumberland Church.

Stop 15: Cumberland Church

From Farmville, turn right onto Route 45 and drive about four more miles to Stop 15.

Lee reached Cumberland Church by mid-day on April 7th and once again prepared to do battle with units of Union General Humphrey's II Army Corps. Fighting in earnest began at 3 o'clock in the afternoon and lasted until dark. Thus Lee's army would once again be forced to march through the night. At about 9:30 that evening Lee received the first note from General Grant suggesting that the time had come for General Lee to surrender his army. After a short conference with General Longstreet, Lee decided that the time had not yet come and, sometime after 11 o'clock on the evening of March 7th, the Army of Northern Virginia began to move out of Cumberland Church, heading west toward Appomattox Court House.

Meanwhile, General Grant, along with General Wright's VI Corps and the Army of the James, had arrived in Farmville. Without waiting for a moment he ordered Meade and Wright to set off after Lee. Generals Ord, Gibbon and Sheridan were sent out in a more southerly direction.

Appomattox Court House National Historic Park

From Cumberland Church, continue on along Route 638 to the junction with Route 636. Turn left onto Route 636 and drive for about 18 miles to the junction with Route 24. Turn left onto 24 and drive for about eight more miles to the Appomattox Court House National Historic Park.

After the Civil War the tiny community of Appomattox Court-house became something of a backwater and was finally abandoned altogether in 1892. Appomattox Station, on the other hand, grew and became prosperous due to its position on the railroad. A group of Union veterans formed the Appomattox Land Company in the late 1880s to develop the area. Fortunately, however, their plans never came to fruition. Slowly but surely the little village deteriorated until in 1930 Congress passed a bill that provided for the building of a monument at the site of the old court house. The monument was never built, but the idea had been kindled and in

1934 it was suggested that the entire village be restored to its wartime condition. The idea was received with enthusiasm and a bill creating the National Historic Park was signed into law on August 3rd, 1935. The land was quickly acquired, but the project was interrupted by World War II. After the war work on the project began in earnest and the park was opened to the public and dedicated on April 6th, 1954.

The reconstructed village looks much the same today as it did in 1865. The old buildings, all lovingly restored, include the McLean House, where the surrender took place, Meeks' Store, the Woodson Law Office, the Clover Hill Tavern, the jail, the Kelly House, the Mariah Wright House, the Isbell House, the Peers House, and the Surrender Triangle where the Confederate regiments laid down their arms and furled their banners. Before you begin your tour of the village, it's a good idea to spend some time in the reconstructed Court House, now the Visitor Center, where you will find all sorts of interpretive exhibits, maps, photographs, and an audio-visual slide presentation. There's no established route to follow, so you can wander the village as much as you please. Take plenty of time and enjoy yourself.

Your visit to the park concludes your tour along the route of General Lee's retreat from Petersburg. Before you leave, however, you might like to visit the site of the Battle at Appomattox Station

Union soldiers pose outside Appomattox Court House, 1865.

Appomattox Court House

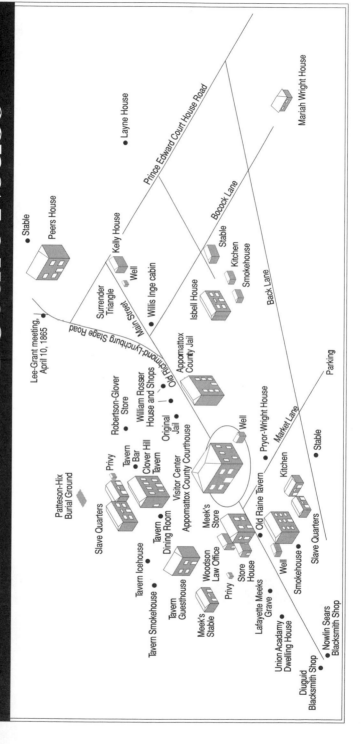

a few miles away in the modern city of Appomattox, where General Sheridan captured General Lee's supply trains, thus forcing Lee into the surrender he still didn't really want.

For more information, contact the Appomattox Court House National Historic Park, PO Box 218, Appomattox, VA 24522. Telephone 804-352-8987.

Additional Reading
from Hunter Publishing

BATTLEFIELDS OF THE CIVIL WAR 1:
A GUIDE FOR TRAVELLERS
$11.95, ISBN 1-55650-603-1, 310 pp

"For each battlefield, combat descriptions are keyed to a map, so that with book in hand you can pinpoint the action. Fortunately, Mr. Howard is no retailer of dry facts; his accounts of battle are fast-paced and riveting. He also gives information on accommodations, dining, and sightseeing in each area." Passport Newsletter.

This, the first book of the series, covers in depth the battles of 1st and 2nd Manassas, Shiloh, Antietam, Gettysburg, Vicksburg, Chicamauga, Ft. Donelson, Stones River, Fredericksburg, and Lookout Mountain. You will find here both the story of the battles themselves and a fieldguide to touring the battlefields today.

INSIDER'S GUIDE TO WESTERN CANADA
$15.95, ISBN 1-55650-580-9, 205pp

".... The lively, sometimes whimsical text makes reading a pleasure... major sites and attractions are intelligently discussed; there's an emphasis on fine arts and performing arts, and culture...." Travel Books Worldwide.

INSIDER'S GUIDE TO EASTERN CANADA
$15.95, ISBN 1-55650-581-7, 256pp

"... text and abundant photographs [are] so outstanding.... This would make a fine addition to most libraries." Library Journal.

Filled with history, tour information, local museums and galleries, where to shop, where to eat, these are the most complete guides to Canada in the bookstores. Superb color photos and maps complement the text. Complete accommodation information, from the most luxurious hotels to places for the traveller on a shoestring budget. As with all the books in this series, a free pull-out color map makes planning your days easy.

Among other guides in the Insider's Guide series:

FLORIDA $15.95, ISBN 1-55650-452-7, 256pp
HAWAII $15.95, ISBN 1-55650-495-0, 230pp
NEW ENGLAND $17.95, ISBN 1-55650-455-1, 256pp
MEXICO $18.95, ISBN 1-55650-454-3, 320pp
RUSSIA $17.95, ISBN 1-55650-558-2, 224pp
CALIFORNIA $14.95, ISBN 1-55650-163-3, 192pp
INDONESIA $15.95, ISBN 1-55650-453-5, 224pp
TURKEY $17.95, ISBN 1-55650-283-4, 209pp
INDIA $16.95, ISBN 1-55650-164-1, 360pp
NEW ZEALAND $15.95, ISBN 1-55650-624-4, 224pp
AUSTRALIA $15.95, ISBN 1-55650-653-8, 224 pp

BEST DIVES OF THE CARIBBEAN
$15.95, ISBN 1-55650-644-9, 342pp

A unique guidebook written by experienced divers and snorklers – Joyce and John Huber. Covering the most well-known islands such as Antigua and St. Maarten/St. Martin, and the more secluded ones like Anguilla and St. Eustatius. Sites are rated for visibility and outstanding marine life and every skill level is considered. In addition, this book tells you where to find the most diver-friendly resorts, the best restaurants, where to stay, and gives contacts for equipment rental and English-speaking tour operators. Color photos and maps throughout.

BEST DIVES OF THE WESTERN HEMISPHERE
$17.95, ISBN 1-55650-250-8, 320pp

"... for serious underwater enthusiasts who want to get in as much bottom time as possible... Best Dives is probably the only guidebook they'll need." Caribbean Travel & Life Magazine.

"... [Best Dives] opens a new world of discovery to anyone with a facemask and a desire to look beneath the water's surface." Pacific Stock, Hawaii.

Best-selling scuba and snorkelling guide to Florida, California, Hawaii, the Caribbean and Latin America. Over 200 sites listed. Color photos and maps throughout. Tips for handicapped divers, restaurant recommendations, money-saving tour packages, sightseeing. Dive in!

ADVENTURE GUIDE TO THE HIGH SOUTHWEST
$14.94, ISBN 1-55650-633-3, 384pp

"... a conscientious and beautifully written guide...."

Hiking, mountaineering, trail riding, cycling, camping, river running, ski touring, wilderness trips – a guide to enjoying the natural attractions of the Four Corners area of Northwest New Mexico, Southwest Colorado, Southern Utah, Northern Arizona, and the Navajo Nation and Hopiland. Includes all practical details on transportation, services, where to eat, where to stay and travel tips on how to cope with the harsh terrain and climate. The most adventurous guide to this region on the market. Maps.

ADVENTURE GUIDE TO THE ALASKA HIGHWAY
$15.95, ISBN 1-55650-457-8, 228pp

Everything you need to know about driving the highway, plus all the worthwhile sidetrips en route. This wonderfully written book also covers the Klondike Highway, Alaska Marine Highway and the Top-of-the-World Highway. Maps.

ADVENTURE GUIDE TO COASTAL ALASKA &
THE INSIDE PASSAGE
$14.95, ISBN 1-55650-583-3, 288pp

How to travel the coast of Alaska on the state's official Marine Highway. From Bellingham WA up to the Aleutians and Kodiak. Color photos and maps.

Among other guides in the Adventure Guide series:

COSTA RICA 2nd Ed. $15.95, ISBN 1-55650-598-1, 470pp
PUERTO RICO 2nd Ed. $14.95, ISBN 1-55650-628-7, 304pp
CANADA $15.95, ISBN 1-55650-315-6, 320pp
VIRGIN ISLANDS 3rd Ed. $14.95, ISBN 1-55650-597-3, 280pp
EVERGLADES & THE FLORIDA KEYS $14.95,
  ISBN 1-55650-494-2, 192pp
BAJA CALIFORNIA $11.95, ISBN 1-55650-590-6, 280pp
BELIZE 3rd Ed. $14.95, ISBN 1-55650-647-3, 288pp
DOMINICAN REPUBLIC $14.95, ISBN 1-55650-629-5, 250 pp

THE GREAT AMERICAN WILDERNESS: TOURING AMERICA'S NATIONAL PARKS
$11.95, ISBN 1-55650-567-1, 320pp

The 41 most scenic parks throughout the US including Acadia, the Great Smokey Mountains, Yellowstone, Hawaii Volcanoes, the Grand Canyon, Big Bend, the Everglades and many more. This tells you where to stay, where to eat, which roads are most crowded or most beautiful, how much time to allow, what you can safely skip and what you must not miss. Detailed maps of each park show all the surrounding access routes and special sections tell you how to make the most of your time if you only have a couple of hours.

CANADIAN ROCKIES ACCESS GUIDE 3rd Ed.
15.95, ISBN 0-91943-392-8, 369pp
The ultimate guide to outdoor adventure from Banff to Lake Louise to Jasper National Park. This book covers walking and canoeing routes, climbs, cycling and hiking in one of the most spectacular regions on earth. Maps, photos and contact numbers.

WHERE TO STAY IN NEW ENGLAND
$11.95, ISBN 1-55650-602-3, 512pp

"... isn't just your usual B&B or hotel listing, but a selection of almost all hotels, motels, country houses, condos and cottages for rent in the region.... Highly recommended: much more comprehensive in scope than competitors." Reviewer's Bookwatch.

Over 5,000 places are listed in this all-inclusive guide. Brief descriptions are supplemented by address, phone number (toll-free when available) and prices. Special sections are dedicated to chain hotels and deals they offer to business travellers, school groups, government workers and senior citizens.

Among other guides in the Where to Stay series:

AMERICA'S EASTERN CITIES $11.95, ISBN 1-55650-600-7, 416pp
AMERICA'S WESTERN CITIES $11.95, ISBN 1-55650-420-9, 416pp
MID-ATLANTIC STATES $12.95, ISBN 1-55650-631-7, 446pp
AMERICA'S HEARTLAND $13.93, ISBN 1-55650-632-5, 572pp
SOUTHERN CALIFORNIA $12.95, ISBN 1-55650-573-6, 394pp
NORTHERN CALIFORNIA $12.95, ISBN 1-55650-572-8, 280pp
AMERICAN NORTHWEST $12.95, ISBN 1-55650-683-X, 320 pp
FLORIDA $12.95, ISBN 1-55650-682-1, 384 pp

HAWAII - A WALKER'S GUIDE
$13.95, ISBN 1-55650-215-X, 184pp

Packed with unforgettable adventures in Kauai, Maui, Oahu, Molokai, Lanai and Hawaii. A practical guide to the most scenic walks to suit all travellers, from easy strolls of a few hours to multi-day excursions. Maps and color photos.

TRAVELER'S GUIDE TO THE GALAPAGOS ISLANDS 2nd Ed.
$15.95, ISBN 1-55650-640-6, 256pp

Comments on the 1st edition:

".... Boyce's excitement and knowledge mix to produce a comprehensive and responsible guide." Booklist.

".... An excellent resource both for exploring the archipelago and for trip preparation." Great Expeditions.

".... Just on the market and badly needed.... Boyce's effort is likely to be a definitive work." San José Mercury News.

Barry Boyce, a relentless adventure traveler, shares his knowledge and experience of travel in this amazing archipelago. Unlike any other book on the subject it orients the reader to various touring options on both yachts and cruise ships, from specialty tours such as photography and bird watching, to general tours covering history and sightseeing. Companies offering tours are described, analysed and price structures are included. Fax and toll-free numbers put you in direct contact to make planning easier.

ARIZONA, COLORADO & UTAH: A TOURING GUIDE
$11.95, ISBN 1-55650-656-2, 160pp

A compact guide written for those eager to see the unforgettable attractions of these three states. Driving tours begin in the state capital and cover the museums, parks, zoos and historical buildings in each city. They then lead the reader out into the fascinating land of giant arches, pinnacles, natural bridges, canyons and deserts for which the region is so well known. All the sights are described, along with the best routes to reach them whether on a daytrip or as part of a month-long tour. Accommodations and attractions are listed with opening times and fees. State and city maps make planning easy.

STATE PARKS OF THE SOUTH
$13.95, ISBN 1-55650-655-4, 224pp

This book takes you to 250 state parks in Georgia, Alabama, Tennessee, Kentucky and Florida. From small ones that are largely undiscovered by the public, to others whose names you will recognize – each offers something unique. History, lectures on the ecosystem, lodges, camping, local attractions, activities, maps and photos put this book above any other available in terms of practical tips and usability.

All of these titles plus thousands more are available from Hunter Publishing. To receive our free color catalog or to find out more about our books and maps, contact Hunter Publishing, 300 Raritan Center Parkway, Edison NJ 08818, or call (908) 225 1900.